With compliments

Arthur Du Cros.

WHEELS OF FORTUNE

A SALUTE TO PIONEERS

WILLIAM HARVEY DU CROS.

CHEVALIER DE L'ORDRE NATIONAL DE LA LÉGION D'HONNEUR.
CABALLERO DE LA REAL ORDEN DE ISABEL LA CATÓLICA.

" MAN OF FAITH AND VISION, WHO ALLIED INVENTION WITH
COMMERCE, AND THEREBY FOUNDED A WORLD-WIDE INDUSTRY."

[Frontispiece

WHEELS OF FORTUNE

A SALUTE TO PIONEERS

By

SIR ARTHUR DU CROS, BT.

With an Afterword

by

ARTHUR ROY DU CROS

BARRISTER AT LAW

LONDON

CHAPMAN & HALL LTD.

11 HENRIETTA STREET, W.C.2

1938

PRINTED IN GREAT BRITAIN BY THE WHITEFRIARS PRESS LTD.
LONDON AND TONBRIDGE
BOUND BY G. & J. KITCAT LTD., LONDON
Flexiback Binding Patent No. 441294

THE LURE OF SPEED

" Soon shall thy arm, unconquered steam, afar
Drag the slow barge or drive the rapid car ;
On on, wide waving wings expanded bear
The flying chariot through the fields of air,
Fair crews triumphant, leaning from above,
Shall wave their fluttering kerchiefs as they move,
Or warrior bands alarm the gaping crowd
And armies shrink beneath the shadowy cloud."

Dr. Darwin, 1791.

" Now there is nothing gives a man such spirit,
    Leavening his blood as cayenne doth a curry,
As going at full speed . . .

    .   .   .   .   .

What a delightful thing's a turn-pike road !
    So smooth, so level, such a means of shaving
The Earth as scarce the Eagle in the broad
    Air can accomplish . . ."

Byron.

" Speed, and the range of God's skies,
    Distances, changes, surprises ;
Speed, and the hug of God's winds
    And the play of God's airs,
Beautiful, whimsical, wonderful ;
    Clean, fierce and clean,
With a thrust in the throat
And a rush at the nostrils."

William Ernest Henley.

THIS book has been written to honour the memory of Robert William Thomson of Edinburgh, inventor of the Pneumatic Tyre in 1845 ; John Boyd Dunlop of Belfast who in 1888 successfully applied the pneumatic principle to the wheels of cycles ; Charles Kingston Welch of Tottenham, London, and William Erskine Bartlett of Springfield, Massachusetts, who by their inventions of 1890 made pneumatic tyres detachable and practicable for all forms of transport, and William Harvey du Cros of Dublin, man of faith and vision, who allied invention with commerce, and thereby founded a world-wide industry. Pioneers all, and makers of history, they enriched the world without hurt to any.

CONTENTS

vii

LIST OF ILLUSTRATIONS

FOREWORD

Here, in peaceful surroundings of surpassing beauty, almost fifty years after the events recorded, I have found a melancholy pleasure in recalling the cavalcade of figures who, in creating a great new industry, left a mark on the world which will endure through the ages. Shortly before he died, my father expressed a wish that the story of the Pneumatic Tyre invention and industry should be written, a desire also voiced by others who were closely associated with him in the movement. The papers which then came into my possession and my own recollections have enabled me to record those events of the closing years of the nineteenth century and their impressive sequel. Nothing was ever published by my father's pioneer company, which, its mission accomplished, has now ceased to exist, nor by anyone on its behalf ; but as numerous inadequate and misleading statements have appeared, and are still appearing even from the pens of technical writers, which may, in the absence of a true dispassionate record of the facts, come to be accepted, I have endeavoured to produce such a record in the interests of historical accuracy. History should not be altered by being ignored or distorted.

Every man who has had the smallest share in the evolution of the pneumatic tyre is entitled to his full meed of credit for helping to give to the world an invention that has proved of incalculable service to the human race. We are nearing the fiftieth year of the founding of a great industry. Most of the men who played their parts in those far-off days are no longer here, and for the others the sun is nearing the west. They can look back along the road they have travelled with feelings of pride and gratification. They have done something for humanity ; something to make the world better than they found it. All honour, even to the least amongst them. The names and portraits of many appear among the appendices.

This story of those golden days of invention and business achievement can make no claim to have been written by an expert in any branch of science, or by one with a precise knowledge of the intricacies of the legal and technical fields ; but it has been born from the knowledge of one whose life has been bound up very closely with the happenings of which it tells, and who is the last survivor who was within the inner circle of those events.

In writing this story after nearly fifty years I have discharged a duty laid upon me, and have done nothing rashly or impulsively, for, like a recent writer, " long experience has taught me that it is better to sleep on what you are going to say than to be kept awake by what you have said."

In the writing of this chronicle I have been helped by the works of other writers and must give myself the pleasure of mentioning, in particular, that monumental work, " The World on Wheels " by H. O. Duncan (from which several illustrations have been taken), " The Early History of Motoring " by Claude Johnson, " Ten Years of Motors and Motor Racing " by Charles Jarrott, and " Bartleet's Bicycle Book " by H. W. Bartleet.

I have not commented upon the posthumous work of Mr. Dunlop, a book remarkable for its " forgotten men," published in 1924, which I have only recently read, but

have included among the appendices (p. 277) a review
of it by T. W. Murphy, who was a close friend of the
inventor and a literary confrère of R. J. Mecredy.

During my researches I have profited by Press comment of past years and have re-read with feelings of
nostalgia the writings of old friends of the Press who
have passed beyond the Bourne, among them E. J.
O'Reilly, J. McCarthy, Jack Dunbar, R. J. Mecredy,
Jimmy Percy, J. Mackenzie, Charlie Wheelwright,
Edmund Dangerfield, Henry Sturmey, W. McCandlish,
Jack Urry, James Nisbet, E. Campbell. " May the sod
rest lightly on them." Whether they were kindly or
critical, they always wrote with a good heart and with
their living contemporaries, " Faed " Wilson, H. W.
Bartleet, Fitz Russell, T. W. Murphy, F. Percy Low,
G. Lacy Hillier, F. F. MacCabe, and others, contributed
nobly to a mighty work.

Dated this forty-ninth anniversary of the founding of
the first Pneumatic Tyre Company, on November 18th,
1889.

ARTHUR DU CROS.

Florida del Mare,
  St. Jean—Cap Ferrat,
    A. M. France.

CHAPTER ONE

THE BIRTH OF AN INVENTION

I

THE early history of England was written in tales of bodily prowess and courage. Once power and fortune were to be gained by feats upon the battlefield or by venturing into strange and undiscovered lands, but, by the nineteenth century's close, the world was mostly tamed and charted upon the then fashionable " globes " ; history is no longer made by the individual qualities of courage and endurance alone ; in these more sober days of business democracy, clear thinking, far-seeing opportunism and ready decisions are needed to mould the destiny of man. Inventors and scientists write for us in mysterious symbols and equations, and by the rightness of scientific theories and their practice are reputations won and lost. The lives of ordinary folk which once were subject to the whims of rival princes and potentates, to-day respond to the demands of science and industry, and our very movements are made at their dictates.

This book forms a part of the new history, for the revival of the pneumatic tyre was one of the first steps forward into the new era of which we are as yet upon the threshold ; an era that is dominated by speed, by a rapidity of communication which has changed the old political and social values beyond all recognition, and by an ever present uncertainty as to what may portend from the air. Around this innocent invention cluster tales of sport and adventure, of fortune and misfortune, of bitter litigation and high finance.

The birth of an invention is a phenomenon that is frequently shrouded in doubt, for it is noticeable that the minds of men of ability turn in the same direction, and, as often as not working upon different and isolated methods, arrive at similar conclusions. When the time is ripe for some new discovery the revelation frequently takes place in the minds of men strange to one another and

working far apart, so that the task of the historian who has to decide who was the first, amongst the genuine claims of sincere and brilliant men, often themselves astonished that their ideas have been conceived by others, is no light one, even if it were not complicated by a host of irresponsible claims that

ROBERT W. THOMSON, C.E.

inevitably arise. So it has been with many inventions, and what seems clear to the layman is often obscure to the more erudite historian, and the greater his erudition the greater his difficulty in determining the truth.

This is not the case with the invention of the pneumatic tyre, but its origin is by no means devoid of strangeness, for the pneumatic principle was invented twice, with an interval of forty-three years between the two inventions, and has never been improved upon in principle in the ninety-three years since it appeared in the Patent Office. That the same idea should occur to two minds

2

of strangely different calibre is a comment upon the apparent chance upon which the progress of our civilisation depends. The first and true inventor, Robert William Thomson, believed in the future of this principle which he discovered and patented in the year 1845, but he was destined to see himself apparently proved wrong and his invention sink into the limbo of forgotten things ; the second inventor, John Boyd Dunlop, with only a limited faith in the principle he unavailingly patented in 1888, was also destined to see himself proved wrong in that the invention swept across the world. Yet from the inspiration of his brain Thomson gained nothing for himself, and even his name is forgotten by the public, if they ever knew it, while his unconscious imitator, Dunlop, who devised a way of exploiting the lost treasure, had no valid patent, but with the aid of brother inventors gained wealth for himself and others and a name which will be handed down as that of one of the world's benefactors. Truly a case of the first being last and the last being first.

This history is an attempt to show why the pioneer failed and those following in his footsteps succeeded, and who were the men behind the phenomenal results which have been achieved.

II

Although Thomson failed to obtain commercial success for his pneumatic principle, it would be the very reverse of the truth to say that he or his tyre was a failure. Indeed, he is an example, of which there are many among Scotsmen, of how courage and moral uprightness can achieve success with little else to aid them, though it must never be forgotten that Thomson was endowed with a scientific and technical mind of surpassing ability ; but with this alone, and lacking the other qualities, he could never have occupied the place he did at the head of his profession as a civil engineer.

He was born on June 29th, 1822, at Stonehaven, Kincardineshire, where his father was the originator and proprietor of a small factory. Thomson Senior cherished a hope, not uncommon among Scotsmen of comparatively humble station, of seeing his son become a minister of the Church, but the boy himself was so averse to classical studies that this project was perforce abandoned, and young Thomson in 1836, at the age of fourteen, was sent to Charleston, U.S., to be educated as a merchant. This second parental attempt to shape a career for his son proved no more successful than the first, and on his return two years later the boy was permitted to pursue his natural bent and embark upon a course of self-education with the assistance of a friendly weaver with a mathematical turn of mind.

This education, supported by periods of practical experience in workshops in Aberdeen and Dundee, was soon to bear fruit, and at an early age he conceived the idea of the ribbon saw, and while employed by his cousin, Mr. Lyon, the builder of Dean Bridge, devised a method of firing mines by electricity, which earned for him the commendation of Faraday himself. Later he evolved a fountain pen and submitted a design for the Crystal Palace Exhibition of 1851, showing the catholicity of his activities.

At the age of twenty-two he was caught up in the whirl of the railway enthusiasm of that time, but although this brought him a brief period of prosperity, the ensuing panic again left him free to follow his inventive genius, nor in later years, with the recovery of confidence, did he return to railway activities.

At the age of twenty-three he discovered the principle of the pneumatic tyre, and recorded his final specification in a masterly and fully-illustrated document on June 10th, 1846, the claims of which are reviewed in detail in a later chapter. In his early experiments in 1847, animal-drawn wagons were fitted and tested in the streets and parks of London in a series of costly and well-thought-out experiments, in the course of which side-slip, skidding and other problems were studied and dealt with. These were not speed trials, but were mainly intended to demonstrate how easily loads could be drawn, motion maintained, and noise reduced, when wheels were fitted with air tyres. They showed in the result that the improvement in tractive effort by the use of pneumatic tyres as against iron tyres varied from 60 per cent. on smooth surfaces to over 300 per cent. on rough roads, so that their advantages were well known and understood by Thomson and many others.

Thomson was confronted with the fundamental difficulties that the miracle effected by Goodyear and Hancock by the vulcanisation of rubber had only been patented two years before his tyre and did not come into general use until some time afterwards.

He was compelled also to carry out his experiments on heavy vehicles, lacking as he did the all-important aid of the cycle, or of any light road vehicle, for which there was a popular demand. In his day the cycle as we know it had not been born, and he was obliged, therefore, to think in terms of the only vehicles available, and these circumstances forced him in the beginning to resort to leather for his treads and to build up his tyre by hand instead of machinery. Nor was it wholly or readily detachable. Although the outer tread could be unlaced, there were over seventy security bolts being used to fasten it to a wheel to avoid creeping, a mode of fastening which was incidental and did not affect the principle of the patent.

But above all, Thomson was hampered by the fact that commercially the market was too limited to justify manufacture on a sufficiently large scale to be economically worth while. He was an inventor, not a philanthropist.

Nevertheless, by 1850 he had succeeded in producing a fairly satisfactory light carriage tyre which he himself continued to use until the end of his life. The *Mechanics' Magazine* of 1849 (Vol. 50) (see Appendix, p. 297) commented upon the improvements on his earlier tyres " which are of a very marked character." It was still hand-made, but the leather cover had been replaced by a specially made canvas with an inner rubber tube and with a tread of vulcanised rubber which showed not the " slightest " sign of wear after considerable use. The engineer of the journal had made a series of dynamometer tests with a brougham (see illustration, p. 188), and of these results and the other qualities of the pneumatic tyre he wrote in eulogistic terms, reciting their advantages and adding his confident expectation that " these wheels will speedily come into general use."

But the use of pneumatic tyres on horse-drawn vehicles, where speed and vibration are secondary matters, could not be popularised by Thomson and has never been popularised since. Had the horse been possessed of the gift of language it might well have been otherwise. A large number were made by the first of all

Pneumatic Tyre Companies,* subsequently founded by William Harvey du Cros in 1889,† and from 1894 onwards were successfully used on carriages by the Prince of Wales, afterwards H.M. King Edward VII, the German Emperor, the Duke of Connaught, Joseph Chamberlain, A. J. Balfour, Lord Lonsdale, and many other notable people ; but they gradually disappeared as had Thomson's, and mainly for the same reasons, that the company was unable to induce an adequate commercial demand, and the cost of marketing and maintaining the diminutive quantities of tyres required was prohibitive, points which have not been sufficiently weighed by writers on this subject.

Thus, despite the fact that Thomson's efforts had attained considerable success, they attracted but little public and no sporting interest, and this combination of unfavourable circumstances ultimately proved too much for the pneumatic tyre. It was Thomson's misfortune to have been too far ahead of his time. He failed for reasons beyond his control ; the obstacles in his way were insurmountable, and had the du Cros-Dunlop combination of 1889 been confronted with the same set of conditions their tyre too must inevitably have been abandoned.

III

Two years later Thomson had migrated to Java, not to return to his native country for ten years. The purpose of his sojourn there was to advise upon and erect machinery for the manufacture of sugar, and among the strange and somewhat primitive conditions prevailing there he found

* For convenience this Company will be referred to as the " Founder Company."
† Publicly known as Harvey du Cros.

new scope for invention. To this period belongs his steam crane and his hydraulic dock. In 1862 he returned to settle in Edinburgh, where he perfected the elliptic rotary engine, conceived in his early youth, and also invented his variation of the road steamer upon which, from that time forward, he concentrated most of his energies.

His interest in the pneumatic tyre had not diminished, although the patent had expired, as is evidenced by the fact that, when he was visited at his home in Moray Place

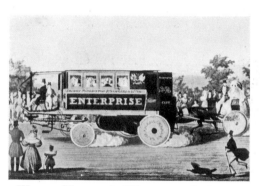

WALTER HANCOCK'S " ENTERPRISE," 1822–23.

on August 2nd, 1871, by the well-meaning but unfortunate Emperor of Brazil, Pedro II, who was deposed in 1889, he personally demonstrated the pneumatic tyres which were fitted to his own brougham when driving the Emperor to the engineering works of Mr. Tennant for the purpose of inspecting his own road-steamer, to the warmly-expressed gratification of that potentate. This was but seventeen years before the date of the patent by Dunlop who, in 1871, was thirty-one years of age.

Thomson's tyre invention was no mere paper patent. He was convinced that it contained all the essentials of success, but he had learned that the cleverest invention in the world cannot be established without a profitable market. The cycle did not arrive in his lifetime, but his

8

patent had stated that his pneumatic tyre was " peculiarly applicable to carriages propelled by steam on common roads," and he therefore set himself to encourage a double market by continuing the crusade to convert all road users to the use of motor traction and passenger motor trains.

In his early lifetime, Gurney's, James', Walter Hancock's and other steam motor 'buses were running regularly in and out of London, but progress was being hampered by rough roads, excessive vibration, unsatis- factory springing, and penal laws and tolls, although Hancock's motor coach, "Enterprise," 1822–23, received the warm com- mendation of Frederick Bramwell many years later when addressing a critical audience of experts in mechanical science. The average speeds, however, of ten miles an hour or so

GOLDSWORTHY GURNEY.

were not sufficient to attract universal passenger traffic, and as to profits it is certain that the early pioneers were better scientists than they were commercial men.

Church was running a steam coach service between Birmingham, Bristol and London, carrying fifty passengers ; while Davies was announcing that his two-ton coach would seat eighteen passengers, travel at from eight to twelve miles per hour, and " to guard against the inconvenience arising from smoke, charcoal and coke will be the only fuel used, and for the safety of passengers, the tubular boiler has been put to ten times the amount of working pressure." Finally, about 1840, these early pioneers were vanquished by repressive conditions and the growing importance of the railway. But they were not first in the field, a claim which has been made for Richard Trevithick, Jnr., who, in 1801, it is said, had the honour of carrying the first passengers on the first steam horseless carriage to move on a common road.

CHURCH'S STEAM COACH, 1838.

A Frenchman, M. Cugnot, produced in 1 7 6 9 a humble two - cylinder locomotive, the first of the steam lorries, capable of $2\frac{1}{4}$ miles per hour, which was seriously encouraged by his Government for military uses.* It is still to be seen in the Conservatoire des Arts et Metiers in Paris. This engine was an advance, although not a striking one, for while negotiating the corner of a street near the spot where the Madeleine now stands, it toppled over and, it has been unkindly said, was thereupon seized by the authorities and locked up, together with its inventor, to keep them out of further mischief.

In the motor traction field Thomson's problems were the reduction of weight and vibration, the attainment of greater speed, and the saving of wear and tear on the engine, problems which, towards the end of his life, he

* See p. 12.

solved to an appreciable degree by the steamer he designed, coupled with his adaptation of the solid rubber tyre, for which he claimed a patent in October, 1867. Speeds of over twenty miles an hour were obtained, and the extended use of passenger motor trains on the roads had become a definite possibility ; many were built in the 'seventies and put into daily use in India and elsewhere, giving good and economical service year after year in the transport of goods and passengers. Thomson's efforts were strangled

RICHARD TREVITHICK, JNR.

when in sight of success by the passing of the criminally stupid legislation of 1861 and 1865 which eventually drove motor traction from British roads,* although the

THOMSON'S "ADVANCE," 1870.

Scotsman of June 3rd, 1870, recorded of the practical trials then made " a new era in locomotion, so far as our large towns and public roads generally are concerned, has begun," and that the system was safe, unobtrusive, " perfectly under control and can be regulated as nicely as a watch."

Thomas Hancock had successfully fitted solid tyres to horse-drawn vehicles in 1846 when, in recording their advantages, he stated that " they have lately been

* See p. 188.

patronised by Her Majesty," but Thomson was the pioneer of solid rubber tyres for heavy traction use, the remarkable success of which was being discussed by leading scientific journals in Europe in 1868, and by the *Mechanics' Magazine* on October 2nd of that year. For his road steamer they were of special design and huge in size, having a thickness of 5 inches and a width of 12 inches, and four weighed 3,000 lbs., and to assist them to withstand the enormous strain, they were later protected with armour or metal clip shoes, a combination giving excellent results. These tyres were made for him in his own city of Edinburgh by the North British Rubber Company from moulds still in their possession, yet this company does not appear ever to have thought of producing Thomson's pneumatic tyre.

CUGNOT'S STEAM CARRIAGE, 1771.

Towards the end of his life, which occurred upon March 8th, 1873, at the early age of fifty-one, Thomson suffered greatly from illness, but he continued to work until his death, nor did the virile quality of his mind, which was capable of contributing something of value to every branch of contemporary thought, weaken in the least. Upon his death he was remembered by his friends as a cultivated and charming companion, a fascinating conversationalist and a sympathetic listener, and as a worthy President of the Scottish Society of Arts, which office he had held since 1868.

* See p. 10. From " The World on Wheels."

From the brain of this man had come, first, the pneumatic tyre, and then a workmanlike solid rubber tyre, which took its place and held sway until it in turn was forced to yield the precedence again to the air tyre, even in the case of the heaviest transport.

MICHELIN'S PNEUMATIC RAILWAY WHEEL.

It is a remarkable proof of the foresight of this early pioneer of the automobile that fifty years before the advent of the internal combustion engine he prophesied not merely the use of motor vehicles combined with pneumatic tyres, but also the application of these tyres to the railway, which although longer delayed, has likewise been fulfilled with the evolution of the Michelin trains in France and other countries. These have progressed beyond the experimental stage into daily use, carrying up to 100 passengers, with an

THE FIRST RAILWAY CARRIAGE, 1825.*

* From " The World on Wheels."

13

annual distance record to their credit of close upon five million miles.

There was a remarkable divergence of view on this subject between Thomson and Dunlop ; the former,

THE MICHELIN TRAIN, 1937.

with his unlimited vision, had illustrated in his patent in 1845 railway wheels fitted with pneumatic tyres, while the latter, in 1909, with all his intervening experience, stated that he " would never dream of applying an air tyre to the wheels of railway wagons." *

* *Cycle and Motor Trader*, September 18th, 1909.

CHAPTER TWO

THE EVOLUTION OF THE CYCLE

I

To the advent of the cycle we owe the resurrection of the pneumatic tyre in 1888, fifteen years after the death of Thomson, and it is interesting, therefore, to glance at its beginnings and consider its bearings upon the respective fortunes of the two inventors. Four years before the birth of Thomson, that is, in 1818, the Dandy or Hobby Horse, the "Draisine" of German invention, and the first *steerable* wheeled machine to be bestridden by a human being, was introduced into England from France, where it had been known

THE DRAISINE

for some years in a more crude form under the name Vélocifère. The *English Mechanic* in 1868 recorded :—

"The Dandy Horse was propelled by the feet upon the ground, and, after a good speed had been obtained, the feet were temporarily rested upon a small projection at each end of the front axle until the horse required further propulsion. Fox, Sheridan, Pitt and other notabilities of the period, patronized the velocipede in St. James' Park, taking their constitutional daily on the Dandy Horse, after a hard night spent in the House of Commons or around the gaming tables."

Be that as it may, the Dandy Horse can hardly be said to have been ridden, since there was no mechanical means of propulsion. Machines for ladies, with the decorous dropped frame similar to the present-day ladies' bicycle,

A HOBBY HORSE SCHOOL, 1819.

were introduced a year later, but, as used by the " Dandies " of the period, the machine was in fact no more than an aid to walking and enjoyed a limited vogue as a curiosity and a new hobby, from which doubtless the better-remembered name of Hobby Horse was derived.

It is a matter of interest that there should be in the vestibule of the historic church of Stoke Poges, memorable as the resting-place of Thomas Gray, the poet and writer of the famed " Elegy Written in a Country Churchyard," an ancient stained heraldic or allegorical glass panel depicting a machine of the hobby horse type, bestridden by a figure pushing with his feet, while he blows a trumpet. The panel is of ancient Dutch origin,* and

* From " The World on Wheels."

portions of the window bear the date 1643. It originally came out of the Banqueting Hall of the Old Manor

House, which adjoins the church and dates back to very ancient times, where Queen Elizabeth was received by Coke, and Charles II was imprisoned, the home of the Penn family from 1760 to 1840.

It was not until about 1839 that the first known attempt was made by man to propel himself on wheels without the aid of his feet on the road. Then Kirkpatrick MacMillan, a Scotsman of Courthill, Dumfriesshire, made the discovery that two wheels placed in line could be safely

KIRKPATRICK MACMILLAN,*
Inventor, Builder & rider
of the first bicycle
Year 1839† ©

* Born 1810 ; died 1878.   † By the courtesy of *Cycling.*

propelled and balanced. He was no engineer, but a man in humble circumstances, who devised, and rode, the first bicycle to be actuated by pedals. These pedals were not attached to the axle of the front wheel as in later days, but to a series of cranks and levers by which a fore and aft *rear wheel* drive was obtained and the machine was fitted with a brake for the first time. Made of wood and iron, and clumsy and heavy as it was, yet MacMillan's was the first bicycle built in Great Britain, the forerunner of the rear driven bicycle of the " safety " type, albeit not of rotary action and somewhat after the manner of Heath Robinson's drawings in its appearance. It was not patented, and although copied by others, comparatively few were produced and it never achieved popularity, being but little known outside its inventor's district of Scotland. MacMillan still holds one record, that of being the first bicyclist to be prosecuted by the police and fined, a distinction which he achieved at Gorbals in 1842 for knocking over a child at the finish of a forty-mile ride.* His machine was five years before the

KIRKPATRICK MACMILLAN'S LEVER-DRIVEN BICYCLE. DATE 1839–1840.

date of the pneumatic tyre patent, and it seems reasonable to assume that had Thomson considered it or the hobby horse practicable for general use, he would have employed them for experimental purposes. Had he done so, cycling might have been popularised by the early Victorians.

* *Glasgow Herald*, June 10th, 1842.

Over twenty years were to pass before the next fundamental step was made in the advance of the cycle, and
visitors to Bar-le-Duc (Meuse, France) will probably
be familiar with the grandiose monument to Pierre
Michaux *et fils*, natives of that town, which was unveiled
in 1894 to
commemorate
on behalf of
" the grateful
bicyclists of
France " their
work and the
achievement in
1861 of fitting
cranks with
pedals to the
front wheel axle
of the hobby
horse for the first
time. Michaux
père was a coach-
builder, and
later a cycle
manufacturer in
Paris, and is said
to have obtained
his idea of a

MICHAUX MONUMENT, BAR-LE-DUC.

pedal and crank from the grindstone. He died in 1883.
With this development the era of the well-named bone-
shaker had dawned, and crude as it was and unpractical
for general use, it nevertheless was the seed from which
sprang the high or " Ordinary " type of bicycle.
    A great impetus was given to the sale of boneshakers

19   C 2

by an event reported in *The Times* of February 19th, 1869, which described the first record made on the classic London to Brighton road on a two-wheel velocipede by John Mayall, Jnr., as a great feat, the time being not less than fourteen hours. This was the first long ride and the first athletic record, which survived, however, for less than a month, being beaten on March 6th, 1869, by the Brothers Chinnery, of the London Stock Exchange, who *walked* the distance in eleven hours twenty-five minutes. J. Selby followed in 1888 when he drove the " Old Times " coach, using sixteen teams of horses, from Piccadilly to Brighton and back in under eight hours for a wager of £1,000, a challenge to speed which was taken up first by Frank Shorland in 1890 and subsequently by S. F. Edge, who accomplished the double journey on a safety bicycle with cushion tyres in just over seven hours. They had all been preceded in 1833 by Sir Charles Dance, who created the first automobile record when he drove the distance in one of Gurney's steam coaches in just over five hours, while the giant automobiles of to-morrow upon the motor highways of the future will no doubt accomplish the distance in thrice as many minutes, only to be eclipsed again by the airplane ; the lure of speed is never satisfied.

JOHN MAYALL, JNR.

To the work of Michaux and to the foresight of an

Englishman, Rowley B. Turner, who brought the bone-shaker to England, was due the introduction of the cycle manufacturing industry into Coventry in 1868 (a city which, as its history shows, possesses a peculiar talent for the absorption of new industries) and with it the all-important market which was afterwards to ensure the commercial success of the pneumatic tyre.

The Ordinary bicycle weighing up to and over 80 lbs., its front wheel getting larger and larger—in the middle 'seventies James Starley made and his son William rode one of a freak type as high as 96 inches—and its back wheel smaller and smaller, was pioneered in England, among others, by Dan Rudge, of Wolverhampton, and Jack Keen, of Surbiton Hill, who were probably the first, in 1870–71, to build what might be called high light machines, although Thomas Humber also was early on the scene. The Ordinary attained its zenith in the late 'eighties, when it had been slimmed down to under 20 lbs. for racing and raised to 60 inches or higher, and wonderfully well it looked, although accidents on the road were so frequent and painful that many, and in some cases successful, attempts were made to produce it in safer form by means of gearing and other devices.

JACK KEEN.

The evolution of the dwarf machine was also proceeding gradually. MacMillan's conception had been lost sight of, but his low-wheel type of cycle progressed laboriously through many stages in many forms at the hands of many designers, notably James Starley and Henry Bate, until there emerged the rotary action, the rear-wheel chain

JAMES STARLEY.

drive, and in 1879 Harry J. Lawson's " Bicyclette," seven years after the death of Thomson and nineteen years after the expiry of his pneumatic tyre patent. Lawson had appropriately introduced the word " safety " for the low bicycle, as distinct from the more dangerous Ordinary, a machine never really suitable for ordinary people despite its name.

Henry Bate's " Shadow " and H. J. Lawson's " Bicyclette " were the progenitors of the modern safety bicycle, which, from 1884, with the aid of a host of clever designers, notably the Starley family, Humber, Hillman, Linley and others, was being improved, apparently with little legal interference on patent grounds, and challenging the precedence of the Ordinary bicycle. Ball bearings, the diamond frame, equi-sized wheels, tangent spokes, hollow forks (an idea evolved, it is said, from the scabbard of a sword) and

STARLEY'S STATUE.

tubular frames were being used, solid rubber tyres had long since been in general use, having been applied by Scott and Goodyear as early as 1855, and experiments were being made with hollow non-inflated rubber or cushion tyres, patented by Macintosh in 1884, but with features which had been described by Thomson in 1846.

The French monument to Michaux has its parallel in Coventry in the memorial to James Starley, a man of many inventions, including the differential gear, and recognised as the father of the English bicycle.* His nephew, J. K. Starley, may be said to have " set the fashion to the world," and commercialised the safety cycle with his " Rover " machine of 1885.

" Conger " Walsh.

II

When Dunlop appeared in 1889 the manufacture of cycles was already a well-established industry and the demand for all types was growing enormously ; the struggle for supremacy between the high and low bicycle was at its height, but the pneumatic tyre tipped the scale and the Ordinary machine went down to extinction, to the infinite regret of the sporting public. Attempts were made to stem the tide by fitting pneumatic tyres to high machines, but to no purpose, although

* Born 1803 ; died 1881.

" Conger " Walsh put up records in 1891 for 100 miles, twelve hours and twenty-four hours, none of which has ever been beaten. The despised Hobby Horse had forged ahead to become the King of the Road for speed, convenience and cheapness of travel, and, true to British conservatism, the best-hated vehicle on it.

TOURING IN THE 'SIXTIES.*

It is somewhat disconcerting to reflect that there is but a small minority of people living in 1938 who from their own experience can speak of cycles and the conditions of cycling in 1888. To the younger generation my bone-shaker built in the 'seventies, with its steel tyres, would be merely a museum curiosity. Just as my own genera-tion is unable to realise a world without the railway the steamship and the telegraph, so present-day cyclists know nothing of the vast difference between pneumatic and

* By the courtesy of *Cycling*.

solid-tyred machines. Yet in those days the contrast between the old Ordinary with its " bootlace " tyres and the pneumatic safety, with its " pudding " tyres, was the difference between a Derby winner and a Shire horse.

H. L. CORTIS.   DICK HOWELL.

No more thrilling or memorable sight could be seen than a closely-fought finish between the racing giants of the day on these high glittering machines. Tall fellows

W. A. ILLSTON.   J. ADAMS.   G. GATEHOUSE.   H. SYNYER.

mostly flashing round tracks already beginning to be built for speed, riders elbow to elbow or overlapping, a clump of colour, every man striving all out for the few inches which meant victory or defeat. Excited crowds roared for their favourites. Jack Keen, Dick Howell,

H. L. Cortis, J. S. Whatton, Ion Keith Falconer, George Gatehouse, Percy Furnivall, Fred Osmond, an outstanding champion, Herbert Synyer, England's most graceful rider, Johnny Adams, Jack Morley, F. P. Wood, W. F. Ball, W. A. Illston, Teddy Mayes, of England; and,

FRED OSMOND.

P. FURNIVALL.

FRED WOOD.

across the water, E. S. McKay, who was to meet his end in a struggle with a lion, R. J. Mecredy, unique as a champion in the tricycle, safety and ordinary fields, P. P. Kilkelly, a potential world beater, Sam MacAdam, W. McCourt, and Charlie Williamson, the Synyer of Ireland. In a class apart were the long-distance men, giants of the road and path, among them Montague

Holbein, G. P. Mills, Frank Shorland, T. A. Edge, Harry Green ; all those names and many others were household words, their owners sportsmen in the truest sense of the word, who are still remembered with admiring affection by their fast lessening band of contemporaries.

The safety took away much of the glamour of cycle-

F. W. SHORLAND.   G. P. MILLS.   M. A. HOLBEIN.

racing, although infinitely the more effective machine, and what the result would have been had they been in demand and available to Thomson must for ever remain a matter for conjecture. Had he lived to the not abnormal age of sixty-six he could have chatted over this interesting problem with Dunlop himself.

Apart from the racing track, cycling before 1888, with its excessive vibration, was not everyone's pleasure, being indulged in mostly by the athletically-minded, since winter roads generally consisted of two deep ruts filled with water, between ridges of loose stones, and summer roads were rough, thorny and dusty beyond belief. Even macadamised roads in the light of to-day would appear but a parody of our modern roads, the only compensation, and a great one, being the absence of motor-cars, a privilege only enjoyed to-day by the Bermudians. The supposedly safe solid tyre, which was usually cemented

27

into a grooved rim, had a habit of coming off at unexpected moments and depositing the unhappy rider upon the ground. None the less, to those who were young and keen, early cycling was a cheap and exhilarating, if strenuous, form of recreation, ensuring healthy hours in the country, opening up new scenes, new experiences, new friendships and promoting a social club life which was a happy feature of those placid times. But then cyclists paid a higher price for these benefits in nervous

exhaustion, aching heads and stiffened muscles, while no woman would attempt the bicycle, and but few the safer tricycle, when even the majority of their men-folk were disposed to flinch from the ordeal.

Nevertheless, there was a daring young lady of Dublin, whose name should appear on the tablets of fame, who took a first step in the emancipation of women in the early 'nineties, when she rocked the city by appearing in public riding a man's bicycle with habiliments to match. To say that tongues wagged and heads were shaken would be an understatement : for it was universally assumed that the perpetrator of this enormity had condemned herself to a lonely existence, if not life-long spinsterhood. It is probable that none of the consciously élite of Dublin ever spoke to her again, yet in her own way she helped to loosen the shackles from women's freedom and gave a sporting lead to the feminine world, which was to be emulated by the

Lenglens and Earharts, the Mollisons and Battens, and all those others who, by their initiative and enterprise, were to expand the outlook of women and advance their status.

That, in outline, is the process of evolution of the bicycle up to the year 1887, when it occurred to a Belfast veterinary surgeon to apply to it the pneumatic principle.

A DU CROS TEAM—OLD STYLE.

CHAPTER THREE

AN HISTORIC RENAISSANCE

I

JOHN BOYD DUNLOP was born at Dreghorn, in Ayrshire, in 1840, of tenant farmer stock, and was, therefore, a contemporary of Thomson, only eighteen years separating their ages and sixty odd miles their places of residence.

JOHN BOYD DUNLOP.
Died, October 1921

He studied in Edinburgh and migrated to Ireland whilst in his early twenties. Quite early in his life someone chanced to inform him that his entry into this world had taken place two months before his mother expected it. This piece of information affected the whole of Dunlop's life, for he became convinced that his health must have suffered as a consequence, and accordingly shrank from travel and strenuous exertion of any kind. His faintly stooping walk suggested one recovered from an illness and his low-toned voice was almost that of an invalid. He was prone to confide his misgivings as to his constitution and the suspected cause, and these misgivings coloured his outlook and appeared to depress his mentality. He wrote : " When I made the first tyres for my son I was in failing health," * and again, in 1892, " I have always been handicapped by an extremely delicate constitution, so much so that I resolved to retire from active practice when 52 years of age." Yet despite all these forebodings he enjoyed consistently good health, and remarked in 1921, " although I am now in my 81st year, I am happy to say I am still hale and hearty and feel as young as when I was fifty." Though never robust, he never had a serious illness till in October 1921, at the age of eighty-two, he died unexpectedly, almost suddenly, as the result of a chill. When he produced his pneumatic tyre in 1888, although only forty-eight years of age, he was full-bearded and even patriarchal in appearance, of medium height, and slow and deliberate in his manner.

I first made Dunlop's acquaintance at the North of Ireland C.C. Sports held on the grass track at Ormeau Park, Belfast, on June 1st, 1889, when I found him to be a diffident and gentle-mannered man, quietly confident

* *Irish Cyclist*, March 2nd, 1910.

as to the success of his tyre by reason of its scientific construction, and insistent upon its superior speed qualities on grass and rough surfaces. Later I came to know him very well when, in 1892, he came to reside on my father's estate at Blackrock, Dublin, and we were frequently in each other's company and formed a valued friendship, although thirty years separated our ages. He was a most interesting and informative companion, devoted to his home, which was presided over by his wife, a simple, practical woman, wholly preoccupied with the care of her husband and their son and daughter, who were inseparable. This son, Johnnie, became nearly as well known as was his father, and his untimely death in April, 1920, was not only a terrible loss to this intimate family circle, but by robbing the world of a most promising personality, left it so much the poorer.

DUNLOP AND SON.

Dunlop's mind, like Thomson's and many others, had been revolving for years round the problem of anti-vibration. That the subject was an ancient one may be seen in the Cairo Museum, where there reposes a carriage of the chariot type fitted with leather anti-vibratory tyres unearthed from one of the tombs of the Pharaohs. As a veterinary surgeon, Dunlop's business was concerned with locomotion, but it is not recorded that he used solid rubber tyres to ease his horses' daily round, although he was experimenting with a more humane type of collar. Several versions were current as to the manner in which he evolved his first pneumatic tyre, although Dunlop's own account was simple.

It was that the sources of his inspiration were the cycle and his ten-year-old son, Johnnie. Belfast streets are, or were, intersected with tramlines and partly paved with granite setts, and although practicable, the risks to a solid-tyred cycle by this fiendish combination were rightly objected to by all cyclists, including Johnnie (who was by no means the cripple romanticists would have us believe), who complained of the excessive vibration and had a natural ambition to get his wheel in front of his cycling schoolfellows in their daily meetings in the public park. This being confided to his father, set him moving as to how best to gratify his son's desire for comfort and speed. Thus spurred to action, Dunlop met both these demands by reproducing the air tyre, thereby becoming the second man to apply this principle to wheels, and the first man to see the practicability of fashioning rubber and canvas into light, even frail, tubular form for the wheels of the new light vehicle, which had grown up since Thomson died, and for which there was a commercial and increasing demand.

This was not " the first pneumatic tyre in the world " as Mr. Leslie Burgin, Minister for Transport, has stated, but, nevertheless, it was an epoch-making event. In the safety bicycle with its small wheels, Dunlop found the perfect medium which enabled him to solve the problem " for light vehicles, at any rate," as he said himself. Possibly someone else may have thought of it, but then nobody did it, and in this world it is only the people who do things or get them done that matter. Henry Sturmey, a one time leader of the cycling and motoring worlds, has recorded that ten years before this he himself had " conceived the idea of an air tyre " but that as a patent at that time cost £40 more than he possessed, the idea remained an idea and an idea only. Winwood Reade, a brother of Charles Reade, the writer, and himself the author of "The Martyrdom of Man," prophesied in 1872 the advent of " three inventions which perhaps may be long delayed, but which possibly are near at hand. . . . The first is the discovery of a motive force which will take the place of steam ; secondly, the invention of aerial locomotion which will transport labour at a trifling cost of money and time to any part of the planet . . . and, thirdly, the manufacture of flesh and blood from the elements by chemical process." Such speculations are impressive as examples of prescience, but until they are translated into reality they add nothing to the wealth of the world.

All honour, therefore, to Dunlop for achieving the Thomson-Dunlop tyre, for this was a dual inspiration. Bricks can now be made without straw, as the Pharaohs seemed to expect, but even to-day they cannot be made without material, and when Dunlop resuscitated and applied a past invention, and saw what few would believe, *that it would wear on a cycle*, he not only provided the material which was to lead to developments far beyond the cycle industry, but he opened up fresh fields for the many clever brains which were to follow and expand and perfect his work. Incidentally he added the word " pneumatic " to the world's vocabulary as applied to tyres.

II

Once the idea had occurred to Dunlop of a hollow tube inflated with air under pressure attached to the periphery of a wheel so as to present a cushion of air to the ground, the task of carrying out a rough experiment in his own back yard was an easy one. Perfectly vulcanised rubber and suitable canvas material were readily procurable, and for this experiment Dunlop harked back to the Dark Ages, for he used a solid disc of wood instead of a spoked wheel, to which he nailed the necessary pocket of linen which enclosed the inflated rubber tube. This was not intended for use, but merely to compare the bouncing and rolling properties of a wheel so fitted with those of a wheel shod with the usual solid tyre. He found, of course, that the one being hollow and resilient was as lively as a tennis ball, while the other, being solid and hard, was as lifeless as a cricket ball ; the difference being comparable to that between a boxing glove and a clenched fist. So far so good.

The experiment next progressed to the building up and fitting of a pair of tricycle wheels, for which Dunlop made and used wood rims, of elm, an American importation in later days, the tyres this time being made up in more shipshape form, and substantial enough to stand a riding test on the road. The canvas pocket containing the rubber tube was protected from wet by outer rubber strips, which were afterwards thickened on the running surface, the whole forming a " D " section tyre with the rim to which it was taped and stuck by rubber solution with the aid of flaps formed for the purpose on the inner canvas jacket. A simple but rather ineffective non-return valve was provided for

35

inflation (but not deflation), which Dunlop had made the subject of a separate patent, as too was his method of

swathing the tyre on to the rim, from which it was referred to in after days as the " mummy " tyre, or, alternatively, the " rag," to differentiate it from developments of a later date.

It was a highly creditable achievement by a man who was not an engineer or a cyclist, had no confidant outside his own family, and who worked it out with his own hands with only the appliances available at his home and business premises, just as the first

JOHNNIE DUNLOP AND THE FIRST
PNEUMATIC TYRES MADE, 1888.

telephone had been produced from the odds and ends lying about his place by Bell, and the cinema machine and other devices by their inventors.

A preliminary secret trial at night by Johnnie was so convincing as to comfort, smooth running and speed, that the first convert was immediately made, and in its subsequent history it never happened that anyone making a first trial on a properly inflated pneumatic tyre needed a second one to be convinced of its superiority. When I first rode it over the streets of Dublin it took me just one turn round " Nelson's pillar " to be convinced that granite setts and rough surfaces had lost their terrors for good and all.

" A pleasurable experience that can never be repeated by the ancients and is denied to their successors." I was on velvet for once in my life. Then was produced the first bicycle, one wheel of which, and its original tyre, is to be seen in the Royal Scottish Museum in Edinburgh, and is reputed to have covered 3,000 miles. The rear wheel was removed from the machine and sent to Paris in an endeavour to maintain Dunlop's claim for a French patent which, however, was unsuccessful.

JOHNNIE AND THE FIRST PNEUMATIC-TYRED BICYCLE.

The annals of invention teem with interesting episodes and stories of the odd sources from which inventors have obtained their inspirations. For instance, a man stood waiting for a street-car in Washington ; he picked up a hairpin from the sidewalk, idly bent it around his fingers. It suddenly occurred to him that this piece of wire, properly bent, could be used to hold papers together. That marked the birth of the paper clip, a lone effort which brought a large fortune. And every school-child for a century has been familiar with the tale of James Watt and his kettle, an incident, by the way, claimed by other countries and ascribed to other inventors.

One such story has clung persistently to the Thomson-Dunlop tyre since its inception fifty years ago, Dunlop being credited with attempting, as his first experiment, to utilise a length of garden hose as a tyre for his son's cycle, and the story, which in itself is in no way derogatory, has never died, notwithstanding frequent and even vehement denials, both verbal and in writing, in later years by Dunlop, who characterised it as a " myth," and childish at that.

Nevertheless, Dunlop came very near to describing a hose pipe when he wrote, " at length it dawned on me that the problem . . . might be solved by means of a triple tube of rubber, canvas and rubber distended with compressed air."

The story is as old as the patent itself, being even sponsored, it is said, by Dunlop himself on occasions, and no doubt had its origin with the late Sir John Fagan, one of Ireland's most distinguished sons and a commanding figure in the surgical world. He was a founder of the Belfast Children's Hospital, one of the great teaching hospitals, twice President of the Ulster Medical Society and one of its few honorary Fellows, a distinction which he shared with Lister, before he gave up his surgical practice in Ulster in 1897, to the dismay of his friends and patients, to occupy the post of Inspector of Reformatory and Industrial Schools. In recognition of his forceful and successful methods in that position he was appointed medical member of the General Prison Board, and afterwards became a deputy Lieutenant for the County of Dublin, and was knighted in 1910. He had a fine presence, a gracious manner and was regarded by his students with deep respect and affection. He died, aged eighty-six, on St. Patrick's Day, 1930.

Sir John was a frequent caller at the veterinary establishment in May Street, for Johnnie was his patient and Dunlop was his " vet," and was wont freely to relate to his friends that in attending Dunlop's son, he had suggested that cycling would be an excellent form of exercise for his particular case, but that it would be better still if they could mitigate the " jarring " which he deprecated and of which Johnnie complained. Dunlop first tried a hose-pipe filled with

SIR JOHN FAGAN.

water as a tyre (the use of water was claimed by Robert Scott in his Patent 16805, October 1891, and he was not the first), but with unsatisfactory results, and witnessing this, Sir John, having experience in his work of the practicability of air cushions and mattresses, suggested the use of air instead of water. Then followed Dunlop's experiments with the miniature disc wheel and enclosed air tube.

Sir John never in any way sought to claim credit for himself for his contribution, but frequently related the incident as an interesting fact, and I have verified his statement as being still within the personal recollection of intimate friends of his and emphatically vouched for by them, by his distinguished son, Lieutenant-Colonel Bernard Fagan, D.S.O., and by other members of Sir John's family. They certainly regard it as an indubitable fact that these two minds working together for a merciful purpose hit upon and revived the long-lost principle of the pneumatic tyre, a circumstance which must silence for ever the doubters, if any be left, who were wont to suggest that Dunlop had been assisted by knowledge of the Thomson patent. The medical advantages were stressed in the prospectus of the Founder Company, which claimed that the air tyre was " most indispensable for ladies and persons of delicate nerves."

The late Henry S. Doig, in an article in the *Sunday Dispatch* (inaccurate though it was in some of its details), referred to the " charming little story " of the garden hose, the father and the son, and added " I treasure it the more, for Mr. Dunlop himself told me, to my great delight, that it was perfectly true," a statement which is also within the recollection of others now living.

Whether Dunlop's idea was wholly original or not, seems to be beside the question, for the fact will ever remain that, however it came about, he it was who first put the pneumatic principle into everyday use by evolving the cycle tyre, and for that he has earned and received the commendation of the world.

CHAPTER FOUR

RIVAL CLAIMS
I

FOR the purposes of comparison I have set out in essence the claims made by the two Scotsmen in their patent tyre specification.

THOMSON	DUNLOP
10th December, 1845.	*31st October*, 1888.

"An improvement in carriage wheels which is also applicable to other rolling bodies.

"The nature of my said invention consists in the application of elastic bearings round the tyres of the wheels of carriages, for the purpose of lessening the power required to draw the carriages, rendering their motion easier and diminishing the noise they make when in motion.

"*I prefer employing for the purpose a hollow belt composed of some air and*

"An improvement in Tyres of wheels for bicycles, tricycles, or other road cars.

"To afford increased facilities for the passage of wheeled vehicles—chiefly of the lighter class such for instance as velocipedes, invalid chairs, ambulances —over roadways and paths especially when these latter are of rough or uneven character as also to avoid the sinking of the wheels of vehicles into the ground when travelling over boggy soil or land ; and likewise for the tyreing of wheeled vehicles generally, in all cases where elasticity is watertight material, such as caoutchouc or guttapercha and inflating it with air, whereby the wheels will in every part of their revolution present a cushion of air to the ground or rail or track on which they run.

" *The belt may be made of a single thickness of india-rubber or guttapercha in a sheet state and then enclosed in a canvas cover.*

" A pipe through which to inflate the elastic belt with air was passed at one place through the tyre of the wheel and fitted with an air tight screw cap.

" Figure 8 shows a side view of a pair of railway wheels. The elastic belts are also particularly applicable to carriages propelled by steam on common roads. The comparatively small amount of power required to propel carriages, the wheels of which are fitted with these belts ; the steadiness of their motion, the absence of all jolting and consequent security of the machinery from injury, the

requisite and immunity from vibration is desired to be secured, and at the same time *ensuring increased speed in travelling* owing to the resilient properties of wheel tyres according to my invention.

" In carrying out my invention, I *employ a hollow tube tyre of india-rubber surrounded with cloth canvas* or other suitable material adapted to withstand the pressure of air introduced and contained within the tube tyre as hereunder mentioned.

" The canvas or cloth being covered with rubber or other suitable material to protect it from wear on the road. Said hollow tube tyre is secured to the wheel felloes—say by a suitable cement or by other efficient means—and is inflated with air or gas (as the case may be) under pressure, being introduced to the interior of the hollow tube tyre through a small duct formed in the rim of small damage the carriages will do to roads, the absence of nearly all noise, *the high speed that may safely be attained and the great gentleness of the motion, will, I think, enable steam carriages to be run on common roads* with great advantage both for carrying passengers and goods."

the wheel and provided with a non-return valve."

In view of the disclosure in Thomson's specification, the following amendment to Dunlop's Patent specification was granted in 1892 at his own request on the ground that his original claim might be understood to cover more than he was entitled to, *i.e.*, the compressed air principle as applied to tyres :

" I would have it known that I make no claim to the construction or use of any tyres, which are not in accordance with the description set forth in the last preceding paragraph of this specification, commencing with the words ' In carrying out my invention ' and ending with the words ' with air or gas under pressure.' "

It will be seen that Thomson's vision was unlimited ; he ran the whole gamut and specified that his tyres, or " Aerial Wheels," as they were called, could be used not only on bath chairs, but on railways and especially for motor vehicles, at high speeds, illustrating his ideas with copious drawings, while Dunlop, whose patent contained nothing that was not in Thomson's, showed but one drawing, and more modestly claimed that his invention was made chiefly for the lighter class of vehicle.

It is a coincidence that Thomson, foreseeing the puncturing difficulty, claimed that he could use a number of air tubes " clustered " together in one tyre, each supplied with its own screw-down valve, or alternatively an air tube divided into a series of isolated sections, the removal of an air tube or section being provided for by an opening in the side of the cover secured by lacing. Dunlop also claimed the employment of " tubes," presumably for the same purpose, but without mentioning it or making provision for removal.

As regards the more technical aspect of Thomson's pneumatic tyre, I have reproduced his own final patent specification (see Appendix, p. 300). It will suffice, therefore, to point out here one or two further points of difference or resemblance between his and Dunlop's tyre.

Thomson used a cap as his valve to retain the air while Dunlop had a one-way valve (Patent No. 4115, March 1889), which could not be deflated, neither of these devices being fully effective. Dunlop also protected his method of sticking his tyre to the rims (Patent No. 41168, March 1889).

Thomson, who obtained a French patent in 1846 and an American patent in 1847, described his air tube as being of several thicknesses of canvas, each saturated with rubber solution on both sides, and laid one upon the other, all being thus cemented together and crudely vulcanised, *or as an alternative that it might be made of a single thickness of indiarubber in a sheet state and then enclosed in a canvas cover*, thus describing the actual method subsequently employed by Dunlop, a fact which is constantly ignored. Dunlop applied for a patent in France for the air principle, but in no other foreign country.

The steel-studded tread, many years later to become a popular non-skid *innovation*, was also a feature of

44

Thomson's tyre to provide an " improved bite " on the road.

While Thomson made ingenious provisions against puncturing, cutting and skidding, yet his tyre was put together by hand so as to form a permanent part of the wheel in practice, as was Dunlop's, and experience has since shown that by this method they could not have

THOMSON'S AERIAL WHEELS.

possessed the strength and durability to withstand the weight and strain of heavy road traction. Not being detachable, their tyres could not be vulcanised in manufacture into one homogeneous whole under heat and pressure, even if that method had been known and available.

Wheels fitted by Thomson with specimens of his earlier tyre, and sold to Lord Loraine, of Albury Park, Guildford, may be seen at the Science Museum, South Kensington, to which they were lent by me many years ago. A set of these tyres came into the possession of the Founder Company, having come to light before all hope of amending Dunlop's original patent or obtaining its amendment to give it the scope of a master patent had been abandoned. Accordingly, when this occurred, it was suggested to Dunlop that, in view of the possible bearing of Thomson's old wheels and tyres on the validity of his patent, he should purchase them, but to this he demurred, and in February 1895 the Board authorised up to £500 to be paid for these ancient relics to Mr. Joseph White who had forwarded the wheels.

II

Usually an invention leads to a whole crop of ideas for improvements or alternatives, some good and many bad, but this was not the case with Thomson's patent, which had no imitators even though it was much used in public, had always been available to searchers in reference libraries and the files of the Patent Office and was described and illustrated in the *Mechanics Magazine* of March 17th, 1847, and again in 1849 (see Appendix, p. 297).

Dunlop was not the only person to re-discover Thomson's ideas, for in addition to the studded tyre, two tyres were marketed in the early 'nineties by two companies based upon claims made by Thomson in his 1845 patent ; one called the " pleumatic," embodying his method of expanding the tube with a spongy material to minimise cutting and puncturing, and the other, the Kerry tyre, reproducing his laced opening as a means of access to the tube.

Thomson was well remembered by the engineering profession, but although his tyres were running on the streets of Edinburgh up to 1872, there is no record that his patent was discussed in public prints after 1849 until a leaflet was published, apparently in 1887, the year in which Dunlop began his pneumatic tyre experiments,* by William O. Aves, of the Barbican Works, London, E.C., a student also of anti-vibratory methods, and a pioneer and improver of the bicycle, who obtained six patents between 1875 and 1891 in connection with wheels and tyres. The late H. Hewitt Griffin, the well-known compiler of bicycling, motoring and other statistics, and an authority in these fields, drew attention in *The Irish Cyclist* of February 9th, 1910, to Aves' leaflet which was on the subject of anti-vibratory wheels and was entitled " The following are selected from the eighty specifications of ' Elastic Wheels ' filed by inventors at the Patent Office between the years 1772 and 1887."

There were four inventors " selected," including " Robert William Thomson, civil engineer, of Adam Street, Adelphi, London, 1845," and drawings of each were shown.

Dunlop's invention had become generally known in 1889, two years later, but Aves remained silent, as Griffin pointed out in the following qualified statement which he made :—

" The leaflet does not bear any date (*i.e.*, of issue), but must have been printed in 1887 in relation to a patent of his own. I received the sheet at the time of its issue, but could not trace it or remember details. A day or two ago I unwrapped a parcel of old MSS. relating to work I was engaged on in 1884/5—statistics of the last (1884) and earlier Reform Bills, done up with these were

* He wrote : " At last I thought of the Pneumatic Tyre. That would be about October, 1887." *Scottish Cyclist, March 17th*, 1909.

several old cycling documents of 1885, and the enclosed (*i.e.*, Aves' leaflet) which had lain perdu for about 22 years. Why Aves did not bring it forward again at the debut of the Dunlop I know not—perhaps he was interested in some other line of invention and overlooked the matter.

" Anyhow, here is the original sheet—issued before the Dunlop was re-invented—and as it must have had a pretty fair circulation, it is strange that it was not brought forward at the time. But for the date on it (*i.e.*, ' between the years 1772 and 1887 ') I would have set it down as at least two years earlier, owing to other documents with which I found it. Anyhow, Aves brought the invention to light—to be re-re-re-found by ' Bicycling News ' (actually by Charles Wheelwright * of ' Sport & Play,' a journal which was afterwards incorporated with ' Bicycling News '). If the original promoters of the first Dunlop had seen it, in 1888, cycle history might have been different."

Both Aves and Dunlop had for long been thinking of spring wheels, and it is to be noted that the leaflet refers to " Elastic Wheels," and not specifically to tyres, and for this reason may not have attracted the general attention it deserved.

Dunlop disclosed his knowledge of the Aves leaflet and the Thomson patent in a letter to the Secretary of the Founder Company dated September 11th, 1890, and subsequently stated that it had come into his possession in Belfast, through Mr. Hunter, a pawnbroker of that city, who had received it from Mr. Redfern, a London patent agent. Dunlop was unable to remember the date upon which he received it, but his letter is revealing as showing his then state of mind.

* See p. 102.

48

I also enclose a leaf which was sent to me from London a few months ago and you will find thereon a description of a patent dated 1845 similar to my first patent. It is doubtful if my first for tyre is valid

You will require legal advice as to which patent is valid if either

Please take Care of my paper indicating old patent

SEPTEMBER 11TH, 1890.

The receipt of this letter was kept secret by the company for obvious reasons and was not entered upon the Minutes.

In a letter to the Press in 1896 Dunlop again reverted to this matter, when he said :—

" A considerable time after the Pneumatic Tyre Co. was floated I received from Messrs. Redfern & Co. a leaflet illustrating four spring wheels or tyres. One of the wheels was Thomson's fitted with his tyre. I immediately forwarded the leaflet to the Pneumatic Tyre Co. This occurred a short time before the old patent was unearthed."

The old patent was " unearthed " and published to the world at large on September 30th, 1890, but it was then no news to the company, or presumably to others who may have known of it since 1887 through the Aves leaflet and the records of the Patent Office, that is if Griffin's facts with regard to its date are facts, which seems, on the face of it, to be the case.

Dunlop acknowledged that " very many engineers and scientists in England were aware of Thomson's invention from the first," and that through the articles published " thousands must have known of it," but he passed his word that he himself had never heard of it until 1890, and had not been influenced by it, and his colleagues who knew him best accepted that, and so my father stated publicly on more than one occasion. As for those who did not know Dunlop and were not so convinced, it is surely one of those things which they can hardly presume to judge. After all, there can be no monopoly of intellect and therefore no end to unconscious plagiarism.

Progress can be compared to a chain in which no one link is of greater importance than the other, and even though Dunlop's claim to the envied position of the first link must be ruled out, yet the chain of progress might never have been forged without him. The inventor, the adapter, the improvers and those who commercialised their ideas were all links in the chain and it is invidious to deny honours to any in a sequence in which all are necessary to achieve the goal. On this reasoning even Charles Goodyear and Thomas Hancock should not be overlooked.*

* See pp. 155 and 156.

CHAPTER FIVE

SPEED THE INCENTIVE
I

CYCLE racing in 1889 was a popular sport, almost comparable with tennis to-day, and a fortnight before my meeting with Dunlop, in June of that year, W. Hume of Belfast, a medium rider only, had carried all before him, against high solid-tyred bicycles, riding the first pneumatic racing safety ever built or used on a racing track and defeating two of my brothers among the rest. This sounds, perhaps, an unexciting event, but on that day history was being made. *Thomson's invention had been publicly exhumed* after its long oblivion and the effect was instantaneous. When it appeared on the track, the dwarf machine, the gearing of which was not even then fully understood by the public, was hailed with a roar of laughter and derision from the crowd, because of its low unsightly appearance, compared with the sleek slimness of their old favourite, the ordinary bicycle.

Everyone who looked upon himself as a wit loosed his shafts at the unfortunate, or fortunate, Hume, but only those who can remember the machines and tyres of those days can realise the amount of reason which lay behind the jocularity of the crowd. But to the stupefaction of the onlookers the ugly interloper outpaced all rivals so decisively that their derision was turned to hysterical applause.

Now two weeks later I was at the same track to put it to a more searching test in a contest for the five-miles bicycle championship of Ireland, and when Hume and I and the rest faced each other at the starting-point, he on his pneumatic safety and I on my solid-tyred safety, the excitement of the spectators was intense, although the result was in their view a foregone conclusion. The foreigner from Dublin would bite the dust. But the

Solid Tyres   Pneumatic Tyres

versus

1st
June,
1889

Arthur du Cros.   William Hume.

unexpected happened once again, and the winning of that championship, with something to spare, under conditions most favourable to the pneumatic tyre, not only upset the expectations of the crowd, but also apparently the claims of the inventor ; a performance which was to be repeated later in the year by J. P. Butler in a fifty-miles road race in the Phœnix Park, when he, on his solid-tyred safety, defeated Hume and other leading riders on pneumatics. As was to be expected, in the face of these results the speed qualities of the tyre, even among experts, continued to be a matter of controversy for many months.

My father and I left Belfast that day with the previous

defeat of my brothers avenged, but with no great opinion of the speed qualities of the new tyre, whatever time might have to show as to its smooth running or comfort, and with no thought of business in our minds. Soon after I again competed successfully against pneumatic tyre riders, this time on a hard fast track, still on my solid tyres, thus upsetting current theories once more, and it was not until later in the year 1889 that by the courtesy of Dunlop my father and I had the opportunity of forming our own opinions. Then, on both grass and hard tracks I tested it for myself, conceding flatteringly long handicaps, and won every championship and every race in which I competed on even terms, reaching a conclusion with my father upon the merits of the pneumatic tyre from which we never afterwards wavered and which riveted our attention upon this development.

On September 14th, 1889, I entered for the ten-mile scratch race for the Surrey Challenge Cup at the Oval; thus did the first pneumatic tyre come to London. As the race was advertised as being open to ordinary and safety bicycles my entry was sent from Ireland and accepted on the advertised basis, but when I arrived on the ground, accompanied by that fine sportsman Jack Dunbar, proprietor of the *Irish Sportsman*, neither of us ever having been in London before, I was informed over the heads of the crowd by George Lacy Hillier, a forthright and deservedly popular figure of imposing presence, and now, with "Faed" Wilson, an octogenarian *doyen* of the cycling world, that safeties had been barred, so that although, as champion of Ireland, I

G. L. HILLIER.

53

represented my country, I should not be allowed to compete. There was such fierce finality about Hillier's words that I felt as Jack must have felt when confronted with the Giant, and we returned to Ireland with a brand new grievance which lasted us for years. Jack Dunbar fairly quivered with rage, and during the next twenty-four hours I received a liberal education in Anglo-Irish expletives which has stood me in good stead ever since ; only, he *would* keep waking me up in the middle of the night to tell me some new ones.

It seems I was the victim of a campaign which was being waged in conservative England against the safety bicycle, for I was not even permitted to enter upon the track to produce the written acceptance of my entry by the Committee, of the cancellation of which no notice had been given, except through advertisements in English cycling papers which did not penetrate to Dublin. The only importance of all this was to delay for half a year the public advent of the pneumatic tyre to London. Time has allayed this particular grievance, but, it being well known that no Irishman can ever be happy without one, and, seeing the rate at which they are now being settled, I would appeal to British and Irish statesmen alike to pause before it is too late, for the thought of an " Eireland " without a grievance is one to make any patriot shudder.

The incident is green in my memory still, because of the derisive hilarity with which I was greeted in the preliminary outing which I had on the morning of the meeting and at every point between Euston and the Oval. Omnibus and hansom drivers, making the most of a heaven-sent opportunity, had the time of their lives ; messenger boys guffawed at the sausage tyre, factory ladies simply squirmed with merriment, while even sober citizens were sadly moved to mirth at a comicality which was obviously designed solely to lighten the gloom of their daily routine. There are many forgotten heroes in history, not the least of whom was the man who wore the first silk hat ; his name, whatever it was, should be commemorated with my own and that of the stalwart who carried the first umbrella, for we all deserve immortality.

Not until April and May, 1890, at London and Birmingham were the superior speed qualities of the air tyre effectively demonstrated against the pick of English riders. Englishmen and their cycling press had remained unimpressed and unconvinced by the successes achieved in Ireland, Liverpool and other places by Irish riders who happened not to be in the first flight. But at the Oval Frank Shorland and G. L. Morris and at Birmingham my brother Harvey and I met and defeated some of the best English scratch riders of the day on equal terms, the former upon their best grass track and we on one of their fastest cinder tracks. Since no Irishman had ever before successfully challenged the bicycling cracks of England, the shock reverberated throughout the cycling world.

I still possess the original telegrams sent to Ireland on that and other occasions, one being from Paris when the tyre made its first appearance over there.

Ashton-under-Lyne : " First, second and third in mile ; second and third in two miles."

Loughboro : " Willie won all the races."

Leicester : " Won all races, second in two. Arthur won Challenge Cup."

Birmingham : " Arthur and Harvey beat Leitch and other best men of England to-day. Harvey beat Leitch in trial heat ; Arthur first in final."

Paris : " Arthur won scratch race handicap and scratch tricycle race ; Harvey second scratch race."

The latter events imbued Frenchmen with the spirit to excel and set their feet on the path which led them to pre-eminence in the athletic field.

Later in the year 1890 a team of six Irish riders, " The Irish Brigade," visited London and swept the boards

B. W. Pigott.   K. N. Stadnicki.   R. J. Mecredy.   F. F. MacCabe.

Arthur du Cros.   Harvey du Cros.
THE IRISH BRIGADE, 1890.

wherever they competed, R. J. Mecredy, a fine Irish rider and sportsman, winning the four open championships for which he entered. That settled it ; there was not a racing cyclist left who did not clamour for pneumatic tyres ; the trouble was to obtain them. A belated effort by the die-hards to have pneumatics " warned off " the track—a unique testimonial in itself—came to nothing ; the tide was flowing too strongly. Of these first rank fliers of those days there are still alive Ernest Leitch, W. C.

Jones, A. G. Fentiman, Lewis Stroud, A. J. Watson, Harry Parsons, A. T. Mole, W. Price, and others.

II

The heated discussions, arguments and controversies which raged throughout those early years, both in the Press and out of it, gave the pioneer tyre gratuitous advertising throughout the world, to the value of many hundreds of thousands of pounds, and contributed enormously to the rapidity and completeness of the conversion of the public. Thus it was that cycles and cycle-racing supplied the medium, the publicity and the demand for the Thomson-Dunlop invention, all of which had been lacking in 1845, and the supreme value of racing as a testing and publicity medium was again to be demonstrated from 1895 onwards in the popularising of motoring and the perfecting of the motor car, the aeroplane and the motor tyre.

Had the pneumatic cycle tyre not proved its superiority on the track from the moment of its first appearance, it would have been laughed at for many a long year, but its racing successes riveted public attention upon it, and convinced the world of its outstanding qualities. So certain were we of the Founder Company of the value of this appeal to the sporting instincts of the British public, that no efforts were spared to develop cycle racing and encourage

J. BURNLEY, TRAINER.

riders. Training facilities under Jack Burnley, a competent trainer, were arranged, a regiment of professional

H. W. BARTLEET.

pacing teams with multiple machines was organised under the command of H. W. Bartleet, to-day's chief authority on cycling history, and one of the earliest members of the company's staff, and placed at the disposal of the great riders of the day. As a result of these thorough measures records were made and broken both on the road and path with startling rapidity, and championships were won until there were no more worlds left to conquer. In 1899 human pacing was superseded by motor pacing and then it was that motor-racing entered the field and began to monopolise

DUNLOP PACING TEAM, 1897.

58

the attention of the company and of the sporting world.

Among the more interesting records accomplished was that achieved by Dunlop himself, who, in 1895, was pronounced to be a professional cyclist by the National Cyclists' Union of England, although he had not then mastered the art of riding a bicycle. Together with his elderly colleagues on the Board of the company he was " suspended " from racing under amateur rules on the assumption that he and they were parties to the financing of amateur riders. Goaded to exasperation by this injustice, Dunlop retaliated by learning to ride the bicycle.

J. B. DUNLOP.

I feel bound to confess to a gnawing jealousy of Dunlop at this time. He was first an amateur, then a professional, and after that an amateur again, while I was only a " tweeney," that is, neither one thing nor the other. This arose when I entered for the Plymouth Cup in 1895, of which I was the holder, and was forbidden to ride by the powers that reigned on no other ground but that my amateur's licence had been arbitrarily withdrawn without notice for no reason given. This being a repetition of the " Oval " method, and one such grievance being enough at a time, I journeyed to Plymouth, and *after* the start of the race was discovered, to the *apparent* surprise of the officials, who were a sporting crowd, tucked well in among the large field of

59

competitors. I meant to win the cup twice, once on the track and once in the law courts. But it was not to be ; I lost handsomely to a sterling little sportsman, A. J. Watson, who, I am convinced, " never tried a yard "

A. J. WATSON.

until he saw that I was out of the race ; he and all true amateurs detested the Star Chamber methods of the ruling body, who promptly suspended me from the society of amateurs and professionals alike. This incident darkened a career otherwise reasonably free from crime, but, as hope dies hard in the human breast, I am still optimistic that the prodigal may yet be received back to the fold in time to snatch another championship or notch up another record. The hope is a fading one, I admit, but I still ride my bicycle—just in case.

Lord Loraine probably holds the record as the first purchaser of a set of pneumatic tyres, and Harvey du Cros gave the highest price ever paid. Hume made the first purchase of a Dunlop-tyred bicycle and the writer scored the first Irish championship to be won — both in 1889. R. J. Mecredy won the first English championship while A. G. Fentiman made the first British record, and the writer again the first world's record, all in 1890. After that records

" JUST IN CASE."

became as unstable as the English summer weather.

Other picturesque records made in those early days were those of Charles Terront, of Paris, and R. L. Jefferson, an Englishman. Terront rode from St. Petersburg (now Leningrad) to Paris in 1893, a distance of 2,000 miles, finishing at the Velodrome in the presence of an enthusiastic crowd, in fourteen days, seven hours and thirty-one minutes. Jefferson, in 1898, rode from England to Khiva, in Chinese Turkestan, across Europe and Western Asia, a distance of 5,482 miles in four and a half months, a marvellous feat of endurance when one considers the absence of roads in many places, the fording of streams and the crossing of deserts and mountains. Both these performances were accomplished on Bartlett-Clincher tyres, which subsequently became formidable opponents of the Founder tyre.

R. L. JEFFERSON.

In view of the world-wide publicity of these times, it is hardly to be wondered at that Thomson's pneumatic vehicle tyres of 1845 were heard of and used by the few, while Dunlop's cycle tyres were known to millions and used by all who could get them, with the result that from the first the inventive brains of the world became concentrated upon the essential problems of improvement.

The historic racing bicycle, the first ever built, which opened the ball at the Queen's College Sports at Belfast on May 18th, 1889, is to be seen in the unique collection of " Old Crocks " assembled by H. W. Bartleet, which forms a museum to itself in Coventry, this machine being still adjusted to suit my own stretch, just as it was for the occasion on which I cleared the boards on it at Cork in

September 1889, and subsequently appeared as a figure of fun at the London Oval. I was the last to ride it.

So far Dunlop had achieved success only upon the racing track, where slipping and puncturing were secondary factors. It remained to produce tyres in quantity which, besides being speedy, would also stand up to rough usage on bad or wet roads and the neglect and ignorance of the average rider ; in this sphere formidable obstacles already loomed ahead. The tyre was non-detachable, and had therefore to be built up piece by piece by hand, thus forming a permanent part of the wheel itself. Although sightly and sufficiently durable, the maximum of durability could not be obtained by a tyre cover so constructed, and not vulcanised in one piece, nor could it be guaranteed against deflation or the danger of puncturing ; it was practical, therefore, only to a limited degree even for cycles. These and other problems were gradually emerging ; everyone was feeling his way ; so far only three or four dozen pairs of tyres were in use from which there had been no time to gauge definite results, and as there were no other testing facilities, progress was necessarily slow and uncertain.

The pneumatic tyre was waiting to be developed and exploited as a commercial article. It was obvious that capital, an organisation and a man of force and vision were now required, if a permanent industry were to be founded, and that pointed in the first place to a limited company.

CHAPTER SIX

A MAN OF FAITH AND VISION

FROM Edinburgh to Belfast and now from Belfast to Dublin the story moves where William Harvey du Cros " was issued in 1846," the same year as Thomson's patent, as he put it himself on one occasion when speaking of that event.

His ancestor, five generations before, in 1704, had settled there, a captain of infantry and a Huguenot refugee from the religious persecution of the French dictatorship of that period, who apparently lost no time in " joining up," as he fought for * Queen Anne under Winston Churchill's great ancestor, who, however, from recent publications, seems to have overlooked his presence.

Not a great deal is known of my father's early years and struggles, for as a boy of fifteen, without money or influence, he chose to leave an unhappy home to fend for himself. Unappeasable differences between his parents, in which his sympathies were on the side of his mother, drove him to this step, combined with the insistent ambition and craving for independence for himself and his family which marked the whole of his subsequent career.

From the crown of his head to the soles of his feet, 65 inches in all, this little man was a fighter who was never known to acknowledge defeat. Not pugnacious by nature, or fond of a fight for its own sake, but somehow he always found himself on the side of the weaker vessel, and could never tolerate the sight or sound of injustice. Therefore his way in life could not be easy.

* See Appendix, p. 293.

Of no particular physique in his earlier years, diffident and therefore aloof, sensitive, and sentimental beneath a formal exterior, a more unlikely subject for the role of Don Quixote could hardly have been found. Nevertheless, he possessed an indomitable spirit and something of the resilience of the pneumatic tyre with which his later commercial career was to be so strikingly associated.

As a scholar he held no place, such learning as he possessed being unwillingly absorbed at the King's Hospital, Dublin (founded by Charles II to be " for ever a Free Grammar School," conformable to that of Christ's Hospital in London), opened in 1675, which my father entered in December 1855 at the age of nine and a half, and left in December 1860. This, " The Blue Coat School," was a continuation of the old " Free Schole of the Cittie," the masters of which, in the reign of Henry VIII, were appointed by the Corporation with the duty of teaching twenty children of the free citizens " in humanytie and others the liberal sciences and frealtyes," and the rights of receiving from the Freeman from 3s. to 1s. 6d. a quarter for each child and for other men's children as they might agree ; for something beyond this they were referred to " the curtesies of the parentes according to their dysposycions." Many great names are inscribed on the Rolls of the School, including in 1588 that of the great Primate, James Usher, and in 1662 that of John, eldest son of Sir Winston Churchill ; there was taught, at least for a time, the hand that wrote, and, it is said, misspelled, the despatches of Blenheim and Ramillies.

In my father's day pupils were nominated and selected, it being vaguely understood, however, that they should be drawn from the families of " decayed gentlefolk " (dreadful expression), whose parents would, in better circumstances, have given their children a good education. With its distinctive dress the school was no blessing to its pupils in one respect, for in those days they were a mark for " idle boys without any lawful calling, precursors of the corner boys who are still with us." Scholars found it wiser to take the air in batches, and a knowledge of fisticuffs was not merely an accomplishment, it was a necessity ; the fact also that the " swaddlers " were Protestant and their assailants Catholic lent additional zest and venom to the game. His name, too, pronounced " du Crow," was a never-failing subject for the wit and derision of tormentors and led to many an encounter, wordy and otherwise, all of which, no doubt, had its influence in the forming of my father's character.

BLUE-COAT BOY.

He left behind him no record of scholarly achievement, but his athletic prowess was remembered.

The one recollection of his boyhood days which never faded from my father's memory was that he had never had enough to satisfy his appetite in those early years, and when as a lonely youth, cut off from his home, he was earning a bare subsistence, the hardships he endured spurred him on to unceasing effort to safeguard those for whom he cared from similar experiences.

Gradually success came to him, and when it did, he took protective measures to secure his descendants from the mischances of fortune, not as a check to ambitions or to place a premium upon idleness, for this he despised, but, because his own forebears having fallen upon evil days in a foreign country, he was generously determined to protect his family from a similar fate.

The measure of his courage, if courage it was, may be gauged by the fact that at twenty-two he had married, worked daily from eight o'clock to six as an unqualified book-keeper, was the possessor of two sons and £90 a year. At twenty-six his home had become enriched by four more sons (soon to be increased to seven), and his bank account by an additional £80 a year. If he was not rich in money he was rich in sons.

" NAN." *

What my mother thought of that she kept to herself, but what she did was to reduce thrift to a science, remodelling for us the clothes of our elders on a diminishing scale, the tallest inheriting first, the shortest last, and generally " manage " the eight of us and create a home which to this day remains the happiest memory of my life.

There are wives and wives, as there are mothers and mothers. They can be helpful and practical, unselfish and cheerful, courageous and devoted, loving and loyal, but it is given to few to possess all these qualities. My

* Died May 1899.

mother was one of these, and at the last a vivid picture
is engraven upon my memory of the sublime and saintly
patience with which for a full year this simple natured
woman waited upon her death from a fell disease, with
no sign of self-pity or fear.

My father by his upbringing was stern and just ; my
mother a gentle influence upon us all. The one was
proud of his sons and rarely showed it ; the other was
devoted to them and could not conceal it. She lived to
share his successes and died at fifty-nine in one of
England's stately homes, but her heart was ever in the old
humble days when she was her husband's best and perhaps
only friend.

A letter is extant which she probably helped to write
and the answer to which she no doubt awaited with bated
breath :—

The application was apparently irresistible, for at twenty-three my father obtained the appointment and with it an ever-growing circle of staunch friends, and his first real step towards the independence for which he craved. The sequel to this incident is contained in an address made to my father nearly twenty-five years after, in which these words appear :—

" Having heard of your resignation of the position of Secretary to the Irish Commercial Travellers Association, we desire on behalf of your friends on the Managing Committee of that body, to express our regret at the loss of your services, which have, for the past twenty five years, been discharged with such signal zeal and ability.

" To your efforts, and the energy and ability you have invariably displayed, is largely due the success which our association has attained in promoting so effectually the interests of the Commercial Travellers of Ireland.

" We have heard with pleasure of your election to the position of Vice President of our Association, so that we shall have in the future the benefit of your advice and judgment, which have proved so valuable in the past.

" We wish to take this opportunity of congratulating you on the commanding position in the commercial circles of our City which you now occupy.

" By your distinguished talents, great business capacity, indomitable industry and unfailing integrity, you have succeeded in establishing, on a firm basis, a new industry which though it has made wonderful strides in the past few years, is still in its infancy ; and in connection with which, thanks to you, Dublin has taken a prominent place in the industrial world, and in your person, the business capabilities of Irishmen have been once more demonstrated."

My father seemed to think more of this testimonial from the old friends who knew him best than of the many honours which he received in after life.

68

Later in life the *Revue Franco-Anglaise* in a personal sketch described him as :—

" A dapper gentleman below the middle height with an expressive physiognomy and lofty intellectual forehead —a man also of robust build that bespeaks his ability to take care of himself. Quite modest and of a retiring disposition, he has also the pleasant open countenance which invites friendship and confidence. His infinite capacity for detail, his judgment of character, his perspicacity in choosing able lieutenants, his exactitude in the manipulation of figures and the most necessary of all attributes of successful men—the ready willingness to listen—render his position impregnable."

CHAPTER SEVEN

WE WERE SEVEN

It was a dubious day for his six sons when Harvey du Cros, of whom they stood in considerable awe, was advised by his doctor at the age of thirty to turn his attention to athletics, as his too sedentary life was impairing his health. He did so with characteristic thoroughness and, as a boy of seven, that is in 1878, I can remember a great display and distribution of prizes at the Dublin Gymnastic Club, a very popular and prominent institution, at which he seemed to monopolise attention, winning the fencing and light and middle-weight boxing championships of Ireland and being there or thereabouts in other contests. In those gentlemanly days of amateur boxing the knockout was unknown, and my father was so extraordinarily light and quick on his feet that his opponents complained with truth they never could hit him.

Years later, when as the father of six he ought to have known better, he founded and trained the Bective Rangers Football Club, and as its captain won the Irish Rugby Championship, the annual contest for which in Ireland at that time out-Donnybrooked the Donnybrook of the old days, earning for his pains the thick ear which his picture shows. The only occasion upon which he ever displayed any inventive genius was when he devised a sort of bridle which he wore over his head to protect his other ear, being received with whoops of delight from the assembled multitude when he took the field. He stopped, however, at patenting it. But in 1887 five of the Bective Rangers team played in the first international contest in which Ireland was ever victorious over England, and at the celebration which followed, their founder was able to produce a topical song which he had written on the doings of the club and sing it, too, without clearing the hall.

Not content with his own successes, he conceived the sinister idea of making his sons champions too, and there commenced a period of travail for them, the memory of which time has hardly dimmed. First, we boxed, or at least he boxed, and repeatedly and vigorously demonstrated every punch known to the cognoscenti, whilst we tried not to remain too passive. My father had a fine straight nose and I don't mind admitting now that for years I practised secretly to reach it, but it was never where it ought to have been and mine always

Harvey du Cros when 35 years old ft.

was, as its slightly bent appearance testifies to this day.

Football and gymnastics were among his hobbies and they had to be among ours too. He had a repulsive theory that the effects of a crash could only be set off by subsequent instantaneous action on the part of the crashee; a lightning reaction was the thing, he said, and

71

a lightning reaction it had to be. And so when one of us executed a faultless volplane from the lofty height of a horizontal bar on to the back of his neck, or was winded, kicked or crushed on the football field, while millions of stars gyrated before him and express trains thundered by his ears, he would return to bare life only to hear " The Governor's " voice like the chirrup of a distant sparrow, saying " Up again, Sonny," and so it had to be.

He was fond of sailing a cockleshell in roughish seas when merely to embark was a feat of unerring skill. To hesitate was to be lost in more ways than one ; " Jump, Sonny," he would say, and unless Sonny jumped he would have resort to the low methods of the Press gang ; nor was his grip on the seat of the breeches ever known to fail.

Then, too, he was a swimmer and we were not ; so regularly on Sunday mornings after negotiating two good Irish miles at a walk, trot and gallop, he would take us out one by one quite regardless of what sailors would describe as weather " moderate to rough." The take-off was into deep water which was black and never still, and we slipped and slithered about in pick-a-back fashion on his bare back as we receded from the safety of the shore. He got peevish if we clutched his neck to strangling point, and when we emerged something more than half-drowned and visibly distended from the intake of salt water he would blandly inquire whether Sonny had enjoyed it, and Sonny swore that he loved it and prayed inwardly that another Sunday might never dawn.

Among his other pursuits my father as far back as the late 'seventies possessed a high bicycle, one of the first in Ireland, which was the apple of his eye. We all shared it ; that is, he rode it and we cleaned it—otherwise we were forbidden to more than look at it. Fortunately he was of short stature and presently, although he little knew it, he was housing a team of three proficient cyclists, with three more coming on. An accident which deprived him of a handlebar could not be explained away, and the harmony of the home for a time was not at all that it should have been.

But my father always expected results and when I became a cyclist officially, I accompanied him from Dublin to Belfast, and back, riding a 42-inch ordinary machine with, of course, the solid tyres of the day ; we covered the distance there, 103 miles, in a single day, and for a boy of thirteen that must, seeing that the first motor-car to cover the same ground in January 1898 took two whole days to complete the journey, have satisfied even such a father as mine. In still earlier years I was taken, as a mere matter of routine, over three miles of the rocky road to Dublin and the cobble-stones of that city to the gymnasium, perched on one leg on the twig of the back step of his ordinary bicycle, clinging for dear life to the spring of his saddle, an experience only comparable with some of the lesser Chinese tortures ; but he never knew that.

The " old man," as he was affectionately called, was ingenious too. His work as a book-keeper lay in a Quaker merchant's shop in Dawson Street, which was one street beyond Kildare Street, where for a time we unwillingly went to school and he devised a plan for checking our punctuality. We had to make the detour so as to pass by his window every morning, and this necessitated our being ten minutes before time. But orders had to be obeyed, truth observed, and this scheme circumvented all in one. It was simple ; observing that tramlines were laid in Dawson Street, we, on late mornings, trotted by on the off-side of a tram and on early mornings sauntered idly up and flattened our noses against his window. I have never flattered myself that he was unaware of this device, but it worked.

There was one thing upon which my father was adamant. If it came to his ears that any of us had evaded a challenge to fight, retribution was sure to follow. To beat or be beaten was his law which caused us to exercise a nice discrimination in the daily route we chose to school, for if the gangs were " out " we had to run the gauntlet and that was no joke. If we executed a strategic retreat my father was quite capable of sending us back through the enemies' lines one by one.

My mother, on the contrary, saw only commonsense in a tactical avoidance of the disturbed area and did not hesitate to advocate her views on peace and with some violence on occasions. Thus we had to steer a canny course between three contending parties, which helped perhaps to develop a certain amount of brain as well as brawn. The loss of my mother's only umbrella has never been forgotten. One of us had been cut off and cornered by our foes, and in a suitable *cul-de-sac* was engaged in a duel *à l'outrance* with their chosen champion, surrounded by his gloating fellows, when suddenly he was assailed by a fierce succession of blows which caused him to see at least three opponents where there was but one before. That was my mother with her best, indeed, her only, umbrella now in several pieces, expressing her views on street-fighting, and, bitter thought, not one blow did she even aim at the enemy. I could see her point of view, if only dimly, but that she failed to share her attentions with the assailant was an injustice which rankled.

My father was a strict disciplinarian about our training, which he supervised with an eagle eye, and lights out was supposed to sound at ten o'clock when all doors were banged, barred and bolted for the night. But as the years went by the breaking of bounds, naturally enough, became the order of the day, or rather night. My brother Harvey and I were fortunate in sharing a room which could be easily scaled from the ground, and it became the conduit pipe into the fortress after latish nights in Dublin four miles away—a distance we could easily cover under thirty minutes. The business instinct was stirring too, and my brother and I fixed a reasonable tariff for the passage through our room of late-comers, which was often the cause of whispered but futile recriminations in the early hours of the morning.

On one occasion my two elder brothers applied for entrance at an unconscionable hour which justified a tariff on the highest scale, but after the usual exchange of courtesies on this subject they were admitted. Removing their shoes they made their way with infinite caution to their room in the upper regions ; a creaking stair was followed by agonising moments of petrified waiting, breathing was almost suspended and the simple act of opening and closing their door occupied minutes of time. Safely in, they proceeded to creep into their one bed in the darkness only to discover my father peacefully sleeping there—or apparently sleeping. After a long interval two pallid figures reappeared in our room below where for a really paltry figure they were permitted to rest on the floor for the remainder of the night. The incident was never again referred to ; my father had a twisted sense of humour, and from all I have heard since he had been young himself once.

When all our ingenuity failed in avoiding detection for some flagrant escapade my father was not averse to showing his skill with the ordinary cane, and that was something to be remembered ; but he was not always in the mood and then he would pass us over, cane and all, to our mother with detailed orders; "Nan," however, having taken us to the torture chamber would whisper to us " to do our stuff " or words to that effect, and amidst blood-curdling cries vigorously attack the innocent and empty bed with her cane ; thus was justice done and honour satisfied.

He once rode in a cycle-race himself in which he started from scratch with R. J. Mecredy, then an Irish champion, and was fond of recounting how he finished first, a yard in front of the redoubtable " Arjay." Then the " Governor " would explain with a twinkle in his eye, that he was mounted on the front seat of a tandem tricycle.

Looking back on my father's methods I find that I thoroughly approve of them, for I have found few, if any, joys in the world to surpass the feeling of complete physical fitness. He had to fight to live, and he trained his boys in the same school ; and in such encounters in which inadvertently I became involved in after-life in one part of the world or another, I have never been fatally or even seriously injured ; but then, I was always a fairly decent runner. We learned to be philosophic whether shattered by defeat or with another championship medal in our waistcoat pocket, and instead of mawkishness in the family there were a couple of hundred prizes, none of which was allowed to be used ; clocks ticked by the dozen and there were epergnes, butter-dishes, salvers, cake baskets and mugs unnumbered.

76

In a home stocked like a crowded jeweller's shop, surrounded by a team of sons with whom he could stage a gymnastic, boxing and trick-riding display deemed worthy to fill the largest halls in Belfast and Dublin in aid of the Irish Cyclists' Association Funds, my father must have reaped some satisfaction from all this tireless devotion to athleticism. And later in life he could always

THE DU CROS TEAM, 1888.

be relied upon to back us up in anything of a sporting or pioneering nature which we might undertake. Whether it was the transportation of a battalion of the Guards to Hastings by motor-car, the first experiment in Army mechanisation, the acquisition of the first airship by the nation, the raising of the first ambulance convoys for the front, or competitions of any sort or kind, the " Governor" would be on hand with his approval and his cheque book.

In all matters he took the philosophic view. " Do your best," he would say, " and whether you succeed or fail you have earned your place among the elect." As T. P. O'Connor was to write in later years : " This Harvey du Cros was a very remarkable fellow."

Our education was another matter. The family exchequer, if it could be dignified by such a title, was balanced to a farthing—there were no half-farthings— and a penny a week each was the amount set aside for our day schooling at one of Dublin's " National " Schools, the odour of which clings to me still. That, and some private tuition, preceded our advent into the business world, my own at the age of fifteen being by way of the Civil Service, the bottom rung, I need hardly say, and that by no means at the first attempt. I was paid 12s. 6d. a week, and while I remained there was one person at least in the department who thought I was worth it. For the rest we were dependent upon our own reading and the lessons we learned from contact with the realities of the world, the oldest and hardest of all schools, for which no school tie has yet been designed. I have ever regarded with respect and admiration, those men, and there have been many, who have risen above the sense of inferiority induced by mean surroundings in early life and a haphazard education. They have accomplished something worth while, even heroic.

CHAPTER EIGHT

THE BEGINNINGS OF A GREAT VENTURE

I

It has been commonly supposed that Dunlop disposed of his patents to or by arrangement with William Harvey du Cros, my father, but that was not the case. He made his bargain and disposed of his rights verbally to a Dublin cycle agent, William Bowden, of Bachelor's Walk, who interested himself at times in finance business ; this was the only occasion upon which Dunlop ever offered to sell his patent. The trio no doubt valued the invention on the limited possibilities of the cycle tyre alone, as Dunlop declared that he did not believe in a commercial future for his tyre for heavy vehicles, and in the form in which he conceived it he was perfectly right.

Bowden, with Dunlop's consent, shared his responsibility and profits with J. M. Gillies of Dublin, then manager of a leading Dublin newspaper, both of them being friends of Harvey du Cros, who was widely known throughout Ireland. My father was a noted athlete, a successful figure in commercial circles, and as President of the Irish Cyclists' Association, the governing body of cycling in Ireland, had an intimate knowledge of the conditions of the

J. M. GILLIES.

cycling world. It was commented at the time that " Had he not been a keen sportsman, he would never have seen, or, having seen, appreciated, the potentialities of the pneumatic tyre."

Dunlop some years afterwards wrote to Bowden : " You arranged with me verbally for the flotation of ' The Pneumatic Tyre Company.' The company was successfully floated and so far as you were concerned the arrangements were carried out satisfactorily."

My father, who enjoyed an independent business position without being exactly a Rothschild, took no part in the bargaining with Dunlop, but the promoters of the proposed new company discussed their position with him subsequently, and invited him to join in the project. Bowden and Gillies recognised in Harvey du Cros the one man possessed of the influence and ability to launch and develop the pneumatic tyre, if he could be persuaded to undertake the task. My father asked for time to consider the proposal, and then *stipulated as a condition of his co-operation, that he should assume complete control, appoint the directors, write the prospectus and make the issue to the public.* And that was exactly what he did, without asking for or accepting any profit from Dunlop, the promoters, or the public.

Thus the great adventure was planned at a time when the only experience of the tyre had been gained from its racing successes and the sale of about fifty bicycles added to such goodwill as had accrued from this first advertisement which began to appear in a weekly cycling journal in Dublin in December 1888.

ANTI-VIBRATION
Look out for the new
" PNEUMATIC " SAFETY
Vibration Impossible,
Sole Makers,
W. Edlin & Co.,
33 Garfield Street, Belfast.

F. W. WOODS,
Director 1889,
died July 1936.

R. J. MECREDY,
Director 1889,
died April 1924.

R. BOOTH,
Director 1889,
died April 1930.

ARTHUR DU CROS,
General Manager
to Chairman,
1892–1930.

PIONEERS ALL

FINLAY SINCLAIR,
Works Manager,
1890,
died April 1937.

[*Facing p.* 81

At this early date, as will be seen, the speed qualities of the tyre *under all conditions* were not fully realised, and were not being emphasised. Anti-vibration and ease of propulsion (the equivalent of speed) were the mainsprings of Dunlop's idea as they had been with Thomson.

This was the Board my father appointed, Dunlop's name as the inventor adding to its prestige :

JOHN BOYD DUNLOP : kindly, unassuming, domesti-
cated.

FREDERICK W. WOODS : direct, single-minded, fearless,
just.

RICHARD J. MECREDY : fair, sporting, enthusiastic,
independent, a pioneer among pressmen.

RICHARD BOOTH : amiable, ever satisfied, ever smil-
ing.*

He asked the investing public for £15,010, but even with the subscriptions of the Directors and their following this was not fully subscribed. The Irish people had been enjoying the fun of the fair, but when it came to a question of money they thought the joke had gone far enough. Winning races in the " black North " was one thing, but winning dividends was another, and, after all, the thing *did* " puncture, burst and slip " as was being alleged with some amount of truth. So after paying their bills the Company was left with less than £10,000 in their coffers, not an extravagant sum with which my father was to found a world industry, the capital of which to-day has soared to astronomical figures. Even my mother, whose financial experience was confined to the balancing of her household accounts, looked at her " Willie " at times

* Portraits of later Directors appear on other pages.

as if to assure herself that he had not gone quietly crazy.

As a safety first measure, Booth's Irish Cycle Agency, representing various leading makes of English cycles, had been allied with the tyre with the object of forcing it upon the attention of British manufacturers and in the belief that if the tyre failed the whole capital of the company

---

Pneumatic Tyre and Booth's Cycle Agency,

LIMITED.

Incorporated under the Companies Acts, 1862 to 1886.

Capital £25,000, in 25,000 shares of £1 each.

Issue of 22,500 Shares,

Of which 7,490 fully paid up shares will be allotted to the Vendors, leaving 15,010 shares which are now offered for subscription.

Payable—5s. on application, 5s. on allotment, 5s. on 1st February, 1890, and remaining 5s. when required.

DIRECTORS.

RICHARD W. BOOTH (Messrs. Booth Brothers), Stephen Street, Dublin.
HARVEY DU CROS, Paper Merchant, Northumberland House, Dublin.
JOHN B. DUNLOP, V.S. (Inventor of the Pneumatic Tyre), May Street, Belfast.
RICHARD J. MECREDY (Editor of the *Irish Cyclist*), Middle Abbey Street, Dublin.
FREDERICK W. WOODS (Director, Woods, Webb & Co., Ltd.), Temple Lane, Dublin.

PROSPECTUS.

---

could be justified by the returns on the cycle branch alone, which proved to be the case in the early days of the company.

Edlin and Sinclair, of Belfast, had been retained by Dunlop to assist him with their technical skill after he had made his first experiments ; and as a reward for their secrecy and valuable exploratory services, without which, as Edlin put it, the " invention might have lain dormant for years," they seem to have expected that some permanent place would have been reserved for them by Dunlop, by whose permission they had made and sold about fifty more or less experimental pairs of tyres during the preceding twelve months, the majority fitted to machines of their own make.

But instead of a proprietary or agency interest it culminated in their little business being taken over by the new company for the trifling sum of £490, afterwards reduced to £400, payable in shares, and that the partners should enter its service. Sinclair's, Edlin's and Dunlop's versions of their arrangements form interesting reading :—

Sinclair said in November 1895 :—

" Mr. Dunlop gave us verbal instructions to make twelve bicycles and six tricycles, with a view of putting his invention on the market. These bicycles were designed jointly by Mr. Dunlop and Mr. Edlin. In placing the order, Mr. Dunlop impressed upon us the fact that he possessed considerable means and contemplated resigning his business in the course of a couple of years, also that should the invention prove a success he would support us in its introduction, and would not allow anyone else to make or supply without our sanction. This was entirely a verbal agreement as we had unlimited confidence in Mr. Dunlop."

Edlin said :—

" We had a verbal arrangement only, with Mr. Dunlop, as to the control of his invention, and when the inevitable company was formed, we had to make the best bargain we could, as our financial resources had become more or less exhausted by the heavy drain of 12 months' experimenting with, and forcing the public's interest in the tyres by means of racing machines, etc., and

G 2

placing on the market the first pneumatic tyres and bicycles and tricycles, all of which were made in our own workshops, and without any outside help whatever." *

Sinclair's statement was endorsed by Dunlop as being " substantially correct," when in a letter to the Press he said " I made a very good arrangement for them with the Pneumatic Tyre Company. Indeed I thought more of their interests than my own."

Finlay Sinclair, who became Works Manager, proved a tower of strength to the company in its early difficult years. A man of sterling character and indefatigable energy, he was held in the highest esteem by his employers and enjoyed the liking and respect of all those in the trade with whom he came in contact. To me he was a valued friend and in all the years of my association with him as his chief we never had a wry word. As he said himself, " hard work is a pleasure when we have appreciative masters." Edlin soon left the company's service, preferring his independence.

II

The name chosen by my father for his company was the Pneumatic Tyre and Booth's Cycle Agency Ltd., and as the only pneumatic company in existence it was the mother and founder of all tyre companies.

My father was not only the founder but also the only executive Director of the company, and remained so until 1896, when my own status of General Manager was changed and I became joint Managing Director with him.

* *Irish Cyclist*, October 27th, 1909.

The first Minute passed by the Board was

The Pneumatic Tyre and Booths Cycle Agency, Ltd.
the first formal
At a Meeting of the Board of Directors
held at 65 Upper Stephen Street 30th Nov. 1889
present

F. Woods . R. J. Mecredy
H. DuCros . R. W. Booth
Messrs. Robt Booth . J. M. Gillies.
were also present

Moved by R. W. Booth seconded by
F. Woods and resolved. —
I. That Harvey DuCros be elected
Chairman of the Board of Directors.

It is interesting now to quote from the modest little prospectus he wrote and issued on November 18th, 1889, remembering that he supposed his company to hold a monopoly throughout the British Dominions, as indeed it did—for six months.

" The manufacture of what is known as the Pneumatic Tyre has up to the present only been carried out on a limited scale, but with the aid of the capital now sought the works to be acquired are capable of fitting large numbers of machines.

" The Pneumatic Tyre is composed of a rubber tube about $1\frac{1}{2}$ inches in diameter, filled with compressed air, which is bound to the rim by a linen casing, and protected by rubber thickened at the wearing part. The air is pumped in through a nozzle with a football blower, and a special non-return air valve prevents its escape.

" The advantages which accrue from the use of this tyre upon a roadster cannot be thoroughly understood

85

except by a personal trial. Vibration, with the consequent nervous exhaustion, which tells more against a rider in the course of a long journey than even physical fatigue, is practically annihilated.

" A cycle fitted with pneumatic tyres runs over rough surfaces with extreme ease, and at a pace which under no conditions could be equalled by any other machine, the expenditure of power being the same. The entire absence of noise is also conducive to the comfort of the rider, and the danger and inconvenience arising from tyres coming off is entirely obviated.

" In another respect most remarkable results are secured by the use of this tyre. All vibration is intercepted between the rim and the ground, and consequently the frame of the machine receives no jar, and will last much longer than the frame of the machine fitted with solid tyres. As a result of this, riders will be able to use much lighter frames (to the extent of 15 lbs. to 20 lbs. in Ireland), with a corresponding increase of speed and ease of propulsion.

" This, taken in conjunction with the absence of nervous exhaustion, and the conservation of power through the machine getting over rough surfaces unchecked, will, it is believed, place the pneumatic tyred machine beyond the reach of competition.

" The company intends making these tyres for the trade, the selection of frames being left to the enterprise of the manufacturers and the requirements of agents and their customers.

" The pneumatic tyre will be most indispensable for ladies, and persons of delicate nerves. There is every reason to expect that a large business can be done in fixing pneumatic tyres to the wheels of carriages, invalid chairs, etc."

Commenting on the prospectus a Dublin journal, with a mixture of *naïveté* and wisdom, remarked :—

" We may mention that the Company only contemplate making tyres and they will require very little plant or capital for working expenses ; and should it be decided to let the patents out on royalty, the Company will be in receipt of a large income absolutely without any expenditure," and added :

" We believe that the tyre will wear, and have considered the question from every point of view. At the worst, the shareholders will receive a fair dividend and at the best, the Company should turn out one of the best paying concerns of the day."

Dunlop upon being interviewed was asked : " Are your inventions fully secured from infringements ? " and replied : " Yes, I consider the patents quite safe."

III

It is difficult to believe that at this time *the pneumatic tyre industry of the whole world* was contained in this little Irish company, which was solemnly making decisions and recording events such as these :—

" Resolved that an advertisement be inserted in the *Irish Times* and *Freeman's Journal* for a Salesman." (Minutes, 7.12.89.)

" Resolved that the Manager be instructed to order a ' Belsize ' Safety with pneumatic tyres." (7.12.89.)

" The Secretary was instructed to reply to a letter and state that we cannot see our way to spare a man to go to Leipsic Exhibition as we are so fully occupied in getting out the tyres." (11.2.90.)

" Resolved that we advertise for a Youth having office experience." (4.3.90.)

"The Secretary read a letter from Coventry asking what accommodation was necessary. Resolved that a room suitable for 20 to 30 workers with office and store would suit our purposes." (2.9.90.)

"That a typewriter be procured and the services of a stenographer engaged." (30.9.90.)

"Resolved that a second sewing machine be purchased for the Factory." (28.10.90.)

"That an additional clerk at a salary of 20/- per week be engaged for the office." (3.4.91.)

"The Board approved of the purchase of a desk for Coventry office." (30.8.92.)

And these letters from Dunlop :—

"Tell Mr. Sinclair not to make the valve-tubes too short as when short the tyres are more difficult to fill. See that the nozzles of the pumps are not too sharp as they are liable to injure the valve-tubes." (1.3.90.)

"I suppose you can't do better now than undertake to put the defective ones right. We have had a large percentage of defective ones here. I would rather we should get them than strangers because we can put them right." (3.4.90.)

"Of course a tradesman would require a little instruction in our method of making the tyres but I have not the slightest doubt but he would do his work better. I don't think there is much difficulty in telling whether rubber adheres properly or not. You could easily tell by trying to pull a piece off after it has time to dry." (3.4.90.)

"I hope you are organising and inviting makers and agents to send men to be instructed in putting on and repairing of tyres." (15.4.90.)

"I hope you have written to Coventry and London relative to the method I suggested for preventing the choking of the valves, also to the importance of rubbing the solution (1st coat) well into the flaps." (15.4.90.)

" Before I went to England, Mr. Robertson (the inventor) was talking about asking the Company to cancel his three years engagement. I would be most willing to do so. We will have little to do in repairs for three or four months and repairing would not afford £2 10. 0 per week for one hand excepting we were very busy." (6.9.90.)

" Our old valve as it is now improved is as good as any if we had only a means of deflating." (11.8.91.)

But there were other early and more significant decisions made by the Board. On December 11th, 1889, the proposal of a group of powerful cycle makers, led by C. A. Palmer of the St. George's Engineering Company, and M. D. Rucker of the Humber Company, that a " licence for supplying and fixing pneumatic tyres should be granted to manufacturers," was discussed, and the answer given " that the Board were inclined to adopt the spirit of the proposals."

On December 12th, 1889, the Board resolved that a licence for the fixing of pneumatic tyres be granted exclusively to a " limited number of makers not exceeding ten " at a royalty of 9d. for each wheel. This dangerous decision if persevered in must have had the unfortunate effect of establishing divided interest and control in the industry, but the negotiators attempting to grasp too much stipulated that the licence should be issued to " four first-class firms only." Upon this the Board recon-sidered their position, and after taking soundings in England resolved on December 27th, 1889, " *to throw the pneumatic tyre open to the trade*," a very wise and necessary resolve.

CHAPTER NINE

A WORLD CRUSADE

I

THE public in Ireland and the cycle trade in England were unbelievers. The ridicule and derision with which the tyre had been everywhere received was still almost universal. Important and experienced cycle manufacturers were just as wrong in their estimates as the man in the street, but all their doleful prophecies were to be falsified. J. K. Starley, the head of the celebrated Starley family, pioneers themselves, said :—

" My own impression is that the outcome of this matter will be a greater demand for larger solid tyres and I think, if made of the best quality, they will prove the best in the end." *

The head of the Centaur Cycle Co. was even more emphatic. He wrote :—

" With regard to pneumatic tyres . . . air cannot be permanently confined in any substance such as rubber, owing to its porosity ; after each successive inflation the power of retention becomes less and less. Add to this the series of accidents arising from punctures and defective valves and this must place inflated tyres out of the running for rough and tumble work, in spite of the theoretical advantages that can be adduced in their favour."

Which recalls that Dr. Dionysius Lardner of *Cabinet Encyclopædia* fame in the early days of steam navigation

---

* *Scottish Cyclist and Motor Cyclist*, April 21st, 1909.

proved to his own satisfaction that no steamer could ever cross the Atlantic.

Cycling pressmen, outside Ireland, with but few exceptions were sceptical, many were hostile, and riders and writers alike were disposed to exaggerate obvious defects and invent others to keep them company, but certain writers, notably R. J. Mecredy, A. J. (Faed) Wilson, one of the earliest and most valued recruits to the ranks of the company (founder of the Cycle Trades Benevolent Fund and other cycling institutions),† and E. J. O'Reilly, wrote like men inspired. The latter recorded in after years :—

E. J. O'REILLY.*

" I remember sitting beside him (Mr. Harvey du Cros) one evening as he read the proof of the prospectus, ' Now,' said he to me, tapping me on the shoulder, as was his wont, ' this is your chance. Put all your money into it.' "

O'Reilly added :—

" Mr. du Cros made no mistake from the start, he saw his goal and he made for it straight. He retired from his own business and gave his life to the work of the new Company. He took his sons from their occupations or schools and put them into it."

But in general the virtues of the pneumatic were denied or " poohpoohed," and indeed with its bulging sides it looked a deformity beside the neat little solid tyre of the day. Certainly no one loved it, as my brother

* Died April 1924.
† Any profits accruing from the sale of this book in Britain will be presented to the Cycle and Motor Trades Benevolent Funds.

Harvey found when, in November 1889, he was exhibiting the tyre to English makers. *The Cyclist* opined that " the tyre should last at least a season."

A leading pressman writing of the Stanley Cycle Show of January 1890 said :—

" The contrast was so extraordinarily striking, and the pneumatic looked so utterly clumsy—according to the cultivated taste of those days—that it is not too much to say that a huge guffaw resounded through the house of glass, and we blush to confess that we joined in the chorus—a confession, by the way, which will be shared by practically every conscientious English writer of that period, including some of the most judicial."

Then the impossible was attempted. There were no cycle manufacturers in Ireland, and the machines made in England were unsuitable for pneumatic tyres. Old established conservative makers were coolly asked to incur the expense and disorganisation of altering their plants and scrapping their patterns for the wider forks and chain stays which would be required in order to market this new and comparatively untried tyre, with all its defects.

Worse still, the tyre was not detachable and the doctoring of a deflated tyre was a task for an expert, of whom there were practically none outside the company, and very few within. Consequently makers and agents were invited to send men all the way to Dublin to be instructed in a repairing process which resembled a modern operation for appendicitis with complications. But worst of all, British manufacturers were to be initiated into these mysteries by the tedious and expensive process of consigning their slimly designed streamlined wheels, the very pride of their hearts, across the Channel only to be returned swollen and disfigured by the addition of a tyre reminiscent of elephantiasis, or so it seemed to them, added to which, they were invited to pay £4 a pair for the insult—£5 to the public—as against a mere fraction of that for their well-beloved little solid tyres.

Remembering that little good had ever come out of Ireland, except perhaps prawns and potatoes, and being chary of new ideas, as is the English way, the trade set their backs to the wall. Their seasonal building had started, stocks had been laid in and contracts taken and they would have none of it. Looking back on it all, who can be surprised ? The idea was as fantastic as the tyre itself appeared at that time, but, nevertheless, they were forced to accept it. The company and other Irish agencies were specifying pneumatic tyres with their cycle orders, racing cyclists were demanding them, tourists would not be satisfied until they had tried them, the papers were full of their merits and demerits, their successes and failures, they were being talked of in other countries and it was a matter of favour to obtain a pair ; the revolution was on and gathering force every day ; the whole of cycledom was awake. Enterprising makers made serious proposals to corner the invention, others were afraid of being left out in the cold, the company was spreading the gospel, and opposition, both in the trade and out of it, was being overborne.

It was gradually dawning upon manufacturers that in the much despised Irish invention lay the seeds of a great expansion of their business which, although a comparatively new one, was fast becoming an outstanding industry. And so it proved. Looking ahead a short two years it was to be recorded that at the annual cycle show in London every day from morning till late at night " a struggling crowd stood six and eight feet deep around the counter and behind it, while Arthur, William, Harvey Junior and G. du Cros with ' Faed ' Wilson and other

officials toiled till the per-spiration ran down their faces," demonstrating the new detachable, born of Welch the inventor. The air tyre brought the bicycle into general use and the trade grew to enormous dimensions. For a time even, cycling became a fashionable craze, and footmen cursed the name of Dunlop who had added the bicycle to the lap dog in their daily routine.

A. J. (" Faed") Wilson.

When my father was inducing his friends and the public to join with him in subscribing their money to exploit an article which to the world at large was only another Irish joke, he certainly did not exaggerate when he wrote in his prospectus :

" Nothing so calculated to revolutionize cycling has ever before been invented. There are, it is computed, about 150,000 cycles manufactured in Great Britain annually, and the number is rapidly increasing. If even five per cent. of these were fitted with the Pneumatic tyre, a profit of 10s. per set would represent a net income of £3,750 from that portion of the business."

Where one bicycle was turned out in England in

pre-Dunlop days, dozens are made to-day of a quality unsurpassed by any country. The bicycle has become the poor man's steed and a boon and a blessing to ten millions of our people in Britain alone. Allied trades have benefited in proportion and similar gains have accrued to all other manufacturing countries, so that the output of cycles is now to be reckoned in millions, England alone accounting for two millions a year, of which quite 700,000 are exported.

Time has had its revenges, and were the old solid tyres to return, the cyclist of to-day would gaze upon them with the same curiosity as he would the bone-shaker of old, a phenomenon which has occurred in the case of other inventions ; for the human eye in time becomes accustomed to everything new.

II

Many months of feverish activity followed the formation of the company, which was submerged in the manifold technical and other difficulties of establishing itself. The tyre had been exploited in Belfast before it was ready, and in practice all sorts of unexpected difficulties, manufacturing and otherwise, were constantly cropping up and being overcome.

Athletics were in the du Cros blood, and in the end they profoundly affected the lives of the seven men who were then left of our family. By my father's decision to devote himself to the pneumatic tyre, based upon the experience gained by us in our cycle racing, the Irish home of the family was dissolved never again to be restored. We began to be recruited into the company one by one within a month of its formation and to lay the foundations of this new industry we scattered to the four corners of the earth, my brothers Harvey, Alfred and George settling in America and Canada, William and Fred in Belgium and France, while I migrated to England, and from these countries, with the first pneumatic tyres in our hands, we quartered the globe wherever a cycle business existed. George du Cros, who appears to be gifted with the quality of perpetual motion, in 1891, at the age of sixteen, made with his own hands in Chicago the first pneumatic tyres ever produced on the continent of America.

ALFRED AND GEORGE DU CROS, U.S.A., 1891.

Dunlop by his adaptation of an earlier invention to a modern vehicle, perfected as it was by his brother inventors, provided the material out of which my father designed and erected the commercial structure. Both these men were influenced by their sons : the inventors were the complement of the industrialist, and each in his own sphere contributed to a splendid achievement, the founding of one of the world's greatest industries. The path was strewn with obstacles and failures, but it led in the end to a most notable victory.

My father disliked talking about himself, or for that matter about his sons. He never aspired to be either an engineer or a financier, and had he been professionally minded in these respects he might never have persevered. As a general rule inventors are not business men and business men are not inventors, and my father could not have made or invented anything to save his life. Beyond being able, at a single glance, to distinguish the back wheels of a cycle or motor car from the front, which was not so easy then as this early illustration shows, I doubt if he or I knew much about their internal economy.

An Early "Pennington." *

But many inventions have run their full legal course without being heard of, for lack of the co-operation of business men of energy and imagination, and it may be an advantage that the men who have to develop such businesses should be ignorant of technical details and, therefore, undeterred by their difficulties.

Harvey du Cros Jnr.

Within a few months my father had visited France, Germany and the United States, arriving in

* From " The World on Wheels."

New York on Christmas Day, 1890, carrying with him the first tyres to be seen in those countries. Connections were established and branches and factories opened.

To Alfred Featherstone of Chicago was entrusted the American development, soon to be replaced by the American Dunlop Tyre Co. under Harvey du Cros, Junior, hitherto General Manager in England, who sailed for America in November 1892.

FRED DU CROS.*

In France Adolphe Clément, the Dick Whittington of Paris and later a prominent and attractive personality, became an enthusiastic convert and investor and partner and continued a loyal friend throughout the whole of his life. The Minutes record in May 1891 that having heard that two of the du Cros Brothers were leaving for America Clément requested that one should be sent to France, and accordingly Fred du Cros undertook the task of initiating the workers into the intricacies of the first or " Mummy " tyre, while Frank G. Fenton acted as liaison officer, one of the earliest and best friends of the company and a fine and popular sportsman. Clément was found dead in his car in the Rue Lafitte, Paris, on May 11th, 1928.

With the German business was associated Herr

* Died May 12th, 1917.

98

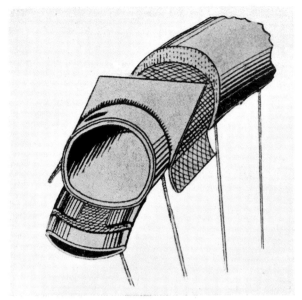

DUNLOP'S " MUMMY " TYRE, 1888.

Heinrich Kleyer, since become a prince of industry in his own country, and formerly a noted racing cyclist, whose masterful methods made it none too easy to run with him in double harness ; but the foundations which were laid were of such an order as fully to justify his restless energy and initiative.

William du Cros, who, with " Faed " Wilson, coined the somewhat inaccurate slogan for the new

FRANK G. FENTON.*

* Died August 1933.

H 2

HEINRICH KLEYER.

tyre " first in 1888, foremost ever since," was ambassador at large on the Continent with headquarters at Brussels, and he and I pioneered through the northern countries, my own travels taking me from Moscow to Lisbon, and back again.

The Dublin Corporation, supported by the Dublin Trades Council, selected this moment to harass the company, taking action against it on the ground of nuisance created by the odour of rubber solution which offended the sensitive nostrils of the dwellers on the banks of the River Liffey. The only solution they would hear of was the removal of the business. The Corporation lost its case at the first hearing, but appealed, whereupon the Board did not wait upon the event but resolved " that in the interest of the company's business it was

WILLIAM DU CROS.*

desirable to move the manufacture of the tyre from

* Died September 1937.

100

Dublin to Coventry." And accordingly this was done, and so it was that tyre-making emigrated from Ireland not to return for forty years.

Perhaps too much stress has been laid upon this incident, and too many stones cast at the Corporation, for candidly it would have been impossible for the company to continue for long to conduct its business from a point so far removed from the centre of the cycle trade, especially with a fixed tyre which necessitated wheels being sent over from England for fitting. As the consumers were in England, the suppliers had to be on their doorstep, but nevertheless the spirit of the attack was plain and would no doubt have harrowed the soul of the Taoiseach in these days of self-sufficiency. It was not to be foreseen that a factory, which has grown into a town, would ultimately be founded at Birmingham, with others in London, Coventry, Rochdale and elsewhere, by the exiles of Erin who followed their trade to England.

III

Then, in the autumn of 1890, our happy dream of success became a nightmare of failure. It was learned from Dunlop that after all he had no patent for pneumatic tyres, notwithstanding that the patent agents employed had, for the purposes of the prospectus, made a search and reported favourably ; he had been anticipated forty-three years before—anyone and everyone could make and import them if they would and could. Not that everyone would wish to, at least not yet : its puncturing, slipping and deflating propensities had not been overcome and were giving pause : the price was high and a demand for the cheaper or " anti-pneumatic " cushion tyre was growing as a safety-first precaution ; although not comparable for speed and resiliency with the pneumatic tyre, it was thought for a time by cautious riders to be more free from trouble and to give better average results in practice. *Wheeling* had written :—

" It is satisfactory to turn from the Irish invention, with its thorns among the roses, to the less pretentious but we believe more generally suitable cushion tyre. No patent stops the way here, no staggering prices, no pump for inflation, no journey to Ireland and back and no monopoly."

But the publication of the Thomson patent, which was made some time later by Charles Wheelwright of *Sport and Play*, seemed the equivalent of a sentence of death, *and was so regarded by the trade and patent lawyers at the time*, despite Dunlop's subsidiary patents. Instead of a master patent and a world monopoly, the company found itself with no patent, little capital, no factories, no technical knowledge of or facilities for rubber making, and a tyre which, good as it was for a first attempt, Dunlop himself described as a " crude beginning," while arrayed against them was the whole strength of the world's rubber manufacturing industry with their half-century's experience behind them. They had only succeeded in putting the rubber makers of all countries into a new business, and setting on foot a competition which would be unrelenting. Their own plant consisted of a half-a-dozen sewing machines in the attic in Dublin, which was their only works, a few wooden racks and a not-too-liberal

C. WHEELWRIGHT.

supply of scissors and other odds and ends. In fact, possessing nothing but a name, they were starting in the race fifty years behind their competitors.

That no decision was taken to abandon the enterprise as a forlorn hope is a tribute, if one were needed, to the dynamic little founder of the business. But he admitted nothing. The anticipating patent might be circumvented, and if not, there remained a slender hope in Dunlop's subsidiary inventions, the non-return valve and the method of sticking the tyre to the wheel; these might hold the position while he was looking round. Dunlop was sanguine also as to the prospects of his " Treadhold "

THE WORLD'S ONLY PNEUMATIC TYRE FACTORY, 1888.

cushion tyre and spring frame cycle, but of these he could never convince my father who was looking much further afield.

The preserve having been thrown open to the inventors

of the world, why should the company not obtain the benefit of the improvements, which were bound to come ? An inventors' Derby had started, for it was not essential to prove novelty when taking out a patent in those days, and for years the runners were to battle inside and outside the courts, litigation which from first to last was to cost this one company, had they but known it, £150,000, and demonstrate that even sound valid patents do not necessarily spell fortune, especially for penniless inventors.

In addressing his shareholders in this crisis, my father said prophetically, " *Some of these days we may unearth a gem in our researches.*" And he did so, and, as will presently be seen, with it in his possession he became the founder of the pneumatic tyre business for the second time. We shall see presently how he did it.

CHAPTER TEN

SUCCESS OUT OF FAILURE
I

IN the course of my life I have come much in contact with inventors in many varied kinds of activity and have had ample opportunity to study their mentality and methods. Mostly sincere men, they begin by convincing themselves of the intrinsic value of their invention, and then armed with an implicit faith in themselves, they set out to convince the world with a fanatical zeal that is hard to resist, but too often their original act of faith is proved unjustified, although rarely to themselves. The results of creative effort, be it in nature or in art, or in scientific invention, are frequently accompanied by a fierce possessive jealousy. This jealousy of the creator gives rise in the case of many inventors to a tendency to belittle the achievements of their fellow-workers in kindred fields and to a distrust of the commercial mind without which their whole invention would be still-born. Just as no animal can recognise the benevolent intention when it is weaned of its young, so no inventor can realise that his interests and those of the business man are, or should be, identical; both need valid patents, both need practical articles to convert the public, the success of the one is inextricably bound up with the success of the other, and yet their relationship is frequently marred by reticence and suspicion.

Naturally there are many outstanding exceptions to these generalisations, but it must be rare to find an inventor so philosophic that when he finds his cherished idea anticipated or improved upon he will spare a word of commendation for his successful rival. Yet in this no less than in other spheres chance plays a leading *rôle*, and it has been the lot of innumerable inventors to find themselves disqualified by anticipation, defective patenting, lack of support or other accidents of fortune.

The first of the many inventors to attract the attention of the Founder Company was Thos. W. Robertson of Belfast, a racing cyclist and a somewhat erratic personality, who was employed from June 1890 for a time at fifty shillings a week to run the all-important and necessary repair department. He was experimenting with a detachable tyre with wired edges, the ends of which were bent over, passed through the rim and fastened with nuts on the outside. It was in use experimentally in January 1891, being probably the first detachable tyre ever to be used on the road, and later in the year was ridden by the great Jiel-Laval in the Paris to Brest contest.

The patent had been applied for on November 29th, 1890, in the joint names of Robertson, for himself, and du Cros, for the company, as Robertson was still an employee up to June 1891. An agreement was made with Robertson to exploit his patent *conditionally upon its proving valid*, and for a time high hopes were entertained that a master patent for a practical method of attaching and detaching a pneumatic tyre had been secured, but fortune was unsmiling and Robertson by a narrow margin missed fame and fortune and joined the throng of the might-have-beens.

We had heard of Charles Kingston Welch, a London man, who claimed the use of endless wires as a method of attaching and detaching covers, for which he had applied for a patent on September 16th, 1890, ten weeks before Robertson.

In the opinion of the company's patent agents, which was unsound as it happened, Welch could not have prevented the use of the Robertson device ; nevertheless, without hesitation it had been decided to buy his patent, and on April 20th, 1891, my father advised the Board from London that he had agreed to pay £5,000 for the British and Belgian rights, £1,000 for the French and £1,500 for the American, all these patents to be valid, this agreement being signed on May 19th, 1891. As ultimately construed by the House of Lords, the Welch was the first patent for a detachable pneumatic tyre ever recorded in the Patent Office.

Among misconceptions which have prevailed in relation to the pneumatic tyre, is one that my father was not the prime mover in the purchase of the Welch patent. But this was not the case. He and all his colleagues, including Dunlop, had been on the *qui vive* for such a tyre, and as a Board were unanimously in favour of a purchase should the opportunity occur. A letter from Welch's solicitor, John B. Purchase, which is among my father's papers, sets the matter completely at rest, if it is of any importance. It states

JOHN B. PURCHASE.*

* Died October 1934.

with regard to claims made by others to have brought about the acquisition of the Welch patent :

" Now I know this to be untrue because as you will remember the patent was purchased by you at my office through me in about five minutes."

I have referred this account of the matter to Mr. Roland Welch, F.R.I.B.A., who collaborated with his brother in the development of the invention and was conversant with the negotiations for its sale, and he has fully corroborated it. Welch did not insist that his name should be adopted for his tyre and Dunlop's retained its pride of place, Welch's being added for a time to mark its detachability.

Purchase wrote in 1897 :—

" Mr. Dunlop's services on the Welch patent were never required and the only occasion on which it was necessary for him to see Counsel was relative to his own patent, the validity of which he strongly upheld up to the very last moment, long after he had heard of the Thomson patent."

Upon the subject of the validity of his own patent, Dunlop's ideas were not always consistent. He has recorded that he became aware of Thomson in the middle of 1890, and in September of that year expressed doubts as to the validity of his own patent (see p. 48).

Subsequently in October he said :—

" When I made my first tyre I was not aware of the registration of such a patent, and indeed it was not until long afterwards that I heard of it. Had I known that such a thing was in existence I would never have taken the trouble to get mine registered, but would have kept it for my son's amusement." *

* *Sport and Play*, October 28th, 1890.

In 1892 he approved the application for an amendment to his patent in which he disclaimed the invention of the air principle, and in 1896 another tyre company of which for a time he was chairman pleaded in a legal case that Thomson was the first and true inventor. Yet in 1921 Dunlop wrote, " There should have been no difficulty in establishing the validity of my patent in face of Thomson's air tyre, which was never made." Finally, in the same publication,* he acknowledged that in view of Thomson his patent was invalid and it may be accepted that, apart from the somewhat nebulous hope of obtaining an amendment to his specification which would render his patent valid, Dunlop's first and last pronouncements expressed his real opinion.

II

All those who use a cycle, an automobile or an aeroplane should know of Charles Kingston Welch, for it is a thousand to one that the detachability of their tyres is the product of this man's brain. He was born at Tottenham, Middlesex, in March, 1861, and was the eldest of the ten children of Charles Welch, who carried on a small engineering business. He was educated at a near-by private day school, but at an early age showed great constructive and mechanical ability and a genius for invention and was given the run of his father's workshop to encourage and develop his natural bent.

He made most of his own toys and many for his boyhood friends, and at the age of about sixteen built himself his first bicycle which was of the penny-farthing type. In those days few ready-made parts were obtainable, so that he had to make practically everything with his own hands, the frame being evolved from gas or steam tubing.

* *The Motor News*, May 14th, 1921.

This machine had tangent wheels which Welch, then little more than a lad, claimed were the first true tangent wheels ever made.

The family were all of short stature, he himself, a cheerful chubby-faced, blue-eyed stripling, being only just over five feet. He formed an attachment when no more than fourteen for the girl who afterwards became his wife, and is now his widow, whose inches were even less than his, this being the prelude to a long and ideal married life. Whenever I saw these two diminutive people in their home in after years the picture of two little love-birds perched side by side on a bough was brought irresistibly to my mind. Welch was a friendly, lucid and rather shy personality, and of all the inventors I have ever met the most helpful and disinterested.

Once his mind was made up Welch was very sure of himself, seldom wavering in his opinions. Having

decided whom he would marry he proceeded to build a tandem tricycle upon which these two small people were constantly to be seen riding through the then grass lanes round Tottenham, and there can be but little doubt that the couple were the inspiration of that most popular of our old songs :—

> " It won't be a stylish marriage,
> I can't afford a carriage,
> But you'll look sweet upon the seat,
> Of a ' tricycle ' made for two."

The machine, which was of lever action with up and down motion pedals, was wholly designed by Welch, who made every part of it with his own hands, including ball-bearings to the crankshaft, levers, pedal-levers and wheels, as well as a band brake which was a rarity in those days. The machine was in constant use for over twelve years and Welch always maintained that it was among the first, if not the first, tandem to be built with both riders facing forward. There was a previous tandem tricycle with the riders back to back. The making of this machine and his first bicycle gained for him a reputation as a cycle maker and engineer, a business which he started but never settled down to seriously, his inclination always being towards invention.

Whatever he saw or heard of, Welch's restless and inquisitive mind invariably went back to first principles. He sought the basic reason, and where a mechanical or technical device of any kind was in question, he would master its intricacies by taking it asunder, and studying its composition piece by piece, being generally prepared with some suggestion for its improvement. He possessed a natural intuition and a wide general knowledge of technical subjects, being a voracious reader of scientific and mechanical literature.

He acquired a fair knowledge of medicine, a good knowledge of lenses and telescopes, and an almost professional knowledge of photography. Being very musical he mastered the technicalities of every form of mechanical musical instrument with which he came in contact, including pianos and organs which he tuned himself. For drawing he had a natural gift, and although he never received a lesson he prepared and finished the numerous and accurate drawings which illustrated his many patents—there were eighteen in his detachable tyre specification alone—as well as the working models and tools required in this connection. Welch became an expert in Patent Law, drafted all his own specifications, and was one of the most imperturbable of witnesses whose candour and truthfulness went far to convince the judges as the results of his cases go to prove.

The records of the Patent Office bear abundant witness to his industry, but perhaps the most ingenious of his early inventions was an improved double driving and steering gear for velocipedes and other vehicles which he patented (No. 6714) in 1884, when he was twenty-three years of age, by which any pair of wheels placed side by side on one axle could be steered without the aid of a third or fulcrum wheel. He applied this to a form of Otto bicycle employing a single chain drive, and not only did he build the first experimental machine and gear himself, which he called the Di-cycle, but made all the jigs, cutters and tools necessary for the purpose. It was accepted at the Inventions Exhibition of 1885, and only failed to obtain a gold medal from the fact that it was not completed in time for the opening weeks.

Punctuality was not one of Welch's virtues, which led his mother, a devout Wesleyan Methodist, to prophesy that he would be too late for Heaven. On one occasion when due in London as a witness in a major patent case he missed his train at Coventry, but ascertaining that it had been despatched one minute before the scheduled time, he descended upon the station-master with such reproaches as his amiable nature would allow, the result being that he became the sole occupant of a " special " which conveyed him, without charge, to Rugby, where he caught a through express to London in time to answer to his call in court.

After many other incursions into the patent field Welch at length invented in September 1890 his detachable pneumatic tyre, which to-day is in general use throughout the world, and the story of this invention can now be told for the first time.

III

Welch had neither pneumatic tyres nor endless wires particularly in mind when he filed his provisional specification, but he spread his net very widely. Subsequently, in his early experiments he started with wires joined by a screw connector, but soon discovered that, with a suitable rim, wires adjustable in length were unnecessary. Of this discovery Mr. Roland Welch has written :—

" On that day I was with King and my father in one of our old workshops, when King came towards us obviously very jubilant and with his eyes sparkling with delight. It was unnecessary for him to tell us he had made a great discovery. He had with him the rim and wire, and showed us that it would go on and off without altering its diameter."

For these experiments, which occupied only two or three days, Welch used an ordinary U-section solid-tyre rim, and the result settled in his mind once and for all the basic principle of the wired-on detachable pneumatic tyre. All that was left to do was to design an outer cover having the form of a saddle or arch in section with two wires inserted through the sides of the arch.

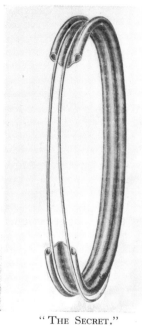

" THE SECRET."

At this point he discovered that an inflated extensible inner tube would provide the arch just as suitably as the solid or cushion tyre which he had had previously in mind, and no other form of tube was ever used. Further experiments proved that upon placing the cover and tube on the special rim he designed, shown above and Fig. 15 of his patent (reproduced in Chapter 20), and inflating it, the wires automatically assumed their correct position on the shoulders of the rim, and the tyre became immovable unless the wires stretched or were broken. They did not come off on deflation. Welch, like Woods with his valve, skipped the slow process of evolution, and produced the perfect tyre in one operation, and it retains its original form to this day.

Anybody might have done it, the thing was so simple,

and indeed Milton might have had it in his mind when he wrote in his account of the Council of Pandæmonium:—

" The invention all admired ; and each how he
To be th' inventor missed, so easy it seem'd
Once found, which yet unfound most would have
    thought
Impossible."

Without any delay, after the preliminary experiments, Welch prepared the necessary drawings and handed them to William Warne & Company, the old established rubber manufacturers of Tottenham (now of Barking), with instructions to make three tyres. Warnes informed Welch that his idea was impracticable, as it would be impossible to make and mould such a cover by existing methods. Welch thereupon set to work to show them how it could be done. He designed and made a wooden " former " or mould in the shape of a ring built in segments, to fold inwards, a very ingenious and accurate piece of craftsmanship. This served as a mould upon which to build up the arch-shaped cover, the plastic rubber was then applied and the former folded inwards to release the tyre. A similar collapsible mould of iron was then made, the built-up cover transferred to this, bound round with canvas and vulcanised, after which the cover was dismounted in the same manner.

The novelty of this idea of Welch's was that of making the moulds to collapse and fold inwards, and thus he, an amateur, was able to teach experienced rubber makers how to tackle their own job. He realised that such a mould was essential to the manufacture of his tyre and patented his invention (No. 10617) in 1892.

Warnes quickly made and delivered the experimental tyres which were fitted to a swing frame tricycle, another patent of Welch's (No. 10239 of 1887), and were found in practice to fulfil all the expectations of the inventor.

In the course of Welch's consultations with William Warne & Company, he offered to sell them his patent, but after consideration they refused to entertain the proposal. What a world of difference this decision was to make to subsequent events ! *Had Warne's reply been otherwise, Harvey du Cros and his Founder Company must have dropped into oblivion and Welch's name would have taken the place of Dunlop's.* With this and the only other master patent for detachable tyres in the possession of two old established and highly efficient rubber manufacturers, there would have been no room for the Founder Company or anyone else who was not licensed, nor, under stress of competition, for *any* middle man, even if he were licensed.

How different was the reaction of Harvey du Cros, inexperienced and unskilled as he was in the technique of rubber making. When the opportunity came to him, as Mr. Purchase, Welch's solicitor, recalled : " the patent was purchased by you at my office through me in about five minutes." That the world-wide business of the Dunlop Company, with its vast ramifications, was built up on the Welch patent, supported as it was by the subsequent acquisition of the Bartlett patent, has never been in question by those acquainted with the facts.

So determined was my father to buy Welch's patent that he sent my brother Harvey to wait on his doorstep until he could persuade him to put us in communication with his solicitor, and pay us a visit in Ireland, a mission which he accomplished successfully. Subsequently, John Purchase became for many years the legal guide, philosopher and friend of the company and for a time acted as a Director of the Founder Company.

CHAPTER ELEVEN

FORTUNES AND MISFORTUNES

I

THERE was much speculation in the shares of the company, " Booth's Babies " as they were called, which fluctuated widely and rose or fell on the market in sympathy with the results of patent litigation and even of important racing and record events. This led to the inevitable crop of mushroom flotations, and for a time in the early 'nineties Dublin became the happy hunting ground of the ubiquitous company promoter. One tyre was as good as another for his purpose, and so long as it was supported by a patent, provisional or otherwise, all was well ; merit did not matter and novelty was left on the knees of the Gods. It was like the railway mania of the 'forties or the Kaffir craze of '95. Everyone great and small had a flutter, and the joke went round that the real capital of Ireland was to be found in the Pneumatic Tyre Company. Queues formed up outside the banks, market prices rose and fell and the city was in a constant state of ferment, companies were as plentiful as blackberries, and little else but tyre finance was thought of or discussed. There were the usual stories which circulate around every boom, of fortunes made and lost, opportunities taken and missed : for a time even clergymen and widows were said to have made money.

The pace, however, was too rapid to last, and of all the tyre companies launched at that time, but few survived for long to tell the tale, and much capital was wasted on inferior devices and barren litigation.

A similar boom arose in cycle history in 1896 under the impetus of the prosperity of the Founder Company, and a hectic rush ensued during which for a brief period fashionable society thronged to Battersea Park on wheels, and prospectuses rained upon a gullible public, many of them based upon doubtful concerns and most of them heavily over-capitalised. The inevitable reaction occurred in due course, when liquidations became the order of the day and the old established well-managed minority alone survived.

But the Founder Company never failed its shareholders. In its first year it paid 8 per cent., and in the five years following on an average capital of just over £100,000 it made net profits of close upon £600,000 and paid dividends at an average rate of 75 per cent. per annum. The £1 shares in 1893 were quoted as high as £22, even though the original issued capital had by then multiplied over three times.

My father's one desire was to please his shareholders, and this influenced him perhaps unwisely to distribute very large amounts. Dividends up to and over 100 per cent. became a commonplace which, however, did not achieve their end; a minority was dissatisfied and showed more interest in the amount of profits retained by the company than in the amounts they received. As a concession to Irish sentiment my father was holding the annual meetings alternately in Dublin and London; those held in London being quiet, businesslike and helpful, and those in Dublin uproarious and injurious.

My father bore this with commendable patience until at length in London in 1898 he informed his shareholders " that last year in Dublin he was baited for five and half hours. He admired his fellow countrymen and appreciated the fact that the chairman-baiting he had been subjected to was mere ' devilment,' and a desire to see how the old man would get out of a tight corner. Years ago, when young, he might have entered into the spirit of the thing, but he was older now, and had upon his shoulders the responsibility of a corporation with something like 20,000 shareholders, and he thought that this was too important to be butchered to make a Dublin holiday."

A shareholder pleaded for an occasional meeting in Dublin and promised a hundred thousand welcomes, but he was met with this pithy comment from my father,

" that he had been promised that before and the hundred thousand welcomes had materialized in a hundred thousand abusive epithets, and a badger baiting for five and a half hours."

And added :

" It was said in my hearing in Dublin that ' I was a fool to have ever come to a meeting there, but I would be a d—— fool to go again.' I have no objection to being the comparative fool, but I will not be a superlative one. If any meeting of this company is held in Dublin, it will be held without me."

That ended it, the Dublin shareholders had had their bit of fun with the old man for the last time and so it happened that the patriots of Dublin, having driven the company out because of their delicate nostrils, now drove the directors away by their indelicate tongues, a result which was received with satisfaction by responsible shareholders whose interests were suffering through these turbulent meetings.

My father had a sense of humour and was eloquent, able, and pleasant as a chairman. He was persuasive and courteous with everyone. To one shareholder who became curious as to the amount of commission being paid to the Joint Managing Directors, and who followed up his question by expressing regret that he should have to refer to so " delicate " a subject, the Chairman suavely replied : " Not at all ; it is a very pleasant one, and the more there is of it the better we like it." Another shareholder, a Mr. Cherry, put a question which developed into a lengthy dissertation to which the Chairman listened patiently and silently for some time, only inquiring mildly at the end whether the speaker had any further questions to put, as he preferred not to make " two bites of a Cherry." Nevertheless, he could be devastating when swayed by a just resentment.

My father's faith in the future of the pneumatic tyre, crude as it was at first, was positively uncanny, for of all those concerned he stood alone in his belief that it could and would be adapted to all forms of traffic. He worked less for profit than for the love of his self-imposed task and the joy of conquest, although Dunlop warned him against being too optimistic, saying that he himself did not depend too much on the pneumatic, which he thought might one day be superseded. Yet in those first years my father was always a buyer of shares when his means permitted and when others closely associated with the business were sellers.

Of him the editor of *Cycling* wrote :—

" The World knows that he converted a Modest Little Company with a comparatively trifling capital into one of the most successful industries of the day. Were it not for his personal influence, and the reliance which all his friends placed in his judgment and foresight, it is quite possible that Mr. Dunlop's invention might have been known only to a small circle for another decade.

" Harvey du Cros inspired confidence in the Company, and imbued its shareholders with much hope for its ultimate success, when it was combating the most determined opposition. In those early days of the Company it may be said that the past reputation of its Managing Director, and the belief that he inspired, were worth many times its capital."

He was direct in his business methods, could present a story in simple form and achieved his success by determination, hard work, thoroughness and above all a firm belief in himself. His was the faith that moved mountains. He united science and commerce and staked his fortune on the result, giving up everything else to devote himself to the task.

His thoroughness led him so far as to undertake to fight a Parliamentary Election in the cause of Tariff Reform—a forlorn hope—at Hastings. He had seen the British cycle industry snuffed out in France and the United States by the operation of punitive duties, and realised the folly and injustice to English manufacturers of the free import system. He scored the first of the only two solitary Conservative gains achieved in the General Election of 1906, and was the only candidate to unseat a Member of the Government, thus releasing for the Empire a great pro-Consul in the person of the Marquis of Willingdon. In due course my father was followed into Parliament by two of his sons who fought in the same cause and represented Hastings, Bow and Bromley, and Clapham.

Harvey du Cros never forgot that he was an Irishman of Dublin, and many a good turn he did on no better recommendation than an Irish accent. Having placed 500 taxi cabs on the London streets with the aid of his sons, " W. and G.," his thoughts turned to the possible hurt of the Dublin jarvey by this modern innovation, for it was conceivable that, as the safety bicycle had ousted the ordinary, so would the taxi account for the outside car.

He refused to import the taxi himself, but offered to send over a sufficient number to open a school of instruction for drivers free of charge and then put them in the way of purchasing by instalments on easy terms. But not at all, it was just another insult to Ireland. The news went round the city that " Ould du Cros is out to best us," and jarveys became united for the first and last time in their lives. But understanding the natural instinct of his countrymen to be " agin " everything new and their slight prejudice against anything that hailed from Saxon shores, my father took this in very good part, but would never have viewed the present fulfilment of his prophecy with any satisfaction.

The *Motor Trader* wrote of him :—

" Mr. du Cros is in most respects a typical Irishman. A man who influences other men so completely has probably many weapons in his mental armoury, but he rarely uses any but one, persuasion. He is one of the most alert and dapper of men—was considered one of the best dressed men in the House of Commons—his manner is quiet with a marked geniality in it, and he is the pink of courtesy even to the humblest caller. Practically a teetotaller, he never smokes, and he has always kept himself physically ' fit.' If the writer were asked what was his strongest personal characteristic, he would probably say, ' Loyalty to his old friends.' He never forgets a friend, and the number of young men to whom he has given splendid starts in business life are legion. Mr. du Cros' career must always remain an example of what can be done by industry when combined with mental power and an indomitable determination not to be beaten by any opposing forces, no matter how powerful."

II

It has been said, and may come to be accepted in the absence of authoritative figures, that Dunlop made very little money out of his tyre, as has so often been the inventor's fate. But this was not the case with Dunlop or any of the inventors with whom the Founder Company dealt. Dunlop received £500 in cash and 3,000 shares for his patent, the latter representing 20 per cent. of the cash capital, and it is true to say that they went to a discount and looked like becoming worthless when, within six months of his receiving them, Dunlop became aware that his patent had been anticipated. Welch with his valid invention came to the rescue, and with this and the impetus of a determined executive the company was successful in restoring and increasing share values. But the shareholders would have received little or nothing in the end in the absence of this combination of circumstances.

In 1896 the capital was valued on the Stock Exchange at £1,400,000, and then the company was sold for £3,000,000 in cash with the condition that its shareholders should have the valuable prior right of taking shares in the new company which was to be floated with share and loan capital of £5,000,000 and additional valuable assets to be bought and paid for by the purchasers and designed to confer upon the company the monopoly for which it had bargained in the first instance. In return for £260,000 of capital Ireland received £3,545,623/12/3, a result which, for a change, was *not* regarded as another Irish grievance.

The courage and confidence of those associated with this operation may be gauged from their commitments and signatures which appeared thus on the prospectus :—

NAMES, ADDRESSES, AND DESCRIPTION OF SUBSCRIBERS.	NO. OF SHARES TAKEN BY EACH SUBSCRIBER.	DENOMINATION.
HARVEY DU CROS, South Hill, Blackrock, County Dublin. *Gentleman.*	66.666 66.667 66.667	Preference Shares. Ordinary Shares. Deferred Shares.
ARTHUR PHILIP DU CROS, Radford House, Coventry. *Gentleman.*	66.666 66.667 66.667	Preference Shares. Ordinary Shares. Deferred Shares.
CHARLES WISDOM HELY, J.P., "Oaklands," Highfield Road Rathgar, Co. Dublin. *Merchant.*	66.666 66.667 66.667	Preference Shares. Ordinary Shares. Deferred Shares.
ERNEST TERAH HOOLEY, Risley Hall, Near Derby. *Stockbroker.*	33.333 33.333 33.334	Preference Shares. Ordinary Shares. Deferred Shares.
ROBERT WATSON, Newfield, Johnstone, Renfrewshire. *Paper Manufacturer.*	33.333 33.333 33.334	Preference Shares. Ordinary Shares. Deferred Shares.
ADOLPHE CLEMENT, 20, Rue Brunel, Paris. *Cycle Manufacturer.*	33.333 33.333 33.334	Preference Shares. Ordinary Shares. Deferred Shares.
MARTIN DIEDRICH RUCKER, Bramlea, Walton-on-Thames. *Director of Public Company.*	33.333 33.333 33.334	Preference Shares. Ordinary Shares. Deferred Shares.

Dated Sixth day of May, 1896.
Witness to the above Signatures,
JOHN B. PURCHASE.
11, Queen Victoria Street,
London, E.C., *Solicitor.*

LIST OF SUBSCRIBERS TO D. P. T. CO., MAY 6TH, 1896.

The *Cycle and Motor Trades Review*, commenting on this transaction, wrote :—

" Mr. R. J. Mecredy [a Director], who was the ever-vigilant watch-dog of the original Company, is the authority for a series of facts which he considered were ' absolutely unique in the history of the companies.' He proved what a gold mine the Dunlop Company was by taking an individual case. A man who invested £100 in

1889 in original shares, and took up the proportion allotted to him of subsequent issues, by 1896 held 1,038 shares, for which he had paid £1,146, and which at the time of the sale were worth £12,658. In addition, he had drawn over £1,700 in dividends ! When the old company was wound up, the names of 100 original shareholders stood on the books."

Had Dunlop retained his original free holding of 3,000 shares he would have received on this basis £380,000 within six and a half years at the small cost to himself of little more than half the dividends which he would have received during that period which amounted to a further £51,000. But unfortunately he had given away half of his holding to Bowden and Gillies, the promoters, as commission for their speculative courage and their acumen in entrusting the task of founding the business to Harvey du Cros, and this extravagant arrangement made a difference to Dunlop of one half of the above amounts. Dunlop was never *au courant* with Welch (who had become the company's technical adviser), and was doubtful as to the validity of his patent. He began to sell out of the company in 1894 at substantial prices, and by the end of 1895 had parted with about four-fifths of his interest, acknowledging later that in all he had benefited to the extent of over £100,000, not a meagre reward even if his patent had been valid. Had Dunlop remained in the company and waited for the favourable decision subsequently delivered upon the Welch patent he would have doubled this amount.

Thus Thomson as the first inventor was out of pocket. Dunlop—for his adaptation of Thomson's idea—received a fortune, and not a penny too much, as things turned out, while Welch's reward of £7,500 for his master idea, although large in proportion to the company's means, was grotesquely small when measured by the phenomenal results, although Welch never repined, since the terms he asked for he received, and more.* Such are the ups and downs of fortune. In considering this it is strange to reflect that under the British amended patent law of 1902, which came into operation in 1905, *no patent could have been issued to Dunlop by the Patent Office, and if there had been no patent there would have been no company*.

The brothers Booth received a consideration of £4,000 in cash and 4,000 shares, which ultimately worked out on Mecredy's basis, which may be taken as correct, to the fantastic value upwards of £500,000, but how much of this they had the faith and patience to wait for, remained their own secret.

Dunlop approved of the arrangements with the Booths by his signature to the prospectus, but many years later became critical of this as well as other matters, saying that, " *If* the Patent proved to be valid, Messrs. Booth Bros. would be multi-millionaires without any special effort on their part." The patent, however, was found *not* to be valid, and Messrs. Booth would have received only £4,000 for their business had they been solely dependent upon it. They were beholden to Welch and other inventors for the rewards which they received, without whom the company must have been stifled under the free competition of the powerful rubber makers of the world.

The only profit my father ever made from the pneumatic tyre business he made by investing in it his own capital, but he did that to the uttermost limit. Subse-

---

* Welch received a voluntary payment of £2,500 for his French and American patents, notwithstanding that they were invalid, making £7,500 in all.

quently he embarked a substantial part of the fortune which resulted in the new motor industry of which he was a pioneer, and became a co-founder of two of the first and most successful of British companies which loom largely in the public eye to-day.

CHAPTER TWELVE

JOHN BOYD DUNLOP

DUNLOP lived a quiet and simple life and when he produced his tyre was contemplating retirement. He was comfortably off and did not give up his profession for the purpose of joining the Founder Company, nor was he exacting in the terms he made for his invention, though greatly over-generous to the promoters with whom he dealt. Yet the reason afterwards assigned for his abrupt resignation from the company in March 1895 turned on a question of money, although the Minutes of the company do not confirm this. They record no differences with his colleagues on this or any other question, and at a shareholders' meeting held about that time at which Dunlop was present, my father stated : "*I want to tell you also that in all our connection there never has been one difference on this Board, and there never has been one Resolution sent to a division since the company was founded.*"

It is evident that if Dunlop had a quarrel with the company or his co-directors, they at least were unconscious of it, which seems to show that it does not always take two to make a quarrel. The Board remained unanimous from the day it was formed to the day that Dunlop resigned, and there are many indications of the high regard entertained for him and the trust reposed in him by his fellow directors.

One such Minute, dated November 1894, reads :—

" The Chairman read a copy of a letter which he had directed the Secretary to send to Mr. Dunlop, stating that it being commonly reported that Mr. Dunlop had some inventions which the Company refused to test, it was desired to now formally tell Mr. Dunlop that this was a misapprehension on his part, that the Company was always more than willing to test carefully any invention of his, and, that they now asked him to submit to the Board any such patents as he considered improvements of his tyre.

" With regard to his son, the Board would be extremely happy that he should enter its service, either now or whenever Mr. Dunlop thought it advisable he should commence, and that as he showed great promise in matters of invention the Company would afford him every opportunity of development when in its service.

" The Directors expressed their concurrence with the sentiments of the above letter and Mr. Dunlop said that if that letter expressed the sense of the Board he had been under a misapprehension for several months past and that he now withdrew any remarks he might have made while under that impression, and expressed himself perfectly satisfied with the action of the Board towards himself."

Another Minute of December 1894 stated that :—

" The Chairman said that if Mr. Dunlop had any new ideas in connection with tyres or business that now was the time to put them forward to be put in force in 1896, and he further said that the Board wished Mr. Dunlop to understand that he was at liberty to order anything he required for experimental purposes."

Yet three months later Dunlop resigned without giving his reasons or discussing his intention beforehand, but complained afterwards that the French company had deprived him of royalties without giving him notice.

Dunlop's French and British tyre patents, the only two he had taken out, were both invalid and never conferred any protection upon their owners. This became apparent in France when it was discovered that Thomson's patent, which Dunlop admitted anticipated his, had been applied for in that country in 1846. The payment of royalties would therefore cease as a matter of course, unless there had been a specific agreement to the contrary, which was not the case. Although Dunlop had not been trained in business, he may have been expected to know that hard-headed Frenchmen would object to continue paying royalties on someone else's patent which had expired in 1860 and that his rights in France had been clearly disestablished by the Thomson patent, as they had been in England. There may be two or more inventions of the same principle but only the first can be valid.

That the reasons which actuated the French company were explicit enough, a letter to Dunlop in May 1897 seems to show :—

" I regret to have to inform you that the judgment pronounced against your patent on the 23rd April, 1896, of which you were duly informed, has now been confirmed by the 3rd Chamber of the French Court, which has now delivered a verdict absolutely against us.

" I regret to add that the judges are very severe on the patent, features of which they saw were disclosed in previous patents and also by actual publication as far back as 1848, and in fact your patent never had the smallest claim to novelty. Under the circumstances, they have declared your claim to a patent null and void."

A year before, Dunlop had been advised by the Company that their French experts " have declared your patent to be invalid," an opinion to which he bowed in his reply, stating : " I am sorry to hear that the French experts consider my patent invalid. I am afraid I could not render them more assistance that I have done. . . . As soon as the Pneumatic Tyre Company's Directors have their minds fully made up that my French patent is invalid I shall be glad to have the same re-conveyed to me."

Dunlop may have become honestly convinced that he had the legitimate grievance in regard to France which he alleged, it was regretted by his colleagues that he did not state this when leaving the Board. His action suggested that they had been guilty of harsh treatment of which it should be said in justice to them that they were quite incapable. It was tacitly felt that as the technical director of the company Dunlop had not acted considerately in resigning at a moment when the company was struggling with the new problem of the motor tyre. This was his letter of resignation addressed to the Secretary :—

" 16*th March*, 1895.

" Please take notice that I shall cease to be and discontinue to act as a Director for the Pneumatic Tyre Company on and after 1st May next. I may mention that I expect my time will be fairly well occupied during the summer considering the state of my health.

" Yours truly,

J. B. DUNLOP."

And this was the Chairman's reply :—

"*April 2nd*, 1895.

" DEAR MR. DUNLOP,

" The directors desire me to say that they accept your letter of 16th March as a legal notice and as such they have inserted it on the Minutes.

" The Directors desire me to say that for their part they are sorry to receive a letter from you couched in this form ; but, on their behalf, I am desired to express a hope that your health will improve and that you will enjoy many happy years and even greater success than that which came to you through your connection with the Pneumatic Tyre Company.

" Yours faithfully,

" HARVEY DU CROS."

His colleagues' views were that the consideration they had always extended to Dunlop entitled them to be informed of his reasons for resigning and to a frank discussion upon them. They had never uttered a word of criticism or reproach when he disclosed Thomson's prior patent to them, and it was realised that they had acquired a monopoly which they neither received nor enjoyed. Dunlop, as has already been said, acknowledged that many engineers and thousands of the public were aware of Thomson's invention, but his assurance that he himself had no knowledge of it until the middle of 1890 was accepted by his fellow directors with a confidence which was not reciprocated.

In the face of this the implied reflection upon their own integrity in connection with French royalties by Dunlop's action was thought to be ungenerous, but no resentment was ever expressed by them, although the proposal of a presentation to him from his old colleagues was not accepted. They were not to meet together again until the occasion of the majority celebration of the foundation of the pneumatic tyre industry in London, fourteen years later, and then for the last time.

There must have been some greater reason to account for this once friendly and amiable gentleman turning away suddenly from the friends who had made him known to the world. It was not a mere question of money, because, apart from the competence upon which

132

he had retired from his profession, the company had endowed him with a fortune.

There is no doubt that the cause of Dunlop's defection went deeper than any financial question. He had voted for the acquisition of the Welch patent and for the payment of royalties to Welch on his fabric and valve patents, but from the day that his fellow inventor joined the company in June 1892, it is doubtful if Dunlop ever knew a really happy moment as a Director. He thought that as his tyre had been superseded he also had been supplanted, and as that feeling grew he could only have been reconciled by the dropping of Welch, with whom from the first he was incompatible and who was now rendering most valuable technical services to the company. The decision in 1892 to adopt the name " Dunlop-Welch " to mark the tyre as being detachable, displeased Dunlop, and other incidents intervened which made ultimate separation inevitable.

There is this to be remembered, that Dunlop had sustained disappointment after disappointment. The revelation that he had been anticipated by Thomson must have been a stunning blow, occurring as it did within a few months of the sale of his invention to the Founder Company. The façade of the Dunlop patent was maintained for a time, and although the company recognised the futility of submitting it to the test of the courts, they were hoping against hope that the lost position might be regained by obtaining a re-issue of the patent, and the Minutes show that their efforts in this direction were unremitting even up to 1896.

It was recorded on January 8th, 1892, " that Mr. Moulton's opinion of our patent was most satisfactory, and by adopting a certain course it could be established

as a master patent." And again on January 19th, 1892 :
" Mr. Moulton was of opinion that the company could
obtain an amendment to their patent specification which
would place them in a non-assailable position, and Mr.
du Cros had instructed Messrs. Haseltine Lake & Co.
to take the necessary steps to that end." The application
for amendment was advertised in *The Times* on March
9th, 1892, and in March and again in September 1892 it
was decided to take the opinion of Sir Richard Webster,
formerly Attorney-General, both on the validity of the
patent and the question of its amendment.

But ultimately these hopes had to be abandoned in the
face of adverse legal opinion, and the opposition which
arose : thus Dunlop's patent finally joined that of Thomson as an interesting but useless relic of the Patent Office.
As a Dublin jarvey would have it, there was nothing left
of his air tyre, except the " climate."

CHAPTER THIRTEEN

JOHN BOYD DUNLOP (CONTINUED)

I

DUNLOP himself worked hard to retrieve the situation in his own way. He was unconvinced that the inherent defect in his tyre—the risk of puncture—could be overcome or that the difficulty of repairing his non-detachable tyre could be simplified. He thought the remedy lay, or partly lay, in other directions, in the production of a cushion tyre allied with a spring frame cycle.

It is curious that Bartlett and Welch in their search for an anti-vibratory device progressed from solid tyres to cushions and from cushions to pneumatics, while Dunlop, having commenced with the pneumatic tyre, was thinking in the opposite direction and experimenting to replace or supplement the pneumatic with cushion tyres and spring frame cycles. He never attempted to produce a heavy vehicle or motor tyre, being convinced, probably with Thomson in mind, that they could not be made a commercial success, which was contrary to my father's unswerving opinion. H. W. Bartleet, a journalist not related to W. E. Bartlett the inventor, in *Cycling* in October 1904 and again in 1938, wrote :—

" One of the most interesting documents which ever passed through my hands was a letter written by J. B. Dunlop to Harvey du Cros soon after the flotation of the Company : it ran, ' I do not think my pneumatic tyre will ever be a commercial success ; but I am at work on something that will be—a spring frame bicycle.' He was referring to a spring frame which he invented after the air tyre was on the market."

This was a case of the reversal of the usual trend of thought, where the inventor had less faith in his invention than the business man who was exploiting it, but Dunlop was perfectly right as regards a hand-made non-detachable tyre such as his, for durability, certainly in heavy tyres, cannot be obtained without vulcanisation in manufacture.

Dunlop, who wavered at times in his estimate of the pneumatic tyre, wrote to my father in August 1890 :—

Perhaps you will see that I am right not to depend too much on the Pneumatic. at the same time I will not leave a stone unturned to improve the tyre

I never was so sanguine about the Pneumatic as you and my opinion is that the surprise is yet in store for the people across the channel,

The latter remark had reference to his spring frame cycle.

He wrote to the company in September 1890 :—

> I have been carefully considering wheels and tyres for some time past and I would not be very much surprised if the pneumatic be superseded in the course of 2 or 3 years It is a question whether we should not try and be first in the field
>
> I dont think the pneumatic will ever be beaten on track however.
>
> Yours truly
> J. B. Dunlop

And again on August 31st, 1891 :—

> I believe that a wheel may be made yet as fast on the track as the pneumatic and probably a compound tyre would be somewhat faster than any.

My father was in no way discouraged by these predictions or by the head shakings of his friends. But all Dunlop's activities were supported by the Board, and numerous Minutes from March 25th, 1890, onwards record the progress which was being made.

The name " Flexible " was ordered to be registered

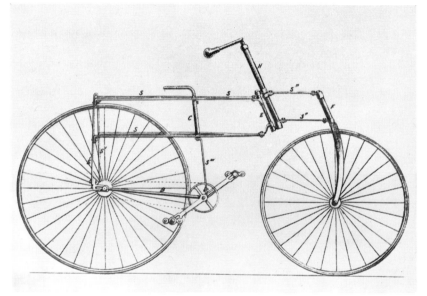

DUNLOP'S PATENT SPRING FRAME CYCLE OF 1889.

as the name for the spring frame cycle (Minute, June 10th, 1890) (Patent No. 16119, October 12th, 1889).

Dunlop agreed to give the company the first offer of his new spring frame machine (Minute, August 19th, 1890).

Letters of authority sealed to take out patent in France and register the trade mark " Treadhold " for Dunlop's cushion tyre (Minute, October 31st, 1890).

The best manner of dealing with the sale of cushion tyres was considered, and it was resolved to place a first order for fifty Dunlop spring frame cycles (Minute, December 5th, 1890).

Chairman reported that Messrs. Moseley and Mr. Dunlop now reported that the cushion tyre had been perfected to their satisfaction (Minute, February 4th, 1891).

Resolved to take out a patent for the " Treadhold " tyre in Germany (Minute, February 17th, 1891).

German application for spring frame patent reported granted (Minute, May 20th, 1891).

Dunlop reported that spring frame cycle now complete (Minute, September 4th, 1891).

It was not until the advent of the detachable tyre that Dunlop relinquished his efforts in these directions, realising that the pneumatic tyre in its improved form had killed all such secondary devices. Cushion tyres after the Welch and Bartlett inventions were as dead as the Sedan chair. His hopes had been again frustrated and the impact of these successive disappointments may have affected his normal kindly attitude towards those with whom he had been working, and certainly on my frequent visits to Dublin from 1892 to 1895 I could not but fail to notice this.

The position was certainly discouraging. Altogether Dunlop had taken out some seventeen patents but, either through invalidity or impracticability, none of these was incorporated in the current pneumatic tyre which was now being made under the valid patents of Welch and Bartlett, with Moseley, Woods and Westwood as important contributors. Even the sale in September 1890 to an American buyer of his United States patent for his method of attachment, which had been agreed, subject to its being valid, at £20,000, half of which sum Dunlop was to receive, was cancelled when the Americans produced a wired detachable tyre almost identical with Welch's. This patent the company was obliged to purchase for a similar amount in order to fortify their position in the States.

II

Events were moving with great rapidity and Dunlop was unable to keep up with them. But although he found himself in this position, he was never without the backers and friends whose efforts had helped him to fame and fortune. That he was unsuccessful with new ideas, or late in the field with them, did not affect their attitude. They had faith in him, trusted him, and looked to him for help in keeping the company abreast and in advance of all competition. Although their feelings of regard for him never changed, the pride and satisfaction which they felt in their own achievements were naturally tinged with regret by Dunlop's withdrawal, while the company was yet in its teething troubles with the motor tyre for the special purpose of which a call of £75,000 had just been made.

The break with Dunlop came four months after a letter dated October 31st, 1894, was received by the Board from Welch resigning from the company on account of " rumours reflecting on his character . . . founded on statements made by Mr. Dunlop." Dunlop at once assured his colleagues that " he never intended his remarks to convey the injurious meaning . . . attached to them," and undertook to make this clear to Welch in a letter which was drawn up and approved by the Board. Although Dunlop had made the *amende honorable*, and Welch replied stating that if he retained the confidence of the Board he would be very pleased to withdraw his resignation, to which the Directors answered that he had " never lost the confidence of the Board," nevertheless this incident was followed by Dunlop's resignation, to the regret of everyone ; *but to the temperamental mind of the inventor Welch's virtues had become the sins of Harvey du Cros' company.*

A case in which the Dunlop Rubber Company was involved as long after as January 1920 was referred to in a personal sketch of Dunlop by T. P. O'Connor, M.P., in which he said :—

" The final chapter of the relations between Dunlop and his associates had just that element of comedy— perhaps also of pathos—which was required to make the great commercial drama complete. For some years the Dunlop Company added to their advertisement of their wares the picture of a tall, very handsome, very stylishly-dressed old man, with a shiny hat, boots that had spats, and who had all the airs of an old beau. A cane and an eye-glass added to the splendour of the figure.

" The picture was so well done and so complete that an advertisement expert would at once recognise it as one of those excellent mnemonics which get for an advertisement that hold on the mind of newspaper readers which it is the business of an advertisement to create."

The company was perfectly innocent in the matter ; nothing was further from the thoughts of those responsible for this advertisement (not, in fact, the Directors) than to show disrespect to Dunlop, or to hurt his feelings in any way. They had acquired the right to reproduce Dunlop's bust and signature as their trade mark, and their business being of a sporting nature, there was added to the bust the body of a typical, genial, lovable type of sportsman which has always had, and will always have, a great appeal for the sport-loving British public. Dunlop, however, chose to regard the figure as " the antithesis of what he really was," and therefore, a satirical caricature

of himself. Accordingly, he took an action against the company, which was settled by an agreement that the use of the advertisement would be discontinued, but only in Ireland, after the current stock of literature had been exhausted, an exception being made in the case of the " Dunlop Road Book " of that day, which on this account now possesses a special interest for bibliophilists. In the course of the case one of the judges remarked erroneously that " the origin of the pneumatic tyre was the tying of a piece of rubber water piping round the wheel of a *wheel-barrow*."

An irrepressible friend of Dunlop, the late Sir " Jimmy " Percy, had the temerity to suggest to him that as a reprisal he " should shave off his beard and deprive the company of its trade mark," a witticism which Dunlop took in quite good part.

It has been one of the strangest aspects of this case that whereas Dunlop never had a valid patent which came into general use, yet he is remembered and acclaimed while the inventions of Welch, Bartlett, Woods, Westwood and others were valid, stood the assaults of time, yielded immense results, and yet with Thomson's are in danger of being forgotten by the public. *Thomson had the patent and no business, while Dunlop had the business and no patent.*

But as Dunlop had been so favoured of the gods and was sensitive himself, it was felt by his friends that it would have but added to his stature had he shown himself more generous and appreciative of the work of his brother inventors and business colleagues, whose efforts had so successfully crowned his own.

With his resignation Dunlop became an onlooker at the great developments which were to lift the tyre industry to the highest plane. He was induced in 1896 to lend his name as Chairman and assist in the promotion of the Tubeless (Fleuss) Pneumatic Tyre Company in an abortive attempt to establish a rival business, in which he invested and lost very heavily. His old company came to law with this new venture on the patent issue and to restrain Dunlop, who, as the original vendor, had agreed to place all improvements at the option of the Pneumatic Tyre Company. In the impending suit it was the contention of the Fleuss Company (and therefore of Dunlop himself) that his patent was invalidated by Thomson's, who, they pleaded, was the first and true inventor.

The case was not fought out, an arrangement being made under which the Fleuss tyre was allowed to be sold under tribute to the Founder Company, but the business was never successful.

It was yet another phase of a curious story that Dunlop should have made this attempt to oust his own name from the position of commercial supremacy to which it had been raised. It really seemed as if, in reward for his brilliant initiative, Dunlop had been adopted by Fortune as one of her favourites and that a benevolent destiny had determined to maintain him on his pedestal by preserving his name for posterity, almost in spite of himself. First, Thomson had been recalled to memory six months too late, next, the law, soon to be changed, permitted Dunlop to obtain a patent without proving novelty, then Warnes had miraculously rejected the controlling patent, and lastly, Welch had not insisted upon the privilege of naming his own tyre.

Had *any* of these events been differently decided the name of Dunlop might have joined that of Thomson, in comparative obscurity.

CHAPTER FOURTEEN

MANY INVENTIONS

I

THE company was always eager to consider anything new, but time was to show that in Britain all patents relative to tyres were to be over-shadowed by those of Welch, coupled with that of William Erskine Bartlett.

Bartlett was born at Springfield, Massachusetts, in 1830, his family, which was of English extraction, having been settled in the United States for 300 years. He was a studious and retiring personality, stood aloof from all public affairs, and shunned everything in the nature of personal publicity. Out of respect for this habit of mind nothing is said here of his happy domestic life, but by the courtesy of his daughter, Mrs. Methuen, his portrait is reproduced.

Bartlett's patent was applied for on October 22nd, 1890, thirty-six days after Welch's application, and, as ultimately developed, embodied the principle of the beaded-edge tyre secured to the

W. E. BARTLETT.*

wheel by means of a hooked rim under which the edges of the cover were held and kept in place by air compres-

* Died 1900.

sion. It always had the advantage of being a tyre vulcanised in manufacture, and was the first detachable pneumatic tyre ever to be placed on the market, as it was, in 1891, Seddon's red tyre being the second, although Robertson's tyre had been ridden experimentally before either of them appeared.

Bartlett, who was a competent and tenacious man of business, was no novice in tyre construction. He had, under the spur of Dunlop's lead, invented a beaded-edge detachable cushion tyre and rim in July 1889, which was designed to remain in position without the use of cement or by wire embedded in the tyre. In concentrating upon the improvement of his cushion tyre, which was to occupy a place between the solid tyre and the pneumatic tyre, but free from the damning drawback of puncturing, it flashed across Bartlett's mind that the device which served for the fastening of his hollow cushion tyre would equally well serve for the attaching and detaching of a pneumatic cover. The lesser idea had led to the greater. Bartlett did not allow the grass to grow under his feet, but early upon the following morning informed his patent agent of this logical development of his original idea, the result being the Bartlett-Clincher patent of October 1890, to which only one minor limitation was ever attached in its own field. The patent was held to be good as regards all tyres containing a separate inner tube, but tyres having no inner tube, of which none was long lived or successful, were held to be outside the scope of the patent.

Bartlett's Clincher tyre patent did not illustrate a true beaded-edge cover ; it showed a thickened straight edge and it was only as time went on that the design gradually assumed its final form. Similarly the edges of Bartlett's first rim were not hooked but only slightly in-turned or dove-tailed, but the many judges who heard these patent cases ultimately held that such departures in detail were in conformity with the patent and that Bartlett covered all forms of beaded-edge covers containing inner tubes.

He had adopted Thomson's pneumatic principle, Dunlop's outer band or cover, and combined the two with a grooved rim. His invention consisted in the method which he described of making an attachment between the edges of the cover and the edges of the rim, using the lateral pressure of the air tube to press the one against the other, and thus produce a grip which consolidated these three component parts of the tyre. In effect, as Fletcher Moulton, Q.C., expressed it, " he made the pneumatic tube act as its own gaoler," thus converting the common enemy—air pressure—into a friend.* Like the man in the fable, Bartlett had appreciated the paradoxical qualities of air, for as the one first blew on his hands to warm them and then blew on his soup to cool it, so Bartlett realised that the air-pressure which could blow the tyre off, might also be harnessed to hold it on.

The next inventor of this type, Golding, whose invention of December 1890 was taken up by Macintosh & Company of Manchester, more truly illustrated a true beaded-edge cover and hooked rim in his patent, but the inventors who got nearest of all in their designs to the tyre as subsequently popularised were Nedderman of England (May 1891) and Jeffrey of America, of 1891–92, whose specifications illustrate almost perfect designs. Nevertheless, their labours were in vain, because in the fierce

* See p. 161.

L 2

litigation which followed, and persisted for several years, it was held that such variations, although they might be improvements, were mere modifications of Bartlett's device, and that if the essence of an existing patent be appropriated as the basis of an improvement, such improvement cannot be used without the licence of the original patentee.

Then came a beautiful invention, that of the Woods valve (Patent No. 4175, March 1891), made by Charles Woods, a cotton spinner and brother of a director of the company. This perfect little device took the place of Dunlop's patent valve, which did not permit of deflation, and as the years went on Woods' valve became practically universal for cycles, being sold literally in millions. Woods asked £1,000 for his invention, and the company being poor, offered him the alternative of a royalty of 3d. a valve, or to purchase all their supplies from him at 11d. each. Woods, however, stuck to his decision and received his £1,000, thus missing a fortune. As showing the trend of prices under scientific construction and mass production, these valves, which in 1891 were sold to the public at 2s. 6d. each, can now be obtained at 3d., while rims and tyres of best quality can be bought by the public at one-sixth of their original price.

CHARLES WOODS.*

* Died August 1929.

II

Among the rush of inventions relating to detachable tyres at home at this time were the Trigwell wired tyre of November 28th, 1890, one day before Robertson's and seventy-three after Welch, another by Dunlop on December 15th, 1890, on the constrictor principle, which was found to detach itself too easily for safety, a wired tyre by Dunlop on April 9th, 1891, which had clearly been anticipated by other patents, including Robertson's, with which Dunlop, as a Director, had been familiar, and many others, including Seddon, Palmer, Smith, Dunn, Sidney, Preston Davies, Heale, Fleuss, Beeston, Turner, Grappler in Britain and Gormully and Jeffrey, Bidwell, Rice and Straus, Stillman, Torrillon, Decourville, Michelin and a large number of others in America and elsewhere.

In all manufacturing countries there was a host of applications for methods of attaching and detaching tyres, causing much overlapping, due mainly to ignorance of what was occurring in the preliminary secrecy period between the dates of application and the issues of patents and the numerous amendments applied for by patentees after publication.

DUKE OF SOMERSET.*
Director, 1896.

The story throughout all the principal countries was much the same with the same characteristics of clashing

* Died October 1923.

inventions, obstinate litigation, trade hostility, public disbelief, and progress by trial and error. But as the founding of the pneumatic tyre industry is essentially a British achievement, its adventures in foreign countries need not be detailed more closely, except to say that legally, commercially and technically the responsibility of directing the policy of the original company all over the world was borne by the management at home, a truly Herculean task.

Generally, efforts were being made by the company to buy up the prior detachable patents in all countries, while at the same time negotiating various agreements with supposedly infringing makers, including Seddon, Preston Davies, Scott, among others, and licensing them to continue manufacturing under royalty. But the company would never allow any other tyre company, whether licensed or not, to adopt the Welch principle of inextensible edges precisely, for it always stipulated that wires, if used, must not be endless, but fastened in some quite distinctive manner. As a consequence a motley collection of methods of attachment made their appearance, including laces, open wires, screws, bolts, levers, all of which being inferior to Welch's masterly device, conferred a selling advantage upon the company in addition to the royalties exacted. In the course of the investigations a mass of patents came to light in various countries, all following hard upon each other's heels, and some of them of considerable merit.

The company investigated various patents for a tyre made non-puncturable by compression, including the Birtwistle, which was bought in March 1892 for £2,500 and experimented with seriously but without success. Probably an efficient non-puncturable tyre, if attainable at all, could only be employed at a sacrifice of other qualities.

The Scott wired patent, another of the winter crop of 1890, thirty-six days after Welch, was purchased in May 1892 for £700, together with a second patent by the same inventor of March 1891, as also the Lindner wired patent for France for under £1,000, these two being acquired as safeguards in an uncertain patent situation.

At the end of 1895, an option of £5,500 was taken on the Golding patent of December 9th, 1890, forty-nine days after Bartlett's beaded-edge patent, in view of its possible validity and priority over that patent, but the option was not exercised and a negotiation to buy the Nedderman patent of May 1891 for the same reason was discontinued, in both cases fortunately for the company.

Major improvements in the details of tyre production have doubtless come from France, Germany and the United States, *but, generally speaking, no foreign inventor or manufacturer working outside Great Britain has ever been first in contributing any novel principle to the advancement of the pneumatic tyre industry.* Their business in both cycle and motor tyres has been founded upon the valid home patents of one Scotsman, two Englishmen, one Irishman and one American, *i.e.*, Thomson 1845, Moseley 1889, Welch 1890, Woods 1890, and Bartlett 1890. Over all these the Thomson air principle still reigns supreme, while Welch has provided the inextensible wired-on principle, the well-base motor rim (Patent No. 22,669, 1892), the cycle rim section and the cord fabric, all of which are indispensable to-day in the manufacture of motor and cycle tyres, a truly remarkable achievement.

I have not observed from the literature of foreign countries any word which would indicate that their tyre magnates have ever fully appreciated all that they owe to the band of pioneers whose achievements it has been my pleasure to record in this book.

CHAPTER FIFTEEN

A LEGAL HARVEST

I

WITH so many minds engaged upon evolving improvements to the immature air tyre, it was inevitable that a tangle of legal claims would arise. So confused and complicated was the position with regard to the protection of the rapidly succeeding series of inventions of this period, that it was only to be clarified by persistent litigation over many years.

The amount of money, time and energy which people were prepared to squander in the law courts was one of the symptoms of the times, and these early tyre cases were fought with a ferocity and lavishness unsurpassed in legal history.

It seems inevitable that the law should lag a step or so behind the main body of social progress (indeed, it is too often completely out-distanced), and at this time the patent laws were in the process of adjusting themselves to the great new burdens which were put upon them by the impetus given to invention from the growth of industrialism. At a time when patent cases were still heard with juries and the Patent Offices of the United Kingdom were not yet amalgamated, the outcome of these actions was even more a matter for speculation, and the opportunities for able advocates were greater than they are to-day : moreover, it is no exaggeration to assert that doubtful justice was meted out by more than one foreign court.

As an instance, in one case a leading firm of foreign rubber manufacturers was offered a licence under the company's patents at a moderate royalty, but carrying with it full co-operation in the building up of the industry in this particular country. They decided, however, that it would suit their policy better to infringe the patent, calculating that by their particular legal procedure a decision in the courts might be delayed for six or seven years, during which they could establish their position and face such damages as might be assessed.

EARL OF ALBEMARLE.
Director, 1896.

Accordingly the legal process was skilfully protracted till it culminated in a long period of consideration by a body of technical experts appointed by the judges to advise the court. After further lengthy delays the experts' advice was duly tendered, and found to support the English company's case on all points. After yet another interval the parties were finally summoned to hear judgment delivered. But it was not to be ; the court assembled with due ceremony, only to inform the litigants that judgment had been postponed, no reason being given. Another substantial lapse of time before the parties were again mobilised, positively for the last time, in order to hear the judges, as one might have expected, uphold the decision of their own experts. But foreign law can be inscrutable and judgment was pronounced against the English company on all points. That was only one more example which suggests that a patent is not a desirable possession for a poor man.

The fact that the Patent Offices of Great Britain and Ireland had not at that time been amalgamated provides another example of the curious twists of fortune which so deeply affect human lives, for when Charles Goodyear of America, after failures which had cost him all he possessed, almost accidentally solved the great problem of the vulcanisation of rubber, by which a sticky comparatively useless product was converted into one of the toughest materials known, with many thousands of separate uses, including tyres, he had not the wherewithal left to patent his invention. He therefore deposited in the United States Patent Office " a claim for record " dated November 6th, 1841, and it was not until 1843 that he was financially in a position to apply for patents in America, England and France.

In the interim, however, during which he was negotiating with Macintosh of England, without, however, disclosing the nature of his process, although samples of the new product had been sent over, Goodyear found that on November 21st, 1843, his patent had been anticipated by Thomas Hancock, a partner of Macintosh. Hancock's patent was attacked on two different occasions, the first in

CHARLES GOODYEAR.
1840.

155

June 1851, and the second, heard before Lord Chief Justice Campbell, twelve years after the patent was applied for. The inventor was called upon to give in evidence a meticulous account of the long series of laboratory experiments carried out single-handed, which had led to the duplication of Goodyear's results.

In both cases the juries upheld the patent on all counts, and Hancock stated subsequently that there was no " document extant which contained so much information upon the manufacture and vulcanisation of rubber as is contained in this specification."

It is remarkable not only that this was a dual invention of surpassing importance, but that it was not, in either case, the inspiration of a moment, but the outcome of months and years of patient experiment and research. The names of such men should not be forgotten.

As a result of the litigation, Goodyear's group were obliged to come to terms with Macintosh, who granted them an exclusive licence for the importation of the over-shoes which had been their main objective. The American group, however, discovered that Hancock, who had patented many other inventions, had omitted on this occasion to make the necessary patent registration in Scotland, so taking advantage of this opportunity, they sailed from New York in the autumn of 1855 to establish the manufacture of their rubber products in Scotland for the European market.

Had Hancock taken out his Scottish patent the North British Rubber Co. would never have come into being in Scotland, and had the Americans been able to find suitable premises in Glasgow, their works would never have been established at the Castle Mills in Edinburgh, which happened to be vacant at that time. As it was, the business was successfully set up, and William Erskine Bartlett, afterwards the inventor of the beaded-edge tyre, was invited by his uncle, Henry Lee Norris, who was the moving spirit in the matter, to come over from America and make his domicile in Edinburgh, which he did in the year 1870, subsequently acting as Managing Director of the company until his death in 1900.

II

If the modern patent lawyer tends to look back upon the patent law of this period as being somewhat chaotic and immature, yet he cannot but look up to the patent lawyers of those days with sincere admiration ; and amongst these there was none greater than John Fletcher Moulton, Q.C. It is frequently said that a great part of English law has been created from the minds of her judges, but it is by listening to eminent counsel upon whose know-ledge and integrity implicit reliance can be placed that the judicial mind is made up, so it can be truly said that it is to Fletcher Moulton, not only in his later capacities as a Lord Justice and Member of Parliament, but also as a leading counsel, that we owe so much of our modern patent law.

By another strange coincidence Fletcher Moulton is connected with the present story, not only through the

fact that he was the constant pilot of the Founder Company through these stormy seas of litigation, but also by the bond of marriage, for in 1875 he married Clare Thomson, the widow of Robert William Thomson, original inventor of the pneumatic tyre.

His career was an outstanding one; he began by proving himself an exception to the rule that

JOHN FLETCHER MOULTON, Q.C.*

adolescent brilliance fades into mediocrity in manhood, for as a schoolboy he was unusually precocious, and his whole academic career, both at Kingswood School and at Cambridge, was strewn with honours and prizes, particularly in the sphere of mathematics. At the Bar, at a time when the competition was less keen and more insular than it is to-day, he was an early success;

* Died March 1921.

158

and the increased number of patent cases, due to the laws of 1883, gave him opportunity to make a name for himself in this branch of the law. No doubt as he watched his steadily growing practice he blessed the day in 1873, the year of Thomson's death, when he decided to turn his back upon school-mastering and became a member of the Middle Temple. After fifteen years he took silk, and for the next twenty years carried on a profitable practice at the Bar. In 1885 he was elected as Liberal Member of Parliament, representing the Clapham Division of Battersea, but owing to the meagre successes of his Party during the next twenty years he did not obtain any advancement, although well meriting it, until 1906, when he was made a Lord Justice of Appeal, knighted and appointed to the Privy Council. He proved himself to be a forceful and independent Judge in the Appeal Court, and six years later in 1912 he became Lord of Appeal in Ordinary, with the title of Lord Moulton of Bank in the County of Southampton.

At the outbreak of the great war Lord Moulton again demonstrated the adaptability of his genius by undertaking the organisation of the Explosives Supply Department, in which he was my chief, which he did with great vigour and efficiency, receiving for his services the K.C.B. and G.B.E. On the afternoon of March 8th, 1921, he took his usual place in the House of Lords, and in the early hours of the following morning he died in his sleep at the age of seventy-seven. That then was the man who was to guide the Founder Company through a vast maze of litigation, which at times reached such proportions that there was virtually a fresh case for every working day in the year.

I have sometimes heard it objected, and this apparently

was the view of Dunlop himself,* that the decisions arrived at by lawyers on questions of science and mechanics are of little value simply because they are the decisions of lawyers and not of scientists or engineers. Yet any mind of average ability is capable of fully comprehending an isolated proposition in any single branch of human knowledge, providing that such proposition is thoroughly and adequately explained. No one who has waded through thousands of laborious and often childish expositions of scientific platitudes which place patent laws among the most exhausting branches of our English legal system will doubt for a moment the thoroughness or adequacy of the explanations in the majority of cases. Unless, therefore, it is held that the minds of the judiciary are consistently below the average, their decisions should be deemed to be of at least equal value with those of engineers or veterinary surgeons. In truth the advantages of a scientific mind are of little assistance in comprehending an isolated set of circumstances of which there is a detailed explanation, but are only of value in the relating of scientific phenomena, and in the deduction of progressive ideas, or in pursuing a continuous line of thought in connection therewith.

III

The first great pneumatic tyre action to be heard was that taken by the North British Rubber Company against Mackintosh in respect of the Golding patent, and was heard for eight days before Mr. Justice Romer in 1894. The judgment then given in favour of Bartlett's company was not appealed against ; there is no doubt that they were fortunate thus easily to hold their verdict. Bartlett

* See Chapter 20.

in his earlier tyres had used an inextensible inner tube of cloth and rubber, and one of the points urged against him was that by introducing the extensible all-rubber inner tube, which he subsequently adopted, his tyre, as originally designed, must have blown off the rim, a defect which could only have been cured by the adoption of inextensible edges, thus invading Welch's territory, or else by adopting the exaggerated beaded edge and hooked rim which Golding and Nedderman were claiming so as to give a greater grip for their elastic tube.

Had Bartlett been held strictly to the drawings shown

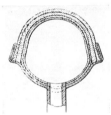

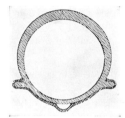

| The Bartlett Clincher Tyre, 1890. | Golding's Tyre, 1890. | The Bartlett Clincher Tyre, 1893.* |

in his specification, he would have been placed on the horns of this dilemma and would have had to confine himself to the inferior cloth and rubber inextensible air tube which he had described in his specification, or else risk infringing upon Welch. But the broad interpretation of his patent by the courts permitted him to accentuate the edges of his cover and bend over the edges of his rim to withstand the extra strain of the all-rubber tube, and thus to approximate to the Golding, Nedderman and Gormully patents. On this all-important point his victory was a narrow one ; the technical evidence was

* These and other patent illustrations reproduced by permission of H.M. Stationery Office.

so conflicting that the court ordered a reference to be made to an independent expert. Bartlett's drawings would not have been sufficient in themselves, but taken with the description of his method and the statement that such method would be used " substantially as described," the courts were convinced of the legitimacy of his claims, and accordingly Golding passed into obscurity, a fate which was shared by Nedderman.

EARL DE LA WARR.*
Director 1896.

Gormully and Jeffrey of Chicago, who, after Bartlett, were first to vulcanise in one piece their highly successful " G. & J." beaded-edge cycle tyre, staged the most prolonged and determined fight in the history of British tyre patent litigation. Their patent in America was dated July 27th, 1891, although they relied as a part of their case in this litigation upon the publication in England of an earlier patent of Jeffrey's dated 1888, which did not, however, form the subject of a British patent. The case between these two American inventors was fought through to the House of Lords, being the first tyre patent case to come before that Tribunal, and lasted for two and a half years (a fact upon which the Lord Chancellor—Lord Halsbury—bitterly commented) before Gormully and Jeffrey were finally relegated to the discards on All Fools' Day, 1898, thus establishing the validity of Bartlett's patent beyond any further question.

* Died 1915.

An exactly opposite result was reached in America, where Jeffrey's earlier patent carried weight, when the " G. & J." Company proceeded against Bartlett and were successful.

It is an instructive fact that the whole of Bartlett's litigation in England turned, in a great measure, upon two or three sentences in his specification, and yet the Gormully and Jeffrey case alone, which was not the first to be fought upon the same broad issues, involved five hundred pages of evidence. Expense was certainly no object in the litigation of the tyre world.

About this time Michelin had introduced a motor tyre of the beaded-edge variety under a claim of novelty. This was an infringement of Bartlett, and Michelin suffered with the great majority, but continued to trade in England through the agency of an agreement under which he was limited to the importation of such tyres as the holders of rights under the patent required for their British trade.

An inaccuracy which may conveniently be disposed of here is that of Michelin's claim to have invented the detachable cycle tyre and used it first for road racing. The mere mention of the date of his patent (1891) should be conclusive, seeing that no less than seven different patentees of detachable tyres filed their claims in 1890. Michelin's came " well at the heel of the hunt," and his cycle tyre of 1891 was substantially a copy of others that had gone before, indeed, Robertson's detachable tyre had been *on the road* in January 1891.

IV

The fighting history of Welch's patent somewhat resembles that of Bartlett. Golding began by raising an objection to the sealing of the patent, alleging " dis-

163　　　　　　　M 2

conformity " and priority for himself, but was overruled by the Comptroller-General. The patent was contested in numerous actions on this ground, and on the grounds of want of novelty, utility, subject-matter and that Welch was not the first inventor.

In cases brought by the Founder Company against Kekeell—heard for nine days before Mr. Justice Caswwich in December 1895 and January 1896—and the East London Rubber Company—heard before Mr. Justice Romer in December 1896—the latter of whom appealed, the appeal being heard by Lord Justice Lindley (Master of the Rolls) and Lords Justices Smith and Rigby, the question of disconformity was decided in favour of the company. In a further action against The Leicester Pneumatic Tyre Company it was held, again by Mr. Justice Romer, that Welch's patent could not be invalidated on the ground of disconformity, that it had not been anticipated, and was good.

This judgment also was appealed against, the appeal being dismissed with costs, again by Lords Justices Lindley, Smith and Rigby, and was taken to the House of Lords, where, in July 1899, it was finally dismissed with costs by an undivided court (Lords Macnaghten, Morris, Shand, Davey and Brampton), which found that the application of Welch's device to pneumatic tyres was " a development that almost inevitably must have been discovered between the provisional and complete specifications."

Welch's patent consequently embraced every form of pneumatic tyre cover held on by wires or any device performing the service of wires, even including edges rendered inextensible by means of solutioned yarns and employing no wires at all.

One case on the latter point against the New Lamb Tyre Company was actually contested and carried to appeal in 1902. The edges of the Lamb tyre were composed of loose strands of yarn forming a thickened edge to strengthen the cover. Although Lamb pleaded that the strands merely maintained the cover in position and that actually it was held on by frictional force, the courts decided that the efficiency of the tyre depended upon the inextensibility of the edges.

The Founder Company had to defend the Welch patent from scores of infringers, for it provided a very ready form of temptation to small people who could make a living out of pirating a few score of tyres every year. It was worse even than horse dealing. No expensive tools were required, all component parts could be easily purchased, and the task of building up

Sir William Goff, Bt.*
Director 1898.

the tyres could be carried out in the back room of a man's dwelling. Writs were served literally by the hundred with uniformly successful results, as people of the type in question had neither the means nor the intention of defending the dishonesty of their actions. The position was rendered more difficult by the fact that when an infringer was stopped under one name and at one address, there was no penalty attached to his commencing operations at another address under another

* Died November 1917.

name. Their final defeat was only brought about by the vigorous action of the two patentee companies and the excellence and cheapness of legitimate tyres, which gradually removed from buyers the desire to deal in the pirated article with its attendant legal risks. Incidentally, quite a number of infringers found a resting place in gaol for contempt of court.

The company in its turn was heavily attacked by the Palmer Company, their onslaught being well advertised and uncharitably timed to coincide with the sale of the Founder Company for £3,000,000 and its subsequent resale to the public.

The Palmer Company, who held John Fullerton Palmer's " all warp " fabric patent of 1889, had acquired the Trigwell wired patent of November 1890, and the Amos Thomas wired patent of March 1889 (amended in 1893 and 1898). The Founder Company held the Welch tangential fabric patents of 1893 and 1894 and were sheltered under agreement by Moseley's Flexifort patent of 1888. They had had the opportunity of buying the Amos Thomas patent, but did not utilise it. Their wisdom and their patents were fully justified when the Palmer attack was repulsed all along the line with costs, after a hearing of eleven days before Mr. Justice Wills, who found in his judgment that Welch did not infringe upon Palmer, but that on the contrary, the latter had been anticipated by the Moseley patent of 1888 and probably by other prior users in England.

It would not be of general interest were I to attempt to deal with the manifold niceties and intricacies of the numerous patent claims of that period, but a deluge of patents appeared which kept the company constantly at law to protect its patent position which it did successfully.

Victories by the company were appealed against without success, and only after ceaseless warfare was it established that no tyre with inextensible edges, whether wired or not, could be made without infringing upon Welch or could be worked without a licence from the company.

The extent of tyre litigation in those years was imposing. At one period Bartlett was attacking Macintosh, Nedderman, Gormully and Jeffrey, Welch and many minor infringers. The Founder Company were at the throats of Bartlett, Macintosh, the New Lamb Tyre Company, Moseley, Seddon, Grappler, Beeston, Bidwell, Neal, Michelin, the Clifton and other tyre companies, besides a host of petty infringers, brisk litigation being also in progress in Germany, France and America. On the other hand, they were being attacked in turn or threatened by Bartlett and Palmer at home, and in America by Bidwell under his valve patent, and Stillman and Rice and Straus under their detachable tyre patents.

Welch had lost his patent in America owing to an irreparable blunder in procedure over there (he had been anticipated in France) and Dunlop had never protected the pneumatic principle in the U.S.A. For a time the Founder Company was left defenceless in the face of the opposition of powerful rubber interests claiming patents of their own, a situation which was partly remedied by their acquisition of new inventions, notably the Brown and Stillman patent of 1892 for £20,000, a tyre almost precisely similar to Welch's. Strangely enough Dunlop in a case taken by Featherstone against the George R. Bidwell Cycle Co. of America in 1892 secured a useless victory for his method of sticking the tyre to the rim, the only win ever recorded for him in any country. After

a careful hearing and a deferred decision, Judge Townsend
of New York declared that the Thomson mode of bolting
the cover to the rim " could not be successfully applied
to a bicycle." Dunlop, under advice, had obtained a
re-issue of his subsidiary patent, and upon an appeal
from the decision of Judge Townsend, heard in 1893,
before the Circuit Court of Appeals, Judges Wallace,
Lacombe and Shipman severely criticised the circumstances of the re-issue, and quashed the judgment of the
lower Court.

How much happier we might have been had Dunlop,
whose provisional specification was drawn by a friend and
contained but $2\frac{3}{4}$ lines, not laid claim to the pneumatic
principle but only to its application to cycles and the
method of employment, although the fact that he did *not*
do so has been quoted as evidence that he was unaware of
the Thomson patent. Many inventors of novel ideas have
had second thoughts about their patents in the light of
later knowledge, and would dearly have liked to turn back

the clock, only realising when
too late that legitimate and
often trifling amendments
would have made all the
difference between validity
and invalidity, fortune and
failure.

Thus at the end of this long
nightmare of litigation there
had emerged two magnificent
patents for attachment which
in their final forms were of
great simplicity and efficiency,

HARVEY DU CROS, JUNIOR.*
Director 1923.

* Died November 1928.

168

PEDIGREE OF THE PNEUMATIC TYRE

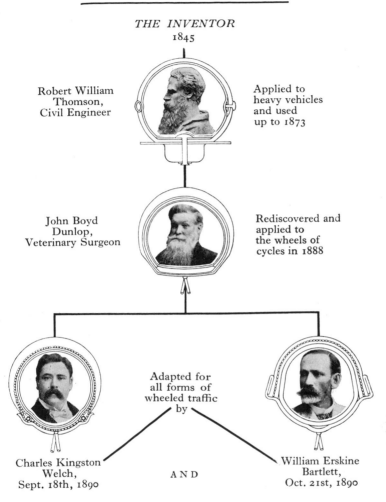

THE INVENTOR
1845

Robert William
Thomson,
Civil Engineer

Applied to
heavy vehicles
and used
up to 1873

John Boyd
Dunlop,
Veterinary Surgeon

Rediscovered and
applied to
the wheels of
cycles in 1888

Adapted for
all forms of
wheeled traffic
by

Charles Kingston
Welch,
Sept. 18th, 1890

AND

William Erskine
Bartlett,
Oct. 21st, 1890

Dunlop's patented method of fastening the tyre to the
rim was discarded in 1892 in favour of Welch's and
Bartlett's inventions, and as applied to motor tyres the
latter method began to fall into disuse after 1920. Consequently the vast bulk of pneumatic tyres throughout the
world are now being made upon the compressed air
principle of Thomson and the wired fastening, cord
casing, and well-base cycle and motor rims of Welch.

[Facing p. 168.

the Welch patent, covering the inextensible edge principle, and the Bartlett patent, that of the beaded edge, both of which in the course of the struggle had been pronounced upon by at least forty British judges in various courts. These stood supreme in Britain as master patents, and in all countries, in whatever ownership, the two systems formed the firm and broad foundation upon which the industry as a whole was consolidated, the wired tyre, dominating the cycle trade (outside America, where the single tube had always held the field), and the beaded-edge tyre the motor trade, until recent years, when its territory has been overwhelmed by its wired rival, even Bartlett's company having bowed before the insistence of the public in this respect.

An interesting and curious commentary on the history of tyre litigation, unsurpassed as it was in volume in any other field, was made by Dunlop when he wrote in 1921 " *I have never taken part in the pleadings of any tyre case, and never appeared in the box in England.*" That would be eloquent testimony, if it were needed, of the ability and success of those who fought the battles of the Founder Company and laid the foundations of the industry and of the fact that Dunlop was doubly fortunate in his advisers and friends and in the position which, through their exertions, he had achieved.

CHAPTER SIXTEEN

ADVENTURES AT LAW
I

THE Founder Company's legal encounters were not confined to the validity of its patents alone. Many suits on other grounds were fought out, including the right to prevent others from using the name Dunlop as a title in combination with other names. Another against Arthur Neal was based on the question as to whether worn out tyres could be re-made without infringement, it being held by the court that work of this nature was not merely a repair, but the construction of a new tyre, and that without a licence it constituted an infringement.

In yet another case against Moseley and others, heard in 1903 before Mr. Justice Swinfen-Eady, the company challenged the right to make and sell separately parts of a tyre for export and to licensees of the company, the defendants maintaining that the patent was for a combination of parts and that the sale of any one of such parts alone, covers, for instance, did not constitute infringement. Both the lower court and the Court of Appeal decided against the company, stating that it would be imposing a burden upon the vendors to ascertain whether the articles sold were subsequently resold legitimately, which " the Law did not impose."

A further point was raised in an action in 1896 against the Puncture Proof Tyre Company, infringement being proved by consent, the question of damages was argued. The net profit made by the Founder Company was put at £1 per tyre, but the court assessed the damages at 2s. 6d. per tyre on the ground that in cases where licences had been issued this was the amount of the royalty demanded by the company : a decision which seemed to place a premium upon dishonesty. Although the company was unbeaten in its main patent actions, decisions such as these had the effect, as time went on, of nibbling at their claims and narrowing their field.

A most important case arose in the early 'nineties when a petition was made to the Board of Trade by a Midland group headed by Mr. Charles Marston, now Sir Charles Marston, the well-known Biblical Archæologist, seeking to compel the company to issue compulsory licences for the manufacture of its tyre to outside groups on the ground that the market demand was not being fully satisfied by the company. This application was defeated after a strenuous and expensive hearing. The company's intensive activity, growing organisation and record of achievement being sufficient to convince the authorities that poaching should not be allowed.

No efforts, fair or foul, were spared to raid the company's preserves, and an outstanding example was that of the famous " Prior-user " case, which in February 1897 occupied nine anxious days before Mr. Justice Romer. The defendants, Marwood and Cross, adduced an immense amount of evidence to prove that a

CHARLES WISDOM HELY.*
Director 1898,

* Died December 1929.

171

wired detachable pneumatic tyre had been made and sold some six months prior to the date of the Welch patent of 1890.

The ball was opened with this letter from the solicitors on the other side :—

" Dear Sir, I am instructed by the Directors of The Puncture Proof Pneumatic Company Ltd., upon which Company a writ has been served by the Pneumatic Tyre Co. Ltd., for an alleged infringement of patents, to inform you that my clients are in possession of evidence of anticipation and prior user of the subject-matter of the patent mentioned in the writ.

" The evidence consists, briefly, of—(1) The person who, in March, 1890, manufactured tyres described in the Welch patent Specification ; (2) those who assisted in the manufacture of the tyre and to whom the idea was communicated ; (3) of persons who used the tyres on journeys upon the road in March, Easter, and August, 1890. The tyres themselves are in the possession of the Company.

" Under these circumstances, I am instructed to demand an instant withdrawal of the writ, and an undertaking not to interfere in any way with my clients in the manufacture and sale of their tyres, and to inform you that on your failing to comply with this demand by 11 o'clock to-morrow, Saturday morning, they will hold themselves at liberty to put the public in possession of the whole of the evidence above referred to as and when they think fit. A copy of this letter has also been sent to the directors of The Pneumatic Tyre Company."

Witness after witness, a score in all, were put into the box to swear with great particularity from their own experience and knowledge to the many occasions upon which the tyre had been ridden, and seen and discussed publicly, their statements being supported by each other, by documents, and by contemporary events of one kind or another.

Although the evidence was mostly of this type, one witness swore that he had been unable to take part in a particular club run on a vital date when he knew the tyre had been ridden, through being incapacitated by an accident for which he had received surgical treatment, his doctor's dated and receipted account being produced in confirmation. Other witnesses fixed the dates by their removals, by their having been sold up, by the riding of the tyre to see a relative who died soon after, and one, a wire-worker, by the supply of the wires with which to make the tyres. The witnesses were all kept out of court, and yet they supported each other substantially in their testimony, although Mr. Terrell, Q.C., stated that he did not ask the court to believe certain of his own witnesses who had not distinguished themselves under cross-examination unless they were corroborated, but pleaded that even if the evidence of some was destroyed, it did not follow that the testimony of all was gone.

As a whole the evidence formed a mosaic, bearing the construction desired, but Moulton took his stand on the fact that everything that was alleged, so far as it was true, had occurred in 1891 and not in 1890, and roundly characterised some of the evidence as deliberately false and generally attacked the *bona fides* of the whole case.

At the end of each day's hearing a band of eager scouts of the company's staff scattered over the scenes of the alleged happenings, seeking to find the flaws in the case by tracking down every statement to its source, and weighing the evidence in readiness for the next morning's hearing. As a result much rebutting evidence was discovered. The bicycles exhibited as having been made in 1890 were proved to be of later date, the valve described as having been used in the supposedly earlier tyre was proved by the alert " Faed " Wilson to have been evolved a year after, and many witnesses were brought forward who flatly contradicted statements " of fact " made by the other side.

Nevertheless, for a long time this case looked very black, but in the end it was broken down when it was proved that some of the witnesses had sworn falsely, and others had been honestly mistaken as to the year of the alleged occurrence.

The judge expressed distrust generally, and said that " it would be a painful thing for me to attempt to analyse the evidence " or to explain why he felt that the case had not been proved to his satisfaction. He wished it to stop there, preferring, if possible, not to give a formal judgment, a course to which Terrell agreed. Accordingly no judgment was delivered, the case, which was perhaps the most exciting and dramatic of the many in which the company was engaged, being smashed by sheer weight of evidence and argument.

GEORGE DU CROS.
Director 1917.

I can do no more than suggest in the compass of

174

this book the immense amount of time, energy and resources that the original members of this industry were compelled to expend at law while building up and consolidating their commercial position, but perhaps sufficient has been said to show with what determination and fortitude they confronted a situation that was at times uncertain and always the subject of attacks.*

II

The honour of inventing the first detachable pneumatic tyre has been claimed for Bartlett, but not quite accurately. He was undoubtedly the first inventor to *describe* such a tyre in his provisional specification, but by the judgments delivered, Welch's patent was held to be both valid and applicable to pneumatic tyres, the situation being that Welch was before Bartlett with his provisional specification of September 16th, 1890, by thirty-five days, and with his complete specification of June 16th, 1891, by thirty-four days.

Heavy litigation was threatened mutually between the owners of the Welch and Bartlett patents on the grounds broadly from the Welch point of view that if Bartlett employed an extensible inner tube which he had not described, and adhered to his drawings, the use of inextensible edges would be essential, thus infringing Welch's claim to cover all forms of inextensible edges : but luckily these threats never materialised, as will appear.

Bartlett, on the other hand, averred, among other matters, that Welch borrowed his idea of including pneumatic tyres in his complete specification, from extraneous sources, and that consequently there was a

* For the latest of which see Appendix, p. 309

want of conformity between his provisional and complete specifications, or in other words, that Welch had introduced into his complete specification an ingredient, the nature of which had not been indicated in his provisional. That this contention was unsound was subsequently proved by events.

The difference in principle between the two inventions is that Welch's wired cover is kept in place by the inextensibility of its edges, which are " floating wires," these being less in circumference than the outer edges of the rims, and resting upon shoulders designed for the purpose. They are held securely in position by the circumferential tension which pulls the wires outwards all round the wheel, independently of any support from the rim, there being no lateral tension on the rim. Bartlett's beaded cover, on the other hand, does not depend for security upon the inextensibility of its edges, but upon these being clinched against or under the sides of the rim and maintained in position by the automatic lateral force of air compression. In short, the Bartlett type of tyre is dependent on the rim for security, while the Welch tyre is independent of the rim.

ROBERT WATSON.*
Director 1917.

Had the threatened actions between Welch and Bartlett been pursued, they would by their magnitude have put all others in the shade; every patent counsel at the Bar of any standing had been retained

* Died August 1929 in his 89th year.

176

on one side or the other, together with a small army of experts, all prepared to back their own side to the limit, as is the way of experts. My father had reported to his Board on July 24th, 1895, that he was " in daily consultation with our legal advisers and experts in this matter, and that the opinion of our counsel was that the Clincher people could not succeed," and that " the case was proceeding in a most satisfactory manner." But in 1896, almost as the seconds were stepping out of the ring, a happy solution was arrived at through the purchase by the Founder Company of the Bartlett patent in dramatic circumstances which to me will always remain a vivid memory.

My father's original company with its £15,010 of cash capital, increased from time to time to £260,000 of Ordinary Shares, had been sold to Ernest Terah Hooley and Martin D. Rucker for £3,000,000; and my father and I, who were being asked to undertake the administration of the new company, stipulated that the threatened litigation with Bartlett should be brought to an end and the proposed new company strengthened by the acquisition of this patent and other assets to justify the increase of capital to £5,000,000, the amount agreed to by the purchasers, £6,000,000, having been vetoed by us. Messrs. Hooley and Rucker appreciated the wisdom of this, and commissioned us to negotiate for the Bartlett patent, for which purpose we travelled to Torquay where Bartlett, who was not a robust man, was staying.

On April 18th, 1896, I sat silently by for hour after hour while these two great protagonists, Harvey du Cros and W. E. Bartlett, fought for their respective sides, with the only result that a complete deadlock was reached. Bartlett, who was about as encouraging as a winter wind in his own city of Edinburgh, as perhaps the circumstances warranted, and knowing what was afoot, demanded a million pounds and conceded nothing after half-a-day's debate, while my father, fortified by the opinion of Fletcher Moulton (which, viewed in the light of after events, was sound) as to the vulnerability of the Bartlett patent, was equally unyielding. Accordingly we separated, but before leaving a working compromise occurred to me with which my father was in complete agreement, so we returned to the fray, proposing to Bartlett that he should accept £200,000, and that the company should grant him a licence to continue the manufacture of his own tyre under a royalty of 2s. 6d. each, with the stipulations that he should not make the Welch tyre, that we should only be permitted to issue one other Bartlett licence and should take over the licence which he had issued in 1894 to the Palmer Tyre Ltd., who were making a beaded-edge tyre.

The upshot was that we shook hands on this bargain, and so it was that the two great governing patents of the tyre world, namely those of Welch and Bartlett, passed into the possession of Harvey du Cros' original company, and the monopoly upon which he thought he had founded the industry seven years before became at last

WILLIAM DU CROS.*

* Alternate Director 1924. Died September 1937.

178

substantially an accomplished fact. The transaction, which was a wise one without being actually essential, was completed without a hitch on April 29th, 1896, and worked out commercially to the complete satisfaction of all parties. The company ultimately received in royalties on the Bartlett and Palmer tyres and the additional licence which was subsequently issued for the manufacture of the "Clipper" tyre, a total sum of over £400,000, double the sum paid for the patent. But Bartlett's company continued to trade very largely and very profitably, a success fully earned on the merits of their production, and having no reason to regret this settlement, which forestalled a contest that could only have been determined in the House of Lords itself. Litigation took place subsequently upon the point as to whether Bartlett's company were entitled to grant a sub-licence to Michelin. The court decided that the latter was merely an agent of the former and that the licence had not, therefore, been violated. This decision of Mr. Justice Byrne was appealed against by the Founder Company and affirmed by the Court of Appeal.

III

"Single" tube or "hose-pipe" cycle tyres were made in many and various forms, and were not subject to patents in England, after the discovery of Thomson's Patent and publication by I. W. Boothroyd about 1891, who produced such a tyre but failed to patent it. They held a foremost place for cycles and light carriages in America, where a patent was granted to Tillinghast in 1893, and but for the innate conservatism of the British public and insufficient propaganda by their sponsors they might well have secured an important position in England as well.

The tyre in its later form was not truly a single tube, but a multiple tyre, the air tube being made as part of the cover, with very resilient results. Contrary to a general impression it was not difficult to repair, and to the ignorance of the English user on this point may partly be attributed the comparative failure of the tyre on the road, though for racing it was temporarily popular.

The improved rim for cycles which was patented by Frederick Westwood in January 1893 has practically held a monopoly since its introduction, the Woods valve of March 1891 being equally tenacious in its hold on the valve trade. It is remarkable that the wonderful utility of all these major inventions was only surpassed by their extreme simplicity.

L. M. BERGIN.*
Director 1917.

There were other outstanding inventions and improvements which went to the making of the pneumatic tyre, the chief of which was that for the application of tangential fabric covers, the forerunner of the modern " cord " or " cable " tyre. This was a lining material having no weft threads crossing the warp, a remarkably effective and important system which added enormously to the strength and efficiency of tyres, particularly of motor and giant tyres. The absence of the weft threads eliminated the sawing, wrinkling and overheating difficulties of the

* Died July 1934.

THE SURVIVAL OF THE FITTEST

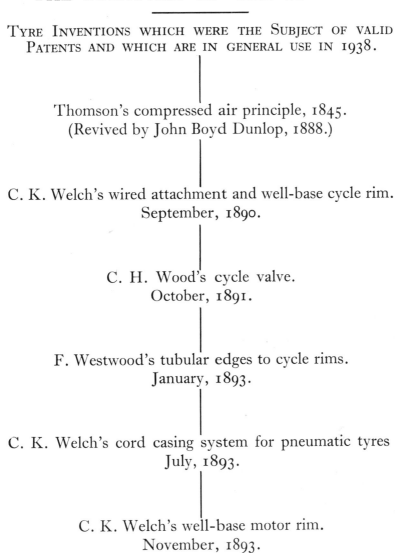

Tyre Inventions which were the Subject of valid Patents and which are in general use in 1938.

Thomson's compressed air principle, 1845.
(Revived by John Boyd Dunlop, 1888.)

C. K. Welch's wired attachment and well-base cycle rim.
September, 1890.

C. H. Wood's cycle valve.
October, 1891.

F. Westwood's tubular edges to cycle rims.
January, 1893.

C. K. Welch's cord casing system for pneumatic tyres
July, 1893.

C. K. Welch's well-base motor rim.
November, 1893.

C. K. Welch's rubber non-skid principle
May, 1894.

woven cloth, and the layers of fabric being impregnated with rubber and superimposed on each other, transversely, contributed to the rigidity and durability of the tyre. The principle had been employed in varying forms and for various purposes by a number of inventors prior to 1888, in which year (Patent No. 11804) it was described and specifically applied for the purpose of preventing or diminishing the stretching of foundation materials by Joseph Moseley of Manchester, who named his system " Flexifort," and subsequently applied it to solid tyres. In 1893 it was applied in a somewhat varied form to single-tube pneumatic tyres by Palmer of America, and great credit is due to Palmer (and through him to the Silvertown Company of London) for helping to focus attention upon a train of thought which gave rise to very important results.

Welch, whose patents (13391, 22589 of 1893, and 4351 of 1894) survived a determined assault by Palmer (the case in which Moseley's master idea, the " Flexifort " patent, was also upheld and Palmer's declared to be invalid in England), was the first to apply this principle to the pneumatic tyre, acting in co-operation with Moseley, and thereby confirmed in its pre-eminent position, the Dunlop-Welch cycle tyre of the day, upon which appeared the words " Welch's Patent Fabric and Moseley's Flexifort Patents," and the trade marks of the two firms. Since then Welch's system has become the universal foundation for all pneumatic tyre covers.

Much credit is due to American energy and enterprise for the adaptation to motor cars of the cord principle and that of the Welch cycle tyre, from 1914 onwards, the latter by the development of wired or inextensible but flexible edges, with straight-sided rims, in preference to

Bartlett's extensible edges and curved rims. With the elimination of rim cutting by the adoption of the Welch method, and the advantages in construction by the use of cord casings, the life of motor tyres was enormously increased, running costs were proportionately reduced and the application of pneumatic tyres in giant sizes to lorries, buses, airplanes and railways was made possible.

Looking back on these events it can now be seen that the chief elements of the most modern motor covers were ready to the hand of the Founder Company from 1901 onwards, when they had become rubber manufacturers, and *were open to all manufacturers* from 1904 onwards, when tyre patents were expiring. It becomes a matter for wonderment, therefore, that these advantages were only recognised and availed of after many years. The explanation, insufficient as it may be, is, that Michelin, being the first in the motor tyre field, and having no licence to manufacture under the wired-on patents, set the fashion with the Bartlett principle, a fashion which was accepted by the public and adopted by all other manufacturers, including the Founder Company, even though the latter held the three Welch Patents which govern all present-day tyre production. Nevertheless, I believe that the Dunlop tyres used in some of the early races were made with cord casings, as it is the fact that the first carriage tyres produced by the Founder Company in 1893 were made on the Welch wired principle.

The first rubber non-skid tread to be used was the invention of William Edwards (Patent No. 11251, June 1892), who placed a series of ridges at right angles to the plane of the wheel round the tread of the cycle tyre, but for a different purpose altogether. He was aiming to minimise a sucking action, which he alleged was produced by the action of the tyre on the road surface, by creating an air space between his projecting ridges and between the tread and the road. The rights were acquired by the Founder Company but for another purpose, that of marketing covers so made, as non-skid tyres, which was done with partial success. Welch patented a rubber non-skid design in 1894 which was adopted generally by others, with a bewildering number of variations of design. For motor tyres it was followed by the revival of Thomson's steel-studded treads in one form or another, and by chains and other devices, until finally every country reverted to the all-rubber non-skid tread which the Founder Tyre Company originated.

A great many inventors, including Dunlop and Welch, endeavoured to produce a true non-puncturing tyre without sacrificing any of the other qualities of the present tyre, but although there have been a legion of such devices, none has, as yet, succeeded, and this ideal would seem to be unattainable.

But the necessity for eliminating the difficulty and inconvenience of roadside motor-tyre repairs was met in other ways, and opened up a fruitful field for the inventor. As Bartlett's rim, which had become the standard form of equipment, was a permanent part of the wheel, it was in England for a time supplemented by an

ALFRED DU CROS.
Director 1918.

183

auxiliary wheel, called the " Stepney," fastened to the outside of the punctured wheel ; that was superseded by a rim with a detachable flange, which in turn gave way to contractible or demountable rims and finally to detachable wheels. These devices, step by step, relegated repairs to the workshop, to the immense satisfaction of the fast growing motoring community.

This community was to provide a second great market for the pneumatic tyre which was to surpass in its extent the first, just as aerial transport bids fair to provide a third as great or greater than either of them.

CHAPTER SEVENTEEN

THE COMING OF THE AUTOMOBILE

I

THROUGHOUT the centuries, many men of many countries have experimented with the known forms of motive power, applied in one way or another, and for one purpose or another. The claims to precedence are as numerous as the prophecies which surrounded this oldest of subjects since Roger Bacon wrote in the thirteenth century :

ROGER BACON.

" We will be able to construct machines which will propel ships with greater speed than a whole garrison of rowers and which will need only one pilot to guide them.

" We will be able to propel carriages with incredible speed without the assistance of any animal. And we will be able to make machines which, by means of wings, will enable us to fly like birds."

But among the host of pioneers and prophets, impractical and otherwise, known to the scientific world, the names that will ever stand forth are of those who, profiting by their own ideas, or the ideas of other inventors, successfully adapted them to everyday usage.

To this category belong the names of the Germans Carl Benz of Carlsruhe, and Gottlieb Daimler of Schorndorf, who were working out their first petrol motors separately, but practically simultaneously, five years

CARL BENZ.*

before Dunlop produced his pneumatic tyre. Both, like MacMillan and so many other inventors, were sons of the people, and neither was the originator of the benzene or petrol motor-driven principle. But they were the practical men who first saw it through, and, by so doing, laid the foundation of an industry which has increased and multiplied as no other industry had ever done before. The two inventors were employing the cycle as a medium for their earliest experiments, before the pedal safety had reached maturity, and as the bicycle and tricycle blazed the trail for the pneumatic tyre so they did also, in some measure, for the motor-car, for they were the first vehicles to be propelled by the new motive force.

To Emile Levassor, the Frenchman, belongs much of the credit for the adaptation of the new principle to motor cars in a practical way, and many of his basic ideas of 1892 still persist in the motor-car of to-day. As the seemingly unattainable ambition of the early aviators was to accomplish a circular kilometre, a

GOTTLIEB DAIMLER.

feat worth a prize of £2,000 performed by Henry Farman in 1908, so it was the ambition of Levassor to perform a journey of six miles, that was three miles out

* Died April 1929.

and back to his works at Courbevoie without stopping, a task in which he only succeeded after eighteen months of unceasing effort. Levassor died in 1897, his life being shortened by a severe accident which he sustained in the Paris-Marseilles race of 1896, and " Papa Daimler," a father, if not *the* father, of motoring, died in 1900.

An Englishman, Edward Butler, showed a petrol-driven motor cycle at the London Inventions Exhibition in 1885—it may have been beside Welch's Di-Cycle—but was " warned off " British roads by our punitive laws, in startling

EMILE LEVASSOR.

contrast to the wise and liberal policy of early French legislation under the protection of which their pioneers were quick to make the most of their unique progressive opportunities in the manufacture both of cars and tyres.

To Michelin is due the credit of being the first to market motor-car tyres in practical form in the later 'nineties, using the Bartlett system ; nevertheless, detachable tyres were fitted to horse-drawn carriages in England at the end of 1892 by the Founder Company, the first of the big tyres after those of Thomson, the French following suit in 1894. It was recorded in a Company Minute of November 8th, 1892, that a dogcart should be purchased for experimental purposes, and this, appearing soon after on the streets of Coventry behind a prizewinner from the Dublin Horse Show in combination with perfectly silent pneumatic wheels made on the Welch model, became the talk of the town.. In August 1894 a paper by me on the subject " Pneumatic Tyres for Carriages " was read before the British Coach Builders' Association, with little, if any, effect on the somnolence of that august body. These light carriage tyres, like Thomson's, gave good service, especially on the buggies of the United States. Being built up by hand, and speed not being in question, they were quite unsuitable for the wear and tear of motor cars, so that Michelin's claim to have produced the first durable vulcanised motor tyre was well founded.

As Dunlop had adapted Thomson's invention to the cycle, so Michelin adapted Bartlett's invention to the motor-car. This success and its influence on the early development of the motor-car is gratefully remembered, and a memorial to this achievement was for years to be found in the fact that in Britain the measurements of all motor tyres were indicated in millimetres. In New York, in 1897, pneumatic tyres were used extensively in single-tube form (a method of manufacture excelled in by the Americans) on the very heavy electrical cabs which were then in public use in that city.

Nor was Michelin's lead in heavy tyres due altogether to the deterrent effect upon motoring in England of the notorious " Red Flag " Act of 1865, under which mechanical vehicles were accompanied by two men preceded by another with a red flag, and limited to a speed of four miles per hour. This and other Acts had effectively crippled the efforts of the pioneers of steam-driven motors and so by wasting thirty valuable years deprived Britain of the lead in the automobile movement which was within her grasp in the earlier part of the nineteenth century. Later, a Bill for repeal was introduced into the House of Commons by Mr. Shaw-Lefevre in 1895,

THE OLD AND THE NEW

ARTHUR DU CROS' DOGCART, 1893

Extract from his Paper read before the Institute of British Carriage Manufacturers at Birmingham, August 27th, 1894 :—

" The diminution of friction when pneumatic tyres are used has been very completely and satisfactorily proved in the Cycling world. The saving in tractional force on carriages has also been ascertained.

Experiments were made with a brougham weighing some 15 cwt. with the following results :—

	Iron Tyres require	Pneumatic Tyres require
Paved Streets . . .	48 lbs.	26 lbs.
Smooth Macadam . . .	40 lbs.	23 lbs.
Fresh-laid Broken Metal .	130 lbs.	37 lbs."

The details of Thomson's activities and experiments were unknown to the Pneumatic Tyre Company in 1894, but these comparative tests indicate the relative merits of the ancient and modern tyres.

R. W. THOMSON'S BROUGHAM, 1846.

*Weight of carriage with its load 15 cwt.

On paved streets the common wheels require a force of	48 lbs.	
The patent wheels		28 lbs.
On clean, smooth, hard, Macadamised road the common wheels require a force of	40 lbs.	
The patent wheels		25 lbs.
On broken granite newly laid down the common wheels require a force of . . .	130 lbs.	
The patent wheels		40 lbs.

* Extract from the *Mechanics Magazine*, 1849, Vol. 50.

but it died with the fall of the Government in that year. Ultimately, the 1865 Act was repealed in November 1896 by a Government measure sponsored by Mr. Henry Chaplin in the House of Commons, through the pioneering efforts of a band of enthusiasts and the Self-Propelled Traffic Association under the Presidency of Sir David Salomons, Bart. It was but seldom enforced in its expiring months against the petrol motor-car, of which the first specimen was imported in 1894 (it is believed by Mr. Harry Hewetson) and of which there were hardly a dozen in England in 1895. In the latter year Hewetson drove his car in London in broad daylight and was duly warned by Scotland Yard " not to do it again," and in the month of the repeal, a belated summons was applied for against H. J. Lawson for being driven in his motor-car in the Lord Mayor's procession without a red flag, this being the dying effort of a lost cause.

SIR D. SALOMONS, BT.*

In the course of the crusade an exhibition of cars was given at the Imperial Institute during 1896 when the Prince of Wales (afterwards H.M. King Edward VII) and a large number of Members of the Houses of Lords and Commons attended, the Prince having his first ride in a car driven by the Hon. Evelyn Ellis. History was to repeat itself in May 1911 when a demonstration of flying on similar lines was arranged at Hendon by Mr. Claude

* Died April 1925.

Grahame White and the writer for the benefit of the Services and our legislators ; thus is progress made, this being the first sortie against the instinctive distrust of flying, or indeed of anything new, which so frequently hampers British progress, which suppressed the steam coach and placed the petrol motor-car at the mercy of Bumbledon for a decade.

England lagged behind in motor tyres partly because she failed to take motor cars seriously in their earliest years, partly through public prejudice, the hostility of county councils, and the strictness of her speed laws under the so-called Emancipation Act, and partly because the Founder Company possessed neither the motoring experience nor the rubber mills which they afterwards acquired. In the official tours of the Automobile Club of 1898 there was not a single car shod with pneumatic tyres, and it was not until 1900 that, for the first time, the Founder Company were in a position to produce a vulcanised motor tyre, either with wired or beaded edges. Their earliest attempts lasted for no more than 400 miles, and only after 1902 did they begin to achieve success with their touring and racing tyres.

The North British Rubber Company alone in Britain were in the doubly fortunate position of being both patentees and manufacturers, but in the absence of motoring experience they resorted to the buying of tyres from Michelin, which were described as " the Clincher-Michelin Tyre, Bartlett's Patent," clear evidence that they were handicapped by fundamental circumstances with which they could not cope and were unable to keep pace with the Frenchmen. As will presently be seen, however, the little Dublin company was soon to overtake the half-century's start in the art of rubber making, which perforce they had had to concede to their rubber manufacturing opponents.

II

The motor field was wide open to everyone and little time or energy was wasted in litigation, there being no valid controlling patent over the petrol motor principle. Apart from patents on special points, which could be avoided, it was doubtful whether any broader claim could have been upheld in a court of law. Its development was infinitely more rapid than that of the bicycle, and, as in the case of the pneumatic tyre, was very largely contributed to by racing.

Speed being the supreme test, it will be of interest to glance at its progressive record. The first motor event in France, Paris-Rouen, eighty miles, for which there were over 100 entries, was held in July 1894, the first arrival being a de Dion steam tractor coupled to a Victoria carriage which averaged no better than 12 m.p.h., less even than the speed achieved by Thomson's 9-ton steamer train twenty-five years before. But in June 1895 the petrol motor disposed of steam cars in the Paris-Bordeaux non-stop race of that year—745 miles, averaging about 15¼ m.p.h. The winner, M. Levassor, of the Panhard firm, used solid tyres and remained on his machine about fifty-three hours, nearly fifty being on the run.

Edouard Michelin was a competitor and used his own tyres, but as they had not yet achieved reliability he only finished ninth, thus being the first man to finish in an international event on pneumatic tyres.

In the opinion which Levassor expressed of the tyre, which Commander M. Grahame White has recorded, he emulated J. K. Starley five years before by declaring that *the result confirmed his bad opinion of the air tyre which might succeed if " filled with hay or straw, but would never work satisfactorily when filled with air."** Unfortunately Michelin's opinion of this pronouncement by his distinguished fellow-countryman has not been recorded. Thus two outstanding leaders in their respective industries, Starley of England, and Levassor of France, with all their knowledge and experience, condemned after trial the pneumatic tyre as an impracticable dream, while the far-seeing man of business and technical ignoramus, Harvey du Cros, prophesied its universal adoption from the moment he and I tested it together. At the moment that Levassor was speaking, Professor Vernon Boys, F.R.S., one of the Founder Company's expert advisers, was prophesying that motor-cars would run on pneumatic tyres, would revolutionise the traffic problem, and improve the sanitation of big cities.

As a pioneer Michelin had to contend with but a modicum of the disbelief and prejudice for his motor tyres which had been manifested in England in respect of the cycle tyre, but it was soon demonstrated that no solid tyre could ever be relied upon to remain on a wheel at high speeds, and no motor engine or chassis, however heavily built, could maintain its efficiency for long without pneumatic tyres. High speeds were only made possible by pneumatic tyres, and to them the millions of users throughout the world owe the motor car, the motor coach and the motor cycle as pleasure vehicles, the latter, with its possible farthing a mile, being doubtless the cheapest form of locomotion in existence.

The autumn of 1896 saw a great advance in efficiency,

* " At the Wheel Afloat and Ashore."

but little increase of speed in the Paris-Marseilles race of nearly 1,100 miles run in sections over ten days, and won by a Panhard car fitted with solid tyres driven by Mayade, notwithstanding that half the competing cars were fitted with pneumatic tyres.

In 1897 all the heavy car international races were won on solid tyres, and it was not until 1898 and 1899 that de Knyff and Charron on their Panhards finally established the pneumatic tyre as being indispensable to success, Michelin again being the maker. These years also saw the end of the steam *versus* petrol war so far as racing was concerned.

Each successive year saw the gradual increase of speed and efficiency of heavy cars in the long-distance international events with averages of 23 m.p.h. in 1897 ; 27 m.p.h. in 1898 ; over 30 m.p.h. in 1899 ; 40 m.p.h. in 1900 ; and 53 m.p.h. in 1901 ; but with foreign cars and tyres always in the ascendant.

S. F. EDGE.

The sequence was broken at last in 1902 in the third year of the Gordon Bennett race run between Paris and Innsbruck, which was won after many adventures by a one-time departmental manager of the Founder Company, S. F. Edge, on his Napier car with Dunlop tyres, who passed the unlucky de Knyff with a broken transmission twenty miles from the finish. This triple win of a British driver, car and tyres was received with enthusiasm throughout the British Empire, and gave much needed prestige and impetus to the English motor trade.

In the Circuit du Nord race of May and the Paris-

Vienna race of June 1902, Charles Jarrott,* one of England's most fearless drivers, was accompanied as

MONTAGUE NAPIER.

mechanician by my brother George, who at that time possessed no qualification for this onerous position other than his love of sport. My brother Harvey was also competing. In these two events every conceivable trouble which could afflict a motor car was encountered, and everything that human ingenuity could devise to keep a car moving was devised, even to the reconstruction of some of the parts, but to his credit, be it said, Jarrott finished in both events, neither he nor his mechanician being recognisable under their filthy disguise of oil and mud—mudguards were a luxury not indulged in. These events were held on the open roads, a madness which the death-roll of the Paris-Madrid race of 1903 brought to a timely end.

With the weather fine, drivers in company could see little but the enshrouding dust although other vehicles, cattle, closed railway gates and unexpected corners might be encountered at any moment. In bad weather the roads were often foggy, muddy and swimming in water, cars pursued a zig-zag course, and side-slips in which they frequently turned completely round more than once were an ever-present menace, especially when entering crowded controls on greasy pavé.

The two races occupied six days, each minute of which

* See Jarrott's " Ten Years of Motors and Motor Racing."

was packed full of incident. Jarrott, ever the sportsman, recorded that the task of sitting on the floor of a car attending to lubrication and other details, and entrusting your neck to the care of another man, was a thankless one, but nevertheless, to use my brother's description, " it was better than steeple-chasing." I remained convinced that the South African War from which my brother had just returned was a picnic compared to the perils of motor road racing of those days.

LORD AUSTIN.

One incident is well remembered. Jarrott was obliged to finish " all out " into the final control, being pressed neck and neck by Marcelin who, driving in Jarrott's dust, could see nothing. There was a large crowd oblivious to their danger, and a Commissaire of Police, attempting to force them back, misjudged the pace of Jarrott's car and was caught by the off-side wheel, being hurled into the air and descending

neatly with his head between my brother's hands who, obeying an old instinct that he must always get rid of the ball, tossed the commissaire back into the crowd, thereby saving what was left of his life. He was carried into a house in an unconscious condition, his clothes in shreds and with all the appearance of a completely dead policeman. Presently Jarrott was sent for by " Monsieur le Commissaire " to face the music, this

THE HON. CHARLES S. ROLLS.*   SIR F. H. ROYCE.†

being his first intimation that that gentleman was still alive. True to French gallantry, however, the interview was to enable the commissaire to apologise in the most profuse manner for having obstructed a " visitor's " car at the finish of such an important race.

Edge's success was short-lived, for he lost to Jenatzy and his continental tyred Mercédes in the following year, mainly owing, but not altogether, to trouble with his

* Killed from an aeroplane, July 1910.
† Died April 1923.

Dunlop tyres, of which no less than seven came off and careered in front of him during the race, certainly the most detachable and fastest tyres ever produced by the Founder Company.

But the writing was on the wall, and those events marked the approaching end of foreign dominance, both in engineering and tyre making, results largely attributable to the sport-loving propensities of the British public, the perseverance of British manufacturers and their policy of concentrating upon reliability and durability in long-distance trials, commencing with the " 1,000 miles of dust " of 1900. It is probable that this event, more than any other, convinced the British people that the motor car was not a freak but had come to stay.

VISCOUNT NUFFIELD.

Under the leadership of " Pa " Austin (now Lord Austin), Montague Napier, F. H. Royce, William Morris (now Viscount Nuffield), Charles Rolls, Sir William Letts and a host of other pioneer manufacturers whose names were concealed behind those of their firms, the British motor industry made up its leeway and has never since looked back. If Thomson, Hancock, Gurney and others could survey these results, what a comment they would supply upon the lack of prescience and intelligence of the legislators of their time and what a testimonial to the grit and tenacity of those who, in spite of penal laws and Free Imports, continued the crusade and carried it to a brilliant conclusion.

There can be no doubt that early racing, sanctioned

CHARLES JARROTT.

by the farseeing French Government and the pressure of intensive competition which it provoked, were of inestimable value in the rapid development of the automobile and tyre industries, affording, as they did, opportunities for tests of the most crucial nature, and elimination of weaknesses through experience of failure.

CHAPTER EIGHTEEN

THE PHŒNIX

I

The march of time brought with it the expiry of the Welch patent, and my father, like a true Irishman, decided that a wake should be held over its tattered remains. He evidently regarded their cremation as a matter for joy rather than grief, and in due time, on September 16th, 1904, a festive company of four hundred assembled, including scores of famous champions of the road and track, the leading representatives of the cycle and motor trades of England, among them men who had violently opposed the company, side by side with its staunchest supporters. Speeches were, of course, the order of the night. Welch sat on the right of the Chairman, taking a sympathetic interest in his own obsequies ; and, notwithstanding the supposed lugubrious character of the function, an air of hilarious cheerfulness pervaded the animated scene. But my father's and my own private view of the event were expressed in the toast to the Guests which I proposed :—

" Gentlemen, referring to the delicate subject of the law courts, I should like to mention that of the many records broken by the Dunlop Company there are two which I think in themselves are somewhat unique. As you know, we have been compelled by force of stern duty to engage in litigation on patent matters to an extent, I think, unknown before in the whole history of invention ; but, on the other hand, we have been engaged for fifteen years in an industry involving transactions to the amount of many millions with many thousands of clients and not once during the whole period have we been at law with one of our clients on a commercial matter. Where uncompromising duty ended and elastic mutual negotiations commenced, we hold this unbroken record.

Well, gentlemen, we are assembled here to-night because we have reached the end of the first volume in the history of this invention, and I can assure you that it gives me and my brother directors the greatest possible pleasure to mark the occasion by this re-union of our friends for the sake of ' Auld Lang Syne.' Whatever the future may hold in store for us, it can never deprive myself and my co-directors of many pleasant memories of the years that have passed, of many difficulties met and overcome and, if I may say so, of duties—often unpleasant, always onerous—which at all events have been carried out conscientiously and with good feeling and with good faith towards all men. Believe me, the possession of patents is not altogether an unmixed blessing. The calls of business in the ordinary course are sufficiently trying, but when they are allied with the bitterness and the jealousies, and I must say also the roguery, which appears to me to inevitably surround a successful invention, then all I can say is that personally I regard their expiry with feelings of relief and feelings of equanimity. As some great man once said, ' We feel now that we can cross the river and rest in the shade.' "

While absorbed in the task of founding this new industry and harassed by its manifold difficulties in England and overseas, the directors of the company had been compelled for twelve years to wade through a welter of litigation in many lands to defend its rights, and were by then weary of it. As must often be the lot of pioneers, we had lived in suspense, always fearing a judgment which might cripple or destroy our efforts, always hoping for a discovery which might build them up, always emerging from one crisis only to be confronted with another. Is it surprising that we come to look upon the courts with the same relish as a funeral ?

An action had been fought for every week in the life of the Welch and Bartlett patents, and although no adverse decision had ever been given against either of them, the litigation cost the companies not less than £200,000. It is a great tribute to the business methods and fair dealing of the company that in transactions running into many millions of pounds, it never found itself in litigation on a commercial question with any of its clients. Now, with our object achieved, other and better foundations were being substituted for the future protection and development of the business. So at midnight on that occasion my father willingly consigned Welch's patent to the flames with these words :—

" Here lies Welch ; he was saddle or arch-shaped ; he rested on a median convexity ; his boundaries are inextensible ; he dies, and yet lives no longer for the few, but for the use of all. According to Irish custom, this is his wake ; these are his ashes. But according to another Irish monumental legend there arises from these ashes a phœnix. *That phœnix is Dunlop, the manufacturer.* Welch is dead—Dunlop lives. He, too, is saddle or arch-shaped ; his median convexity is the world ; his boundaries are extensible—may they extend ! Long live Dunlop, the manufacturer."

Commenting upon this a writer said :—

" At the conclusion of his speech the Chairman, Harvey du Cros, brought this unique function to an end by publicly burning the Welch specification. This was probably the first time that the expiration of a valuable patent was made the occasion of rejoicing and hospitality by the owners. As a rule it is the opponents of the owners who rejoice ! ''

An editorial in the Press recorded :—

'' When one received the invitation to the ' wake ' of the Welch patents, one's first idea was to go in mourning, and so it happened that I spent some time in looking for the black cotton gloves and the melancholy alpaca umbrella that I always wear in times of woe or sorrow. But on second thought I decided to leave them out, for the invitation ran ' in honour ' of the decease of the Welch patents. And it was so. A more resilient and light-hearted party of 400 mourners never paid the last respects to anything.

'' It was a gathering of nearly all the leaders in the trade, and they all seemed to be in the best of form. It was really a remarkable affair as a trade function, and as I sat there in the midst of a goodly company enjoying sumptuous hospitality, I could not help thinking of the small beginnings from which it all sprung—beginnings so small that the history of the Dunlop Company might always serve as a tonic to nerve and hearten waverers in the battle of life. No great invention ever had such a struggle for recognition, or, after that, to retain its foothold.''

II

The reason my father and I were not unduly perturbed by the expiry of the Welch patent was that, having been warned fourteen years previously by the loss of Dunlop's patent owing to its invalidity, such a contingency had long been anticipated and provided for, and this was the key to my father's funeral oration. To make this clear I must hark back to my first association with the company. I was in close commercial companionship with my father at this time, and so remained for twenty-nine years until his death in December 1918 ; years of hearty co-operation and full agreement when he gave me his confidence in family and business affairs to an almost embarrassing degree. This enduring and happy partnership commenced in 1889 when I was absorbed in my racing successes and he was contemplating the founding of the Pneumatic Tyre Company and looking to me to carry on, ultimately for my own benefit, if I wished, or wind up his extensive agency and manufacturing interests in the paper trade in which he had assumed a leading position by his successful efforts in promoting co-operation where previously cut-throat tactics had prevailed. That task I had completed by the middle of 1892, having elected to resign the prospect of a comfortable independence in a business which I did not find compatible.

My father's reception of this intimation was characteristic. He inquired if I had thought very carefully about giving up a settled position, which at my age and in Dublin was one to be envied. I said I had. He then asked me what I thought of doing, and I confided to him my private impression that Australia was a good enough country to make a start in. He asked me what I contemplated doing when I got there, and I said that my thoughts had not extended so far, but that I felt certain Australia needed men like me, and in any case I might run the pneumatic tyre out there. He inquired again if I had thought it well over, and upon being reassured, asked if I had " any objection to the old man thinking it over." To this, with some condescension, I fear, I replied in the affirmative, with the result that within a few weeks my brother Harvey had been moved over to America and I was appointed General Manager of the company with headquarters at Coventry. I was the last of the six brothers to leave and can remember as if it were only yesterday, the kind fatherly encouragement I received from Fred Woods and Richard Booth, Directors, upon my departure from Ireland, never to return except as a visitor.

I have always, therefore, had an intimate knowledge of my father's hopes and fears for the industry, and our long collaboration was to bear important results in the days to come. Our chief pre-occupation was to buttress the company against the day when the Welch patent would expire. We were not manufacturers of tyres, but merely assemblers of their component parts, which we purchased from the most suitable sources, putting them together by hand, and it did not require a Solomon to see that when Welch's patent expired our own days would be numbered unless in the meantime we could keep competition at bay while we put our house in order.

The Welch patent, however, did not protect us from one formidable competitor, the North British Rubber Company of Edinburgh, against whom we were at a disadvantage since they had a tyre as good fundamentally as our own, and no problem of intermediate profits to consider in its production. Had my father and his team been entrenched in that company's position in 1890 with their valid patent and their great rubber mills, knowledge and experience, I cannot but think that we might have barred the entry of newcomers like ourselves into the industry. I have often marvelled how, with all these trumps in their hand, they did not make more aggressive use of the opportunity which was theirs, for by the sheer strength of their position a monopoly was more in their reach than ours, although it is true that the Founder

Company had the prestige and publicity of having been first in the field.

As it was, we camouflaged the position with the trade as best we could by preserving an extreme gravity, pointing out the while that by buying ready-made materials in the open market we only accepted the very best, and were thus safeguarded from the accidents and uncertainties of manufacture. That sounded well enough, and was even put forward at shareholders' meetings as the fixed policy of the company, but it was " all my eye and Betty Martin," the reality being that we had to pay full prices for our supplies, while at the same time building up potential competitors for ourselves.

My father was absorbed in the complexities of the law, to which he attended himself, sitting through all conferences and cases and conducting all negotiations ; in Frank Baisley he had trained an earnest and competent lieutenant, and in Welch, Professors Boys, Hopkinson and others, he had recruited a brilliant team of experts.

F. C. BAISLEY.

Mine was largely the responsibility of making proposals to my father and discussing them with the Board. No one man or superman could have coped simultaneously with the multiple tasks of law, commerce and manufacture both at home and beyond the seas. My father and I were never apart and my proposals which comprised a four-point programme can be summed up in a word which has recently become fashionable—self-sufficiency.

That programme which was to be completed over a series of years was no less than to establish ourselves as manufacturers of rubber, an art of which we were totally ignorant, to search the world for raw rubber and obtain a preferential position if possible, to study the cotton manufacturing industry, of which we knew nothing, with a view to becoming cotton spinners, and to manufacture for ourselves the rims, wheels, wires, pumps and valves required for our business. Simultaneously our normal task of creating a world-wide selling organisation was to proceed : and by these comprehensive measures alone could we secure our place in the sun.

III

The paramount necessity was to build or buy our own rubber mills, equipped with a laboratory and testing department to which we attached prime importance at a time when in England they were prone to be neglected ; and here again sport once more played its part in our fortunes. The company made £2,600 in the first year of its existence and over £70,000 in the next two years, paying 84 per cent. in dividends over the three years, but was not yet strong enough to make proposals for acquiring interests in any of the old-established rubber manufacturing firms, or to undertake responsibilities in this direction on its own account. But there was in Birmingham a family of six brothers of Irish descent who, like ourselves, were prominent in the athletic world and who had been carrying on a general rubber goods business dating back to 1855.

In the 'nineties, E. J. Byrne, Robert Byrne, Fred Byrne and Frank Byrne had achieved international and county honours in rugby football, cricket, and hockey. Fred Byrne was England's full-back in thirteen matches, her captain in 1898 and holds the record for a full-back of having dropped two field goals in international matches. He captained Warwickshire cricket from 1903 to 1907 and knocked up 222 against Lancashire in 1905. His brother Frank, also a rugby international, was a noted golfer, and altogether they were not an easy quartette to tackle at any sort of game. Yet a keen

FRED BYRNE.

football rivalry arose between them and the Irish exiles in Coventry, who included among others three of the most famous Irish international rugby players of their day, Ben Tuke, who played for Ireland in nine matches, H. G. Wells and Jimmy Waites. We were nursing a wild ambition to strengthen the Coventry rugby team until it could wrest the Midland Cup from the Moseley cum Byrne stronghold, or from the " Tigers " of Leicester,

BEN TUKE.*

* Died May 1936.

who between them generally managed to monopolise the trophy, an objective which was achieved after furious contests on many hard-fought fields, in which the spectators and not infrequently the police took a hand, for rivalry was fierce, feeling ran high, and there was Irish blood on both sides.

The day of the final at Rugby in 1896, when little 5-foot Wells, then the fastest three-quarter in rugby football, fed by Ben Tuke at half, ran clean round every man of the opposing side to score the only try of the match, has passed into legend. No man ever refused Ben Tuke an order for tyres or anything else, and Coventry became our closed preserve. We had the pick of the young ladies of the town waiting in adoring queues at our gates hoping to be enrolled where " Ben " was a manager, and had he wished to enter Parliament or become Mayor he would have been carried in shoulder high.

E. J. BYRNE.*

So it was that the kinship of sport and country led to the opening of business relations with the Byrne brothers in 1893, for me the beginning of a forty-five-years' friendship with " E. J.," which still continues ; the first twenty-three in close business association. A community of interests was developed and, as a first step towards creating

* Died November 1938.

THE AUTHOR
AND
FOUNDER OF THE DUNLOP RUBBER CO. LTD.

Facing p. 209.

a direct connection with the rubber manufacturing business and obtaining an insight into its technicalities, I arranged in August 1894 to assist the business of Byrne Bros. with loans and credits to a large amount.

A permanent investment of capital followed in 1896, accompanied by the enlargement of their factory for tyre work exclusively, its flotation as the Rubber Tyre Manufacturing Company, with a capital of £150,000 and £20,000 of debentures, and Harvey du Cros, Junior, and E. J. Byrne as Director and Managing Director respectively, while the erection of a second works nearby, the Manor Mills, was undertaken by the Byrne Bros., for their own general rubber goods purposes. The original works, Para Mill, was now running night and day on supplies for the tyre company, who were also buying very largely from other sources to meet their ever-growing demand.

The company's financial resources and knowledge of the process of rubber making were soon sufficient to enable them to begin to walk alone, and in 1900, four years before the expiration of the patent, I was successful in convincing the Board that they should purchase the Manor Mills in order to commence rubber manufacture in a modest way, thereby beginning to cover our flanks which had been for so long exposed to attack from the North British group. The following year I brought about the acquisition of the Rubber Tyre Manufacturing Company, and by amalgamating our two purchases, founded and named the present Dunlop Rubber Co. Ltd., over twelve years after the launching of the Founder Company, thereby completing the first of our four-point programme.

In parenthesis it is interesting to note the impossibility

in those days of obtaining the services of experienced technical managers trained in the British rubber industry : all such men were principals in the comparatively few manufacturing firms of importance, or were held under strict agreement, and accordingly were not available. The company, therefore, had to serve its apprenticeship as rubber makers, adopted a liberal policy of replacement, and, in course of time, evolved its own technicians, often by trial and error—an anxious and expensive method—but without forfeiting its reputation for fair play, high quality and good workmanship.

I was influenced in the acquisition of the Rubber Tyre Company by the method of manufacturing cycle tyres which they had developed under a very clever American process, the invention of J. Doughty, the merits of which E. J. Byrne had first discerned and impressed upon me, and the English rights for which we agreed he should secure. It consisted of an automatic collapsible metal mould on the lines of Welch's patent former * upon which Welch or Bartlett covers could be vulcanised under high steam pressure and by the addition of certain ingredients finished ready for use in three minutes as against the two hours of the older process. By this process, which is still being used, tyres could be turned out like shelling peas, the cost of manufacture was reduced and uniformity and durability so largely increased that I saw in it another bulwark against the expiry of the patent and advised my father and the Board that the process at that time spelled the last word in cycle-cover production and efficiency.

A matinée was arranged, the Directors travelled to Birmingham, and E. J. Byrne put on a performance which

* See p. 115.

I feel sure he and his team must have rehearsed for many days and nights. It was convincing, and he and I knew each other too well to indulge in any bluffing. The company had the patent tyre, he had the best process for producing it ; a union of interest was indicated, terms satisfactory to both sides were quickly arranged between us, and that union brought about the complete reversal of the company's policy, the removal of its hand-made tyre process from Coventry to Birmingham and, subsequently, the creation of the present magnificent works and community on the 400 acres of Fort Dunlop, a name which I contributed.

Twelve years later, in August 1912, I obtained the consent of 100 per cent. of the shareholders of the Founder Company to the sale to their subsidiary company, the Dunlop Rubber Company, of their goodwill, assets and trading rights, thus conferring full independence upon that company. The old company had decided to rest upon its laurels and to pass the baton to its adequate offspring, who took up the running with all the zest and vitality of youth.

CHAPTER NINETEEN

A PLAN OF CAMPAIGN

I

Side by side with our manufacturing ambitions we had in mind the provision of a part of our own requirements of the raw material, and the company's search for rubber was an exhilarating experience. The Amazon was the main source of supply for best quality rubber, and its upper reaches a far cry and little known. The trade, or rather monopoly, had long been tightly held in a few hands, and interlopers were met by a thousand difficulties, both official and unofficial. Labour was a fluctuating and uncertain quantity, here to-day and gone to-morrow ; facilities there were none, and the ordinary amenities of civilisation were conspicuous by their absence.

With the advent of the pneumatic tyre the production had almost doubled in the period from 1897 to 1912, and immense numbers of men of all races and breeds were now pouring into the rubber regions with the usual result that the native Indians were ruthlessly exploited to their ultimate undoing and reduced to a state of peonage or slavery. We equipped an expedition to explore the possibilities of the Amazon Valley under the leadership of the late B. J. Ebbsworth, but on their return in 1902 we decided that the prospects in Brazil were too

B. J. Ebbsworth.

unpromising, if not intimidating, to justify further action.

Accordingly we turned to West Africa where, in Portuguese Angola on the coast line between the Congo and Cunene Rivers, there flourished a wild bush containing a resinous gum which, when ground and precipitated by a patent process (an invention of the Byrnes), gave a 20 per cent. yield of excellent rubber.

Preliminary inquiries and a small pioneering expedition seemed to promise results, and a persuasive appeal to E. J. Byrne, combined with a spirit of adventure hitherto latent, induced him to accept the hardy *rôle* of explorer, and off he went in 1906 with another stalwart or two, after first, in 1904, negotiating a concession in Lisbon covering an area about the size of Ireland, and sending a preliminary expedition to Angola, which had returned by 1905.

From what I subsequently gathered, the Amazon was a Garden of Eden compared to the places he went, and the conditions he encountered. In recounting his years' experiences, " E. J." prefaced a long series of lurid remarks with the slogan " Never again," to which he returned so often and so insistently, that I believe it took the place of his family motto.

He was in a practically waterless and unshaded country, an interval between showers of a few years not being unknown ; the heat by day was tropical, the cold by night was penetrating, and for transport he had to rely upon the homely donkey. Worse still, when it came to the labour question, Byrne found that slavery was rampant under the polite disguise of " servicaes " or " contract labourers." It made no difference which word was used, men and women were bought and sold for money, forced away from their homes in the interior, rarely to return, shackled and marched in gangs to the

"SERVICAES," 1906.

coast and " assigned " to plantation owners who had requisitioned for them. The humanities were soothed by their being brought before a Governmental Cuvador who, for the requisite licence and other fees, both personal and official, inquired whether they were willing to go as labourers, and whatever the answer might be—if there was an answer at all—each was numbered and registered, and by this piece of official hypocrisy " redeemed " from slavery and converted into a respectable " contract labourer."

Recruiting his labour according to the custom of the country, Byrne trekked north for five days from Mossamedes, started his first camps at Opiambo and Mukungo, separated by a day's march, the latter being watered daily by barrels and donkey transport, and proceeded with the collection of his raw material, in which he was quite successful. It was carried by sailing boat to Mossamedes and from

" E. J." PIONEERING.

thence shipped to England where, after treatment by a specially designed plant and prolonged test, it was found to be quite suitable for our manufacture. Unfortunately, before the organisation was fully established and working, Byrne went down with enteric fever, discipline became relaxed and the " servicaes " began to steal away and become free in fact as well as in name.

Byrne, who at intervals was by now babbling of running brooks and the green meadows of England, was to be carried in an improvised hammock down to the coast, with the prospect, among other hardships, of crossing *dongas* or dry river beds as much as a mile wide and 600 feet deep, each of them a full day's march for his carriers. When he could not be carried he would have to crawl. While nursing his energies in the darkness of his tent for what he knew would be a critical journey, he was roused by his headman for instructions as to what he would like done with his body in the event of the worst occurring, which obviously the headman considered was a foregone conclusion. This, I believe, was " E. J.'s " salvation, for it roused the fighting spirit of the Byrnes. His body would reach home on its own legs, he swore, and in no other way, so revolver in hand he succeeded in keeping a sufficient force together to deposit him at the hospital in Mossamedes, where he lay for some considerable time at death's door, growling at intervals about the disposition of his body.

The upshot was that we turned our backs on the Dark Continent, and when next the collection of rubber came on the tapis for consideration, Byrne was reported as having gone for a prolonged golfing tour, address unknown. Accordingly in 1910 I undertook the exploration of the possibilities in the much more congenial atmosphere of Ceylon, following the beaten track of the pioneers who, as early as 1876, had introduced experimentally the Brazilian seedling into the island, and from thence to the regions beyond. I was soon convinced that rubber growing was an art which we could master and from which the company must benefit if the product gave results comparable with the wild variety.

Having persuaded the Board to take my view, our first estate was purchased in the island. Attracted by my account of the beauty of the East and its balmy climate, the luxury of plantation life in Ceylon, its perfect motor roads, the amiability of the people and the plentifulness of water and other liquids, Byrne was induced to accompany me on a second expedition; but on this occasion I suddenly extended our journey to the Malay, where the conditions, as Byrne forcibly reminded me, bore but a faint resemblance to the rosy picture I had painted of Ceylon. There we examined and compared the possibilities of the two countries, deciding eventually to plant our flag in the Malay. Succeeding years saw the execution of our plan under Byrne's direction, until our area of planted rubber approximated to 50,000 acres by 1919, over every second acre of which we must have toiled and sweated in the tropic sun, not to mention the unplanted area. The era of refrigeration had hardly dawned, and not being a good sleeper and rather finicky at table, I generally left behind a stone or so of good Irish avoirdupois as my contribution to the rough and ready conditions of planting life in those early days. However, in learning that sardines and tea are not the most stable of foods for the strenuous work of pioneering, I also learned enough about rubber and rubber-growing to take up and organise our territories, and thus the second part of our four-point programme had become an accomplished fact.

The magnitude of the subsidiary developments surrounding the pneumatic tyre industry may be partly gauged from the fact that to day this single property is represented by the reclamation and cultivation of over 130 square miles of jungle land, employing 12,000 people or more, a *minute* effort in itself, as compared with the general expansion of rubber growing, and that the yearly output of rubber from the East has grown from practically nothing to 1,100,000 tons, the great bulk of which is accounted for by the tyre industry.

II

Our quest for knowledge in the cotton industry proceeded on similar lines, and was commenced in a small way in 1897 by our becoming associated with the promotion of a small new weaving company, which was to undertake to supply a portion of our cotton cloth requirements, working in co-operation with an old-established doubling concern, the two being under the same management. The arrangement served its purpose in familiarising us with cotton-making processes and convincing me of the practicability and necessity for such a development. But it was not until 1914 that time and means permitted of the founding of the Dunlop Cotton Mills on a scale commensurate with our growing requirements. These mills have since become the largest of their kind in the Empire and hold a commanding position in one of the oldest and greatest of British industries. The enterprise has proved an unqualified success in broadening and strengthening the foundations of the Dunlop Rubber Company, and above all in enabling it, through its experimental departments, to evolve the material which has played so large a part in lengthening the life of tyres beyond all the dreams of the early pioneers.

The third part of our four-point programme had come into being, and the fourth and last presented but one difficulty. The manufacture of inflators and the manipulation of wire were well understood, but we were intent upon securing the master patent for the best form of cycle rim so as to evolve order out of a somewhat chaotic situation and standardise an article which would command the market. This we accomplished in 1896 by the acquisition of the Westwood patent of 1893 and, being already in possession of the Wood's valve patent, we soon became self-supporting in all these profitable departments of the tyre business, to be followed later by the highly essential Dunlop Wheel Works for the production of the perfect wheel for the perfect tyre.

Profiting by their early contact with the thorough-going scientific Teuton, the original " rag tyre " company was convinced of the urgent necessity for experimental and testing departments and made its small beginnings in these directions nearly half a century ago. The advance of motor racing speeds from about 18 m.p.h. in 1894 to Captain George Eyston's 357½ m.p.h. in 1938, when his tyres were subjected to the strain of revolving forty-five times in every second, taken with the increase of motor tyre road mileages from the Founder Company's 400 miles in 1900 to the possible 30,000 miles or more of to-day, tell in themselves the story of that ceaseless, intensive research and testing by which new and improved methods have been evolved and progress assured.

Beginning in a humble way with one solitary heavy-weight cyclist on the road as far back as the early 'nineties, going on to the taxicab fleet of W. & G. du Cros, with its records of millions of miles, this system has so developed that the diagnosis of the constituent elements of a wheel and tyre lays bare their every strength and weakness. Little can be hidden from the magnified eyes of the modern physical laboratory and less still can resist the ingenious and manifold devices of the testing shop, while nothing at all can escape the net of the final tests of time, speed and exposure which are applied by fleets of vehicles under the rough and ready conditions of everyday use. There only remains the human element, a liability to error on the part of the operative, and this can be countered by the watchful experience of the supervisor.

These methods, carried on faithfully from one administration to another, have been the secret of success of tyre making, enabling British industry to maintain its place in world production, the Eystons, the Campbells and the Cobbs to survive to tell the tale of their wonderful exploits, and the new race of birdmen to alight in safety from the clouds. The latter with their aerial clippers, annihilating space and time, have already brought Babylon as near to London as was Brighton in the days of the Regency.

Concurrently with this growing technical perfection, the gospel of the pneumatic tyre had been preached and printed in every land by the Founder Company and its successor, resulting in the ever-expanding markets which to-day are served from a dozen factories and scores of selling centres. All conditions of use, from the frozen regions to the burning deserts, are closely studied and specially catered for, for the watchword of the successful tyre maker must be thoroughness and again thoroughness.

When it is remembered that the Dunlop Rubber Co.,

this child of the first little Founder Company, is now but one of many great international units of a gigantic industry, which itself is dwarfed by the developments that it has brought to many other industries, both new and old, the imagination is staggered by the contemplation of its cumulative effects upon society at large and upon the material fortunes of millions of workers throughout the world, results achieved without the grim record of disaster to other interests which have so often followed in the train of successful inventions.

III

Among the most pleasant of my recollections are the cordial relations which existed between the employees

(1) Shrapnell, (2) Bagnell, (3) Lennox, (4) Sherwin, (5) Geo. du Cros, (6) Large, (7) Siddeley (8) B. Tuke.

(1) Hatton, (2) Patterson, (3) Murphy, (4) Maloney, (5) G. Tuke, (6) Latimer, (7) Pole.

COVENTRY GROUP, 1892.

and the Directors. We had all started practically to-gether and work and play were enjoyed with equal zest. All forms of outdoor activity were encouraged,* for we regarded sport in any form, with its community of feelings and friendships among all classes, as an asset worthy even the attention of British statesmen. To-day " the playing fields of Eton " and all they stand for are being out-rivalled by the playing fields of industry and the Nation, a valuable and significant feature of our modern commercial life.

Our efforts included a company of volunteers for the Royal Warwickshire Regiment recruited from the works in Coventry which saw service in South Africa, and a company of Territorials formed at Birmingham in time

Peters.   T. MacCabe.   R. Carlisle.   Pentony.
M. Scarff.   Lieut. W. du Cros.   Walshaw.

T. Sibary.   Dusson.
A " D " COMPANY TEAM, 1898.
* See Appendix, p. 275.

221

for the Great War, both being officered by members of the staff. Rifle shooting was developed as a sport, and a team to Bisley became an annual event.

A fire brigade, second to none in the Midlands, was

organised. Outings to the Chairman's country home at Cornbury Park, Oxfordshire, were grand affairs attended by every man, woman and child in the Company, and the Anglo-Irish Social Club became an institution in the City of Spires.

When the Company was sold and enlarged, bonus payments amounting to £85,000 were distributed to all its members ; no one was forgotten from the Chairman down. When new issues of shares were made and over-subscribed by the public, the Directors took up blocks of shares in order that for many months after the issues were closed the employees should have the opportunity of investing. A lead was given by the adoption of an endowment scheme on benevolent lines which has since become an important institution, and the workers were always assured of direct access to the higher management for the discussion of their problems.

These attributes of the Founder Company were well known and were the subject of comment in the press. The *Motor Trader* wrote :

" Now and then one comes across a business concern of which the members seem to be a happy and united family. That is one of the characteristics of the Dunlop Company.

" Many of those who started in the business as boys are now holding responsible positions, helping to guide its destinies. In them loyalty to ' the Governor ' is an article of faith from which they would never dream of swerving by a hair's breadth. They know that he is true as steel to his friends of his earlier days. In these facts we have at least some of the causes of the affection with which he is regarded by every member of the staff and by his brother directors."

In the Great War no business institution in the Empire watched over the fortunes of its men and their families with greater care both during and after hostilities, a responsibility which we, in common with a million others, accepted with satisfaction as a national duty.

Another and not the least pleasurable of my business memories is that, controlling, as I did, for many years the expenditure of tens of millions of pounds, yet only on a single occasion was even the suggestion of a bribe made to me, and then it was by a foreigner who I presumed was only following the custom of his country.

In the interests of strict accuracy it should be mentioned in passing that this commemorative tablet to

JOHN BOYD DUNLOP

MEMBER OF THE ROYAL COLLEGE OF VETERINARY SURGEONS PRACTISING IN THIS CITY. INVENTOR AND PATENTEE OF THE PNEUMATIC TYRE IN 1888.

THE PURCHASE OF THIS INVENTION AND THE SUBSEQUENT DEVELOPMENT BY THE DUNLOP RUBBER CO. LTD. INAUGURATED ONE OF THE LARGEST INDUSTRIES IN THE WORLD.

Dunlop which was placed upon his old premises in May Street, Belfast, where he made his first pneumatic tyre, and unveiled in December 1930 by the Lord Mayor, is somewhat inaccurate in several particulars.

Dunlop was never associated with the Dunlop Rubber Company in any capacity. The reference should be to the Founder Company, which through its Welch, Bartlett, and other patents, its system of licensing, and its name and trading connections throughout the world, introduced the tyre and built up the industry from 1889 to 1912. Its name was changed in 1893 to that of the Pneumatic Tyre Co. Ltd., again in 1896 to that of the Dunlop Pneumatic Tyre Co. Ltd., in 1913 to that of the Parent Tyre Co. Ltd. (the name " Parent " indicating that it was the mother of all tyre companies), and later to that of the Parent Trust and Finance Co. Ltd.

This, the Founder Company, was never merged with any other company, and preserved its identity until 1931, when it went into liquidation in tragic circumstances,* yet, although extinct, it worthily survives in its successor the Dunlop Rubber Company. That company was at first a private company created to serve as one of the manufacturing units for the Founder Company, and it was not until twenty-three years after the birth of the latter that the Dunlop Rubber Company entered into its inheritance and so effectively became the sole trading and producing company.†

The commemorative tablet upon Thomson's home in Stonehaven is so simple in its wording that it leaves no room for error, and reads :—

THE BIRTHPLACE OF
ROBERT WILLIAM THOMSON
THE INVENTOR OF THE PNEUMATIC TYRE
BORN 29 JUNE 1822
DIED 8 MARCH 1873

* See p. 258.
† See p. 211.

CHAPTER TWENTY

DUNLOP AS CONTROVERSIALIST

DUNLOP, after he had left the industry, became a prolific letter writer to the Press and was uneasily concerned to assert and defend his claim to have been, if not the first to invent the pneumatic tyre, the first to discover a practical commercial method of applying it, thus providing with Thomson the "seminal principle" of the industry which followed, a claim which was never really controverted by those with whom he was crossing swords or by anyone familiar with the circumstances. But to much else that Dunlop claimed, strong exception was taken by his correspondents, whose object he seemed to think was to "attack" and despoil him of the credit which was his due. Some of the criticisms which appeared were somewhat extreme, but others were both moderate and fair.

It was only in his later years that Dunlop became so supersensitive and made statements which were so untenable for himself and derogatory to other inventors that they mystified his friends and all students of the subject. Writing of Bartlett, Thomson and other inventors, he said " if an inventor has passed away, is that any reason why the truth should not be told?"* There is none so long as it is the truth. Therefore, " let justice be done though the heavens fall."

Until late in his life Dunlop ignored Thomson or dismissed him in a word as " impracticable," stating that if his tyre " had been perfection itself, fitted as it was to

* *Irish Cyclist*, December 29th, 1909.

a brougham, it would have been of no service to anyone," and adding that when Thomson died, " the Press, if it had any recollection of his air tyres, observed a sympathetic and discreet silence."

It is true that Thomson's tyre was impracticable for cycles in its details as Dunlop's was impracticable in its details for carriages or motor cars. It is also true that they both served their different purposes to a limited degree and that they both suffered from the same inherent defects, neither having reliable valves or being detachable or capable of being vulcanised as a whole in manufacture. But they were identical in principle, notwithstanding that Dunlop said with some lack of discernment, " I repudiate the idea of re-inventing such a tyre,"* and while conceding that his own tyre was uncommercial for heavy vehicles would never agree that it was largely impracticable for the rough and tumble of indiscriminate use on cycles until it had been perfected by other inventors.

Dunlop was never a convincing judge of the problems of heavy transport ; he had not studied them and did not believe in the adaptability to it of pneumatic tyres. The main differences between Thomson's and Dunlop's early experiments were those of weights and materials ; Thomson for his heavy wagons and coaches with their large wheels at first used leather, the stoutest material procurable in the absence of rubber, for his casing and running surface, and bolted his tyre to the wheel for security, whereas Dunlop, for his thirty-pound bicycle with its small wheels, was enabled to use " a mere rag of thin cloth and two layers of rubber," as he himself expressed it, and to stick his tyre to the wheel with

* *Motor Cycle and Cycle Trader*, June 23rd, 1916.

rubber solution. In his later tyres Thomson used canvas and rubber as Dunlop did.

Dunlop averred that Thomson was not born too early, but "at the proper time when tricycles were in use," * an obviously erroneous conclusion, since tricycles had not been invented in any practicable form in Thomson's lifetime, and were not in general use for many years later.

Nevertheless, some years after his attention had been drawn to the improved form of Thomson's tyre and the practical tests reported in *The Mechanics' Magazine* of June 2nd, 1849,† and the prophecy that " these wheels will speedily come into general use," Dunlop paid tardy tribute to the genius of Thomson. He wrote in 1921 : " *Thomson was a wonderful man. He was only twenty-three years of age when he invented the air tyre. He conceived the brilliant idea of intercepting vibration before it reached the rim of the wheel. . . . No matter who improved on his tyre, it was his idea . . .*" and after carefully considering Thomson's claims finally added : " *I came to the conclusion that the validity of my patent could not well be upheld in a Court of Law.*"

Dunlop seemed to have become fond of hairsplitting, and rather prone to belittle the efforts of other workers in the pneumatic tyre field. He questioned the merit of Bartlett's invention in its original form, insisting that it was " not a true pneumatic," notwithstanding that it was a tyre inflated above atmospheric pressure, nor yet a " genuine detachable " tyre, notwithstanding that it could be readily attached and detached.

More emphatically still he condemned the " so-called Welch tyre " on these and other grounds, going so far

* *Motor Cycle and Cycle Trader*, June 23rd, 1916.
† See Appendix, p. 297.

as to say that it also was " neither a detachable pneumatic nor a practical article." * Although he had approved of its purchase, he did not believe that Welch's patent was valid on the ground that pneumatic tyres were not mentioned in the provisional specification.

Dunlop persisted to the end in denying that Bartlett invented the beaded-edge cover or that Welch invented the endless wired cover, and clung to an obscure theory of his own, unacceptable to anyone else, that tyres which were made with inextensible inner tubes—a statement which he made but which was inaccurate so far as Welch was concerned—were " not worthy to be called detachable."

Undoubtedly the first Bartlett tyre to be marketed was inferior in all respects, except detachability, to Dunlop's, but not so the original Welch tyre, which was practically identical with the modern tyre except that a different lining is now used. Dunlop *would* ignore the fact that most basic ideas grow and develop and are improved in detail in the light of experience, without affecting the principle ; and even after all these and every other possible point had been argued and disposed of in the courts and these two splendid inventions had been approved and defined by forty or more judges, Dunlop still declined to admit any inconsistency in his views.

He asserted and re-asserted that he himself was " the first inventor and designer of a genuine satisfactory detachable pneumatic tyre " and even that he was " the first patentee and designer of a pneumatic tyre held on by endless wires." His detachable wired patent was dated April 9th, 1891, and the fact that Welch and Bartlett were before him in September and October 1890,

* *Motor Cycle and Cycle Trader*, June 23rd, 1916.

seemed to move Dunlop not at all, nor that the House of Lords had pronounced both these tyres not only to be truly pneumatic and detachable, but entitled to priority over all others of their respective types. He criticised the judges as " judges (not tyre judges) " who " happened " to decide in favour of the patentees and had had " to call in experts, and we all know how experts differ." Yet no adverse decision was ever recorded against either patent.

Most people would be on the side of the British Bench in these matters, but even if Dunlop had succeeded in disposing of Welch and Bartlett, to whom joint honours are due, he would, in order to establish his own claims, still have had to get rid in Britain alone of the Trigwell, Robertson, Golding and Scott tyres which were pneumatic and detachable, all before him and all inventions of merit. Of Robertson he had written on August 31st, 1891, " I am well satisfied now with Robertson's tyre," and in later years that it was " pure bred and was properly detachable," * yet this was a wired patent which as a Director he knew of as being actually on the road in February 1891, two months before the date of his own patent. And he approved of its purchase in order that the company would " have a patent to fall back on in the event of being beaten on the Welch," which he was anticipating, adding the reminder that " in addition mine was in reserve." If his was only " in reserve," he could not have been " the first patentee " as he claimed.

More could be said on this subject were it necessary to insist further upon the obvious.

Dunlop made himself responsible for the statement that his original tyre

* *Irish Cyclist*, January 12th, 1910.

" was not improved upon until it had been in use for four years," adding that " departures from Belfast (*i.e.*, 1889) methods were all changes for the worse until the introduction of the detachable tyre, for which I was responsible." *

No mention here of Welch or Robertson, or the Woods' valve, about the last of which he had written, " our old valve as now improved is as good as any, if we had only a means of deflating." What can be said in the face of these inaccuracies except so to characterise them, if only in fairness to Welch, Bartlett, Woods, Sinclair and others.

Dunlop put forward a claim to have made the Welch tyre practicable by re-designing the rim and cover, whereas Welch, to whom he referred as one who was " considered to be an expert," had nothing whatever to learn from Dunlop. He worked beside me for many years and was one of the cleverest men with his hands I have ever known, competent and self-sufficient to a degree. His complete specification illustrated his rim and cover in nearly perfect form, and it was not until Westwood, by the addition of tubular edges which did not affect the internal section of Welch's rim, reached finality in cycle rims by his clever invention of 1893, that any but microscopic deviations were made. Dunlop, as the Founder Company's technical director, was naturally called upon to approve Welch's designs, which he did in consultation with the inventor, but in justice to Welch's memory it must be said that Dunlop's pretension to have re-designed his rim and cover was quite unfounded. His own conception of what a rim and tyre should be was shown in his own patent (No. 6126 of April 1891), which

* *Motor Cycle and Cycle Trader*, June 23rd, 1916.

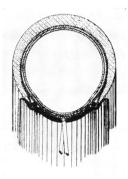 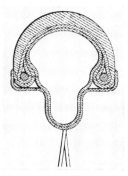

FIGURE FROM WELCH'S
WIRED PATENT, 1890.

FIGURE FROM DUNLOP'S
WIRED PATENT, 1891.

is here illustrated, and although open to the world has never been adopted by reason of their manifest inferiority.

Welch could never be drawn into a controversy, in or out of the Press, no matter what the temptation or provocation might be. A clear thinker, holding sturdy opinions of his own, he might and did on occasion disagree with the technical views of others, but he was always conciliatory and equable and was never known to withhold his advice and assistance when they were needed. A very loyal little gentleman for whom I had a sincere affection. He died on December 7th, 1929, at the age of sixty-eight.

All these points of difference and many others were canvassed publicly from time to time, differences which have now been mellowed by time or silenced by death, and if I appear to drag them back from the limbo of forgotten things it is for the reasons named in the Foreword to this book and also that the " other side " has never before been stated by any original authority. Neither the Founder Company nor its Directors or officials wrote or inspired any of the letters which appeared in the Press from time to time, the company contenting itself with a letter to the *Irish Cyclist* newspaper, written through their solicitors, which stated :—

" Our clients, the Dunlop Pneumatic Tyre Co. Ltd., have called our attention to correspondence in relation to Pneumatic Tyres which has been appearing in the columns of your Journal for many months past, in the course of which copious statements have been made in reference to :—

> The Patents which were the property of this Company.
>
> The Patentees who originated them or claimed to originate them.
>
> And to the general conduct of the affairs of this Company.

" We note with satisfaction that you have now put an end to this correspondence, which, emanating as it did from sources which, as far as this Company is concerned, were entirely unauthorised, might convey an exceedingly erroneous impression. The object of this letter is to officially dissociate this Company, and all its existing connections, from that correspondence, and also from the many questionable statements put forward during its course without any regard to established facts."

CHAPTER TWENTY-ONE

WORLD APPROVAL

I

But as time went on, Dunlop referred to a circumstance which apparently he had overlooked for twenty odd years. In a letter to the Press he said :—

" In your last issue your correspondent in ' Our Notebook ' says he ' remembers how, some twenty-three years ago, Mr. Harvey du Cros, after tremendous efforts to interest a few friends in the invention of the pneumatic tyre, succeeded in forming a little Company with a capital of £25,000. Having accomplished that Mr. du Cros took a sample tyre, jumped on an outside car, and went round the Dublin depots looking for orders.'

" Now from this your readers might be led to conclude that Mr. du Cros was the founder of the pneumatic tyre industry. Before Mr. du Cros had anything whatever to do with the Pneumatic Tyre Company, 50 machines had been sold in the ordinary course of business, and were running successfully in Ireland, 26 were made by Mr. Edlin and 24 by Messrs. Rudge & Co., and when it is remembered that the number of cycles in use in Ireland in 1889 was very small, *it will be readily seen that the industry was on a firm footing before Mr. du Cros was heard of in connection with the pneumatic tyre.*"

The letter was dated in 1912 and, this being the first reference to it since it was written, it cannot be said to have been replied to in hot blood or indeed at all, except by reference to the views of those best qualified to judge.

Dunlop by now had served a dozen years' apprenticeship to commerce, and as Chairman of two public companies his opinion on a business issue should have commanded attention, but he obtained no support for the view he put forward in this letter.

He probably overlooked previous letters in which he had written :—

" Edlin & Sinclair controlled the pneumatic from the early spring of 1889 to August." *

" It is not correct to say that Messrs. R. W. Edlin & Finlay Sinclair were absolutely and solely responsible for the introduction of the pneumatic tyre to the trade." †

And again :

" I have always sympathised with W. Edlin & Co. No outsider could have any idea of the difficulties they had to contend with, not to mention expense and loss of time. I was prepared to stand by them financially. A huge fortune was within their reach, *but they lacked that perseverance which is so characteristic of my nationality.* I told Mr. Edlin that he would make a fortune out of racers alone."

Sinclair would not allow himself to be elevated to the place of his chief. He was a man of rugged honesty and believed in resting his feet on solid ground. On an occasion when he headed a great delegation of employees who desired to make a presentation to Harvey du Cros he had used these words :—

" I am very pleased to be the spokesman for every gentleman present, and to seize this opportunity of expressing my own feelings also. I am proud to say I am one of the oldest servants of the Pneumatic Tyre Company, having been closely identified with it since its inception, and during the past seven years I have enjoyed the warm and generous friendship of Mr. du

* *Motor Cyclist and Cycle Trader*, June 23rd, 1916.
† *The Cycle and Motor Cycle Trader*, October 1st, 1909.

Cros—a friendship which I very highly value and I do not think that any man who has Mr. du Cros' friendship can value it too highly, for I have never met a more loyal-hearted gentleman to his friends than Mr. du Cros, and one to whom it gives more pleasure to do a good turn when he can.

" But apart from this, there is no man who knows better than I do the difficulties that Mr. du Cros has had to contend with and had he not been indeed a man of remarkable foresight, ability, and character, he would have shrunk from it.

" I never wish to have a better general than Mr. du Cros, and I never yet struck a place where ability and hard work were so soon recognised and so well rewarded. We are here, Mr. du Cros, to cordially recognise the magnificent results attending your efforts, and every word contained in the address, which Mr. Hill will read, we fully endorse.

" Irishmen in particular should be proud of you, for by extraordinary perseverance, and in the face of most persistent opposition, your sound judgment and able generalship has not only created a great and thriving English industry, but with amazing rapidity you have established kindred industries in the four quarters of the world.

" In the many—and apparently insurmountable—difficulties which have beset your path, in this great enterprise, you have always shown towards us that even temperament and genial courteous manner which (if you will allow us to say so) has endeared you to us, and made our work a pleasure."

My father was at all times more than generous in his appreciation of the efforts of others and never forgot them. He was the last man in the world to wish to steal another man's thunder, and never sought to do so, or claim any distinction for himself. Over two years before Dunlop's letter was written he had expressed himself

235

with almost exaggerated diffidence * in his presence and that of the other colleagues whom he had appointed to his Board, in 1889, at the international banquet held in London in November 1909, presided over by H.S.H. Prince Francis of Teck, which they all supported by their presence and which was attended by Englishmen, Americans, Frenchmen, Germans, Dutchmen, Canadians, Scandinavians and men from even further afield, given by the cycle and motor trades and clubs to celebrate the coming of age of the pneumatic tyre industry and to mark " their appreciation of the unique services rendered to the cycle and motor industries by Harvey du Cros to whom belongs the credit of turning to every-day use and commercial account the pneumatic tyre of Dunlop's invention." The tribute was from the world to the commercial leader of the movement, and on that occasion, this little man, just out from the shadows and broken in health, stood up and said in tones of surprised emotion,

" I have just realised that this is the most important moment of my life, long as it has been."

This comment was made on my father's remarks on that occasion :—

" It was, I thought, characteristic of Mr. du Cros, that in his speech he should have given credit to all who had been identified with him in the early days of the pneumatic tyre, and taken none to himself. His compliments to every one of his old co-directors were well deserved, and his eulogism of Mr. J. B. Dunlop was graceful and fitting ; but perhaps, what I liked best—knowing something of the facts—was his testimony to the affectionate devotion of his own sons. If

* See pp. 241-2.

ever the saying that union is strength had a vivid illustration, it is furnished by the manner in which Mr. du
Cros and his sons have pulled together—in sport and
business.

" The whole tone of Mr. du Cros' speech seemed to
me to be a sort of kindly, and I have no doubt uninten-
tional, rebuke to those who have seized the opportunity
afforded by this movement to air their jealousies and
somewhat splenetic views and ideas."—*The Cycle and
Motor Cycle Trader*, November 26th, 1909.

Passages from my father's speech and the utterances
of speakers and writers in the Press will best recall the
sentiments of the public and the leading men of sport and
industry of many countries who were then assembled.

II

Mr. Arthur J. Walter, K.C., in the course of his
remarks, said :—

" Your Serene Highness, My Lords and Gentlemen,—
This year we celebrate the twenty-first anniversary of
the pneumatic tyre. We are met here to-night not so
much to think of the future as to dwell upon the past.
Of the future we are assured. Of the past, before human
memory loses touch of the events which have happened,
as human memory is apt to do, we desire to place on
record a brief history of the events of the last twenty-one
years, so far as they relate to the pneumatic tyre industry,
an industry which has conferred immense benefits upon
the industrial world.

" We have to-night 475 guests, and officially represented are the Royal Automobile Club, the Society of
Motor Manufacturers and Traders, the Cycle and
Motor Trades Association, the Stanley Show Limited,
the Automobile Club de France, and the Touring Club

de France. All these, gentlemen, are officially represented here to-night at this historic banquet. But, in
addition, we have here representatives from Great Britain,
France, Germany, Holland, Russia, Scandinavia, the
United States, Canada, South Africa, Australia, and the
Malay States. Truly, if I may say so, a representative
body to assist at our gathering.

"Mr. Robert Thomson on the 10th December, 1845,
described a pneumatic tyre. He was a British inventor.

ARTHUR J. WALTER, K.C.*

But he was born too
early. Really reading
his specification,
which I have had
occasion to do many
times and which I
have recently re-read,
I find it is astonish-
ing to what extent
Mr. Thomson was a
prophet.

"A gentleman
whom we have the
privilege and the
honour of seeing here
to-night, and whose
name will go down to
future ages, Mr. John
Boyd Dunlop, on the
23rd July, 1888, totally ignorant of anything that had
been done before, re-invented the pneumatic tyre.

"Let me pause here for a moment to emphasise,
what I have repeated over and over again, that you
want two things. You want an inventor, and you want
somebody who sees the merit of the invention, and who
has the 'nous' and the energy and the go to make the
public see that the invention is a good one. Many and
many a time have I been asked what I think of an inven-

* Died April 1919.

238

tion, and the question I always ask is ' Who is at the back of it ? ' It is not so much whether the invention is a good one, but whether the people who are going to run it are capable of running it.

" Now it was the good fortune of Mr. Dunlop to attract early the attention of Mr. du Cros and his family. The Messrs. du Cros, Junior, soon found that they had got a treasure ; that there were capabilities and possibilities about that tyre which the ordinary tyre did not possess. Their father, Mr. Harvey du Cros, whose restoration to health and whose presence here to-night we are delighted at, realised the potentialities of that tyre, and being, as those who know him full well, a man who, putting his hand to the plough, does not turn back, he determined that he had there an instrument of benefit to future generations, and he resolved to push it for all he was worth. The flood gates were opened the moment Mr. du Cros had satisfied the world that there was something in the pneumatic tyre.

" Mr. Harvey du Cros was not content with this business being limited to this country alone. He realised that it was an international matter. And so he and his sons wandered over the face of the earth, and not only persuaded the British, but persuaded also Continental nations that the tyre was a thing which had come to stay, and from that grew the great organisations on the Continent, several of whose representatives we have the honour of seeing here to-night. They soon realised what Mr. du Cros had realised and those vast organisations which we now see are the result of the original energy of Mr. Harvey du Cros.

" I have told you also that every invention needs a sponsor, and that sponsor we have here to-night, and we are delighted to honour him—I mean Mr. Harvey du Cros. The names of inventors live in their inventions, but too often the name of the man who has fostered the industry is forgotten after those who lived at the time with him have passed away. Those engaged in the pneumatic tyre industry have determined that no such slur shall rest upon that industry, but that they shall recognise the man who has done so much to foster the industry, who, by his foresight, confidence, sound judgment, untiring energy and commercial ability established this industry on so firm a basis. They desire to present him with an address which I shall have the pleasure of reading to you."

Mr. Harvey du Cros accepted the address and casket amid enthusiastic cheering and musical honours.

M. Adolphe Clément said :—

" Your Serene Highness, my Lords and Gentlemen. I have the honour to announce that I am authorised by the French Government to say that, subject to the consent of His Majesty the King, they have decided to confer upon Mr. Harvey du Cros the Légion d'Honneur."

ADOLPHE CLÉMENT, OFFICIER DE LA LÉGION D'HONNEUR.

A WORLD WIDE TRIBUTE

PRESENTATION MADE TO WILLIAM HARVEY DU CROS, J.P., ACCOMPANIED BY AN INTERNATIONAL ADDRESS CONTAINING OVER 1,000 SIGNATORIES FROM GREAT BRITAIN, FRANCE, GERMANY, BELGIUM, HOLLAND, DENMARK, ITALY, SPAIN, RUSSIA, EAST INDIES, AUSTRALIA, CANADA AND SOUTH AMERICA.

HARVEY DU CROS, ESQ., J.P.

" Your name, Sir, and personality are so intimately bound up with the birth, progress and success of the Pneumatic Tyre, that we desire at this its Twenty-first Birthday to offer you our heartiest thanks and congratulation.

Few of us to-day can realise the difficulties and prejudices which in the early days met you at every turn, but most of us know that it was your keen insight, sound judgment and untiring energy which in spite of every obstacle at last secured success.

It must be a source of neverfailing satisfaction to you that the child you so bravely nurtured has reached so vigorous a manhood. It must also add greatly to your pleasure to feel that in founding what is now a great industry no other trade has been crushed out of existence, but, on the contrary, new sources of wealth and new occupations for countless workmen have been found.

We desire also to express to you our firm belief that in fostering as you did the infancy of the Pneumatic Tyre, you largely contributed to the rapid growth of the Cycle and Motor Industry and greatly assisted the raw rubber, cotton and other allied trades and thus added largely to the sources of our national wealth and the wealth of other nations.

That you may live long to enjoy the fruits of a battle well and honourably fought, and that you may see the industry advance from success to success is the earnest wish and hope of all the undersigned."

November 19th, 1909.

[*Facing p.* 240.

Mr. Harvey du Cros said :—

" When I look round me, and when I heard of the composition of this meeting from Mr. Walter, I felt more charmed than I can tell you. It comprises sportsmen, the governing bodies of sport, and the representatives of those fascinating industries with which my life has been passed. The spirit of the meeting is that of friends, in honourable rivalry in sport and in industrial competition, which is for the benefit of the whole world.

" And the gathering is unique, inasmuch as here are assembled our foreign neighbours and friends bearing generous unselfish chivalrous testimony that our country has contributed an indispensable factor to the sum of their own great achievements in the construction of the homely bicycle, and the magnificent motor. I venture to think, gentlemen, that this meeting is unprecedented, inasmuch as I don't think there has ever been a gathering where sport, industry and wholesome rivalry have been so harmoniously blended as upon this happy occasion. May it be a ' red letter ' day in the annals of our respective industries and a contribution to the amity and good-will of our respective countries.

" If, therefore, I am guilty of the unpardonable sin of pride, I hope that in your minds at least the occasion will be my excuse. I have been specially honoured by you here this evening, but it would not be right for me to accept that honour without qualification. We are met to celebrate the founding of a great industry. It was founded by a group of men, who formed a small company now non-existent. And the founders of that industry were Mr. J. B. Dunlop, who is here, Mr. Robert Booth, who is here, Mr. R. J. Mecredy, who is here, and Mr. Fred Woods, who is here.

" Mr. Dunlop joined the Founder Company because of his faith in his own ideas. If I occupy a prominent position here, this evening, more prominent than theirs, it is due to the extraordinary loyalty of those gentlemen who gave me throughout my career in the founding of this industry the most loyal support that any man ever had. It was because they placed me at the helm, that more kudos has come to me than I am entitled to in this matter. They gave me the privilege of focussing the various inventions upon which the industry rests to-day, and they did me the honour to allow me to deal with foreign countries in an endeavour to found the industries there.

" Mr. Thomson has been referred to ; but the industry as it now exists was not founded upon the Thomson patent, because, as Mr. Walter has said, he lived too soon. It is only bare justice to Mr. Dunlop to say that the industry as I know it, and as my colleagues here all know it, was founded on the tyre produced to us by Mr. Dunlop.

" The day of my meeting with the Thomson patent in the year 1890 was one of the most disagreeable days of my existence. And there is a paradox in the matter ; for although the existence of the Thomson patent was a misfortune to the founders of the original Company, still there is no doubt that if we had known it existed we should never have attempted to found the Company.

" It is impossible for me to express the gratitude I feel to all of you. This gift you have presented to me will be dearer to me than anything else I possess. I am sure you can understand what a pleasure it will be to my sons, who have supported me so loyally, and with such affection, in the efforts to establish this industry, sacrificing their own feelings, and going to live in foreign countries for years, to my temporary distress. But, thank God, they like all my old colleagues, and all those gentlemen who have been associated with the brains of this industry, are all united again, in the closest ties of friendship, and may I say, affection."

Chevalier René de Knyff, representing the Automobile and Touring Clubs of France, said :—

" Appointed by the Automobile Club de France, I

believe the oldest automobile club in existence, and by the Touring Club de France, the most important of all such federations, I have the honour to reply to this toast.

RENÉ DE KNYFF.

" All of you have been associated with the movement from its earliest stages, as has been my privilege, and as cyclists and as motorists, can appreciate the invention placed at our disposal as the result of the genius of Dunlop.

" Dunlop was the creator, but we all know from our experience that the merit of an invention is not sufficient to place it in the position that it deserves. It is necessary to find at the right moment a man full of energy and ardour, who will devote not only his intelligence and his experience, but his faith to the future success of the invention. Mr. Harvey du Cros was the one who placed himself in the forefront of the Pneumatic Tyre Industry. No one could ever describe how great was the struggle and the uncertainty at the commencement, but Mr. du Cros, surrounded by his sons, to whom he is more of an elder brother than a father, knew how to conquer, and to implant in the minds of all the value of the pneumatic tyre.

" I can still recall, as if it were yesterday, on the Courbevoie Track, his sons Arthur and Harvey taking part in the bicycle races, and surprising all competitors by beating them easily, thus laying the foundation for the conquest of the world. I can affirm without fear of contradiction that the bicycle and motor car without the discovery of Dunlop would not have been able to meet with success."

Mr. C. Vernon Pugh said :—

" To me as chairman of the committee which organised this great, and I am glad to say most successful, gathering falls the privilege of having to propose the health of the chairman to-night, and to express on behalf of the organising committee, and those assembled here, our very deep thanks to him for the honour he has done us and the cycle and motor industries throughout the world in presiding over our gathering to-night.

C. V. PUGH.

" Our Chairman's services to sport are well known. His position as Chairman of the Royal Automobile Club is one which he has filled with distinction to himself and with great advantage to that important body."

His Serene Highness Prince Francis of Teck, K.C.V.O., D.S.O., brother of Queen Mary and Chairman of the Royal Automobile Club, who was to die tragically within the year, said :—

" I can assure you it is with great pleasure that I find myself here to-night, and I shall be the first one to publicly congratulate my friend, Mr. du Cros, on the honour which has been conferred upon him by the French Government, and announced in the graceful manner so emblematic of that great nation.

" I came into this room, having, if I may say so, a smattering of the idea of what this industry meant, but I shall leave this room filled and thrilled with all that I have heard. When you consider that wherever you go in life, it may be west or east, it matters not, there is this tyre running, working for ever, expanding for ever, from Continent to Continent, for ever is it moving. And always as it moves is it bringing with it in its trail, success, almost civilization. Always with it is that great force behind it, bearing, as trade does, increasing comfort in wealth, and with the wealth increasing benefit to those who are employed in its enormous ramifications."

H.S.H. PRINCE FRANCIS
OF TECK.*

III

" For the first time, public recognition was made of the immense value of the pneumatic tyre to the civilised communities of the world, and of the splendid services of Mr. Harvey du Cros in founding, fostering, and establishing on a firm basis an industry whose ramifications to-day extend to the furthermost limits of the globe."—*The Cycle and Motor-Cycle Trader*, November 26th, 1909.

" It may be said that it was felt by those who listened to Mr. du Cros' speech on the occasion of the banquet, that his one great desire was to make full and generous acknowledgment of the loyal support he had received from so many, and to do justice to the great abilities of the various inventors whose ideas it had been his privilege to guide to a commercial success that must for ever

* Died October 1910.

245

remain notable in the annals of industry."—E. J. O'Reilly, November 1909.

" We are all agreed that if Mr. Dunlop and Mr. du Cros had not come together the pneumatic tyre would never have made its way. So yesterday's joint celebration was very fitting. There is a peculiar interest in the honour bestowed upon Mr. du Cros by the French Government, for it was owing to the action of another French Government that his family, who were of noble Huguenot descent, had to leave France in 1702. The new Republic has repaired the injury done by the old Monarchy."—*The Globe*, November 20th, 1909.

" Mr. Harvey du Cros saw the great possibilities of the idea commercially and the revolutionising effect it would have upon locomotion generally. He was lucky to find the inventor, to whom he paid the fullest and most generous tribute ; and the inventor was fortunate in finding such an organiser and financier as a sponsor.

" Mr. Harvey du Cros was singled out—and rightly too—to be the guest of the evening, as being the individual who had made this great invention a practical fact in everyday life all over the world ; and he did not fail to pay the most generous tribute to all his colleagues and coadjutors. He made a most memorable speech in reply to the address and presentation—modest as to himself, tactful to a degree, and instructively historical throughout.

" The history of the Dunlop tyre, the tale of the pneumatic and its rapid evolution, will go down to posterity as one of the greatest commercial romances of all time."—*The Standard*, November 23rd, 1909.

" We have had nothing like it in the history of our trades, nor are we likely to see anything like it in our time. It was, in effect, the tribute of the world to a great invention, and to the man who, taking it up to exploit it, founded on it a world-wide industry."—*The Motor Trader*, November 24th, 1909.

" What appealed to me most was the crowd of men

246

who were there merely as sportsmen, and who came to honour a man they had known, above all things, as a sportsman. For it must be remembered that Mr. du Cros was already famous as a sportsman and an athlete long before it began to dawn upon us that he was one of the great industrial geniuses of the age. Men whose noses he punched, whose eyes he blackened, and whose ribs he prodded, from the old gymnasium days in Earlsfort Terrace onwards, gathered round him in the hour of his triumph to show that they had not forgotten those delicate little attentions, and to testify their delight at the amazing success in life of one who never yet turned his back on an old friend.

" Mr. du Cros has had to fight through twenty-one jaded years of endless, tireless labour and has had to endure disappointments and to enter on struggles that would have broken the heart of most men. But he would indeed be hard to please if he did not feel after the wonderful scene and proceedings of last Friday night that it was worth it. He must now be able to realise what it means to live ' one crowded hour of glorious life.'

" One of the joys of the evening was the presence of the veteran inventor, John Boyd Dunlop. It was pleasant to hear the ringing and sustained cheer that greeted the mention of his name. But Mr. Dunlop is one of those fortunate mortals who are ' not for an age, but for all time.'—*The Irish Cyclist*, November 24th, 1909.

" Large as was the company there were few whose names are not familiar as household words in some particular walk of the pneumatic tyre and allied industries of the world. Practically every concern in the United Kingdom actively engaged in the manufacture of tyres, and every motor car and cycle manufacturing company using them, was represented. The tyre manufacturers of the Continent and of America were there, and from every country in Europe men of commercial mark had journeyed to do honour to one whose part in this romantic chapter of history marked him out for honour even more than the men whose inventions were the material out of which he fashioned a trading success, than which nothing more remarkable is contained in the entire history of commerce.

"Like the architects of old, Mr. du Cros builded better than he knew when he persuaded his business and personal friends in 1889 to join him in forming a company to purchase and work Mr. J. Boyd Dunlop's pneumatic tyre patents. He founded a company and created an industry, the violent cessation or removal of which to-day would throw the entire machinery of the world out of gear and well-nigh paralyse the everyday life of every civilised nation under the sun."—*The Scottish Cyclist*, November 24th, 1909.

"There are countless inventions every year, but not one in a thousand ever gets beyond being an invention and becomes something of practical use to humanity. It is therefore as much a question of the commercial man's ability as of the inventors as to whether or not any development shall become useful to the public. At a time when none had faith in the pneumatic tyre Mr. Harvey du Cros staked his fortune on it, and the result has been a new means of locomotion in all parts of the world, with an incalculable effect on the development of the motor-car. In these circumstances it is fit that the Royal Automobile Club and all the other motoring bodies should join hands to celebrate the exploitation of an invention that has worked such a wondrous change and which has been responsible, incidentally, for a wide variety of other inventions enormously useful to civilisation."—*The Morning Post*, November 19th, 1909.

"Mr. Harvey du Cros lived a life of incessant toil. Years ago he had his reward in the material sense, but not till Friday last did he know that public recognition of his great work in introducing a new industry to the

world, that must be his dearest memory in the days
that are still before him. The whole civilised world
was represented, either in person or in spirit ; business
rivals were there, and so were old sporting opponents
by the dozen. Pastime and industry combined to do
honour to a man who had done so much for both. A
member of the Royal Family presided, and honours
were sent by the French Government and afterwards by
the King of Spain.

"Verily, such an acknowledgment of great work
accomplished was well worth waiting for, and it was
evident that Mr. du Cros realized to an almost over-
whelming degree what such a wonderful demonstration
meant."—*The Cycle and Motor-Cycle Trader*, November
26th, 1909.

" But in the hearts of a vast number of his fellow
countrymen, Mr. Harvey du Cros (and with him that
group of clever and enthusiastic sons to whom he has
been, as Chevalier René de Knyff said, more like an
elder brother than a father) fills a very high place. His
recognition of the potentialities of Mr. J. B. Dunlop's
invention was fraught with great consequences, for the
pneumatic tyre revolutionized the cycle movement and
made the motor car and motor cycle possible, whilst,
if all that is meant by these simple facts be considered
it will be seen that one very important industry has been
created, two others have been enormously developed,
and many others have been benefited."—*The Motor*,
November 23rd, 1909.

" The company was to a very large extent one of
veterans, most of whom were in the prime of their
athletic manhood when the Dunlop tyre was first given
to the world. Yet there were moments when the
emotional enthusiasm would have done credit to a great
crowd of schoolboys. There were four remarkable
scenes in the drama of the evening. The first was the
burst of cheering long lived that greeted the first mention

of Mr. Dunlop's name—cheering that must have been as sweet music in the ears of the veteran ; the second was the enthusiasm which greeted M. Clément's announcement that the French Government had decided to enrol Mr. du Cros in the Legion of Honour ; the third, the ovation that greeted Mr. du Cros when he rose to speak, and which affected him so much that he was not quite his old self for a few minutes ; and the fourth, the cheers that rang out when he sat down.

" It was a night that marked the crowning triumph of Mr. du Cros' amazing career, and an event that must be a cherished memory to him for the remainder of his days. The tribute paid to him as the man who had founded a world-wide industry came, not only from England, or the United Kingdom, but from the whole civilised world. In the 850 names on the scroll—presented to Mr. du Cros in a magnificent casket—it is safe to say that every country on the face of the earth that is so far civilised as to know the pneumatic tyre is represented, while the company present at the banquet was as cosmopolitan as it was enthusiastic.

" The whole celebration was significant as a testimony to the wonderful part which the pneumatic tyre has played in the history of the last quarter of a century. It has done more than any other factor to revolutionize locomotion, to develop the cycle and motor industries, and the pastimes identified with them, and, consequently, to help largely in advancing the health, happiness and prosperity of the human race. For the men who created such a revolution no honour could be too great."—*The Cycle Trader*, November 26th, 1909.

" Last, but by no means least, came the guest of the evening, surrounded by his bodyguard of stalwart sons. The scene in the reception room at 7 o'clock was one that completely baffles all my poor powers of description. It was an historic gathering, comprising, with hardly an exception, the men who had built up two great industries.

" Next to the guest of the evening, there was no figure in that big assembly so interesting as that of J. B. Dunlop, for the simple reason that he was the man who had enabled the world to ' ride on air.' Others may have anticipated him, but he alone made the tyre a practical thing. Mr. Harvey du Cros was the driving power behind this great invention, and to his marvellous skill and unique abilities for organisation and administration belongs the honour of making the tyre a household word in practically every civilised country in the world."— *The Irish Cyclist*, November 24th, 1909.

Further Press comments appear in the Appendix, p. 292.

CHAPTER TWENTY-TWO

VALE

AFTER this event my father rested from his labours, and in 1918 was appointed its President by the Dunlop Rubber Company, an office which was specially created for him by the shareholders as a mark of their appreciation of his great services.

He longed for his native country, and as a stricken man returned to Ireland to live with his memories beside the sea which he loved, until he slept quietly away on the eve of Christmas 1918 in his seventy-second year.

OBITUARY

" The death has occurred at his residence, Inniscorrig, Dalkey, Co. Dublin, of Mr. William Harvey du Cros, founder of the pneumatic tyre industry.

" A very prominent personality in the business world, and one of the most ardent promoters of the Entente Cordiale between England and France, he was a descendant of an ancient Huguenot family, whose name is inscribed in the Roll of the French nobles since the twelfth century. In the seventeenth century the head of the family was Francois, Count de la Combe and Sieur de Pradills, who had been page to Henry Quatre and afterwards Captain of his Royal Regiment, his nobility being for a special reason confirmed by the King in Council by Decree of May 7th, 1697. On his death his widow, with their only son, Jean Pierre du

Cros, escaped from France during the religious persecution and settled in Dublin."—*Coventry Herald*, December 28th, 1918.

" With his demise there ended one of the most romantic chapters in the history of commerce. To Mr. Harvey du Cros will always be given the credit of foreseeing the vast potentialities, beneficent and commercial, of an invention the moment he saw it in its crudest and least promising form.

" It is quite in accordance with the conventional conception of the career of a prince of industry that he should start very young, and with his foot on the lowest rung of the ladder. Therefore, when Mr. Harvey du Cros, in a rather rare moment of self-revelation, during an address to the Dunlop employees at Birmingham, recalled the fact that he left home to seek fortune at the age of fourteen, earning a pittance which few lads of the present day would regard as a living wage, the reminiscence seemed perfectly appropriate for a millionaire speaker.

" It was as the Napoleon of the tyre industry that his great commercial ability and directive genius were so brilliantly displayed.

" Beginning active life as a strong-willed, independent boy, insisting on making his own way in the world, young du Cros came of a stock that was by no means obscure in its origin. For five generations the family of du Cros had lived in Dublin, moderately prospering, since the first years of the reign of Queen Anne, when, in order to escape finally from the religious persecutions that followed the Revocation of the Edict of Nantes, Jean Pierre du Cros had emigrated with his widowed mother from Montpelier, in the Hernault district of Southern France, and settled in Ireland, serving as a lieutenant in the English wars of that time.

" Young Jean Pierre du Cros, on leaving the army, married in Dublin, and the five generations of intermarriage with Irish families evolved a happy blend of Celtic fire and Gallic grace.

" No one who ever heard the rich persuasive eloquence of Harvey du Cros, playing upon the emotions of a turbulent public meeting, could fail to recognize him as an Irishman ; while his polished manner, faultless style, and exquisite perfection of courtesy, were fragrant echoes of his paternal ancestry."—*The Motor*, December 31st, 1918.

" Somewhat small in stature, in spite of his splendid athletic powers, and with a face that did not suggest the fighting man—for it had quite regular and handsome features ; it was thin ; the moustache was long and waxed until it looked like that of Louis Napoleon—he might have passed for a man of fashion with no particular strength of muscle, until you considered the splendid depth of the chest, the breadth of the shoulders, and above all, you realised what kind of man he was if, despite the tranquillity of the expression, you looked steadily at the glittering blue-grey eyes. He looked and he was a man of iron nerve."—T. P. O'Connor, M.P., December, 1918.

" Before Hastings knew him he had made a great name as pioneer of the pneumatic tyre industry, and for his development of the wonderful Dunlop business. He came to us as a politician and persistently preached the commercial doctrine of Joseph Chamberlain, and when he won the seat against Mr. Freeman-Thomas he claimed, and not without justification, that it was the first contest won on the Tariff Reform ticket.

" From the first moment he appeared before the Candidate Selection Committee his popularity was secure. He had a wonderful winning way, he was an attractive personality and a witty Irishman. Added to this he was a great sportsman—once a champion boxer —and he possessed a particularly generous heart."— *Hastings Observer*, December 28th, 1918.

" The death of Mr. Harvey du Cros removes one whom it is no exaggeration to call the biggest man in the cycle and motor industries. Though short in stature, Mr. du Cros had a big heart, a big brain, and big ideas, and though his phenomenal success as a commercial magnate made him famous throughout the world, his intimates and all who were fortunate enough to know him in private life will remember him best as a sportsman." —*Athletic News*, December 30th, 1918.

" We stop the press to announce the death, which we do with very deep and sincere regret, of Mr. Harvey du Cros. The sad event took place in the early hours of Saturday morning, the 21st inst., as the result of heart failure. He passed away peaceably in his sleep, and there thus came to an end a life that was marked by strenuous activity.

" Mr. du Cros had reached the age of 72 years, and for some time past he had ceased to take an active part in the management of the great business which his genius had created. He took up his residence in his native land, which he loved so well, and spent the concluding days of his life in quiet enjoyment of the results of his labours." —*Irish Cyclist*.

My father's portrait had been commissioned by the company he had founded and was made by H. Tennyson Cole, to hang in the Board-room as an inspiration to his successors and to keep his memory green.

But it came to my knowledge subsequently it had been jettisoned by the company, which upon being

HARVEY DU CROS, by H. TENNYSON COLE.

approached was not averse to profits by selling it, whereupon it was purchased by and is now a treasured possession of his family. As to who was responsible for this un-English proceeding I am unable to say, but am glad to have had the assurance of the present Chairman, Sir George Beharrell, that he was not aware of it, and feel sure that everyone will agree that those who reap where their predecessors have sown should be content to think of and act towards those who have passed away with the consideration which is their due.

II

After the death of my father and the manifold and exacting activities of the war, I found myself with but one ambition which has been well expressed in the lines :

> " Free am I to come and go
> But Fate moves thee so—and so."

After thirty years of successful struggle, and regarding money as of secondary importance, I was satisfied and wished no longer to be master of other men, but only of my own time. So I sought to substitute for the chains of executive control the less onerous responsibility of consultant and adviser, leaving freedom to gratify an early ambition as well as to indulge in the first clear break from business since I had entered it as a lad. " 'Tis not the miles we travel but the pace that tells," and this old thought of seeking out peaceful places, remote and unvisited by war or tyres (if possible), took practical shape in November 1919 when I put forth in my small boat for a leisurely progress to the back of beyond.

Alas, it proved to be an unfortunate interlude, for largely through unwise speculation and inadequate finance, aggravated by executive and technical weaknesses, as well as falling prices and widespread depression, which affected other great tyre firms, potential losses of over £8,000,000 eventuated within one short year and bid fair to bring down the Dunlop Rubber Company for the creation of which I had been responsible. But its foundation had been widely and deeply laid, and by the untiring exertions of a reconstructed management it was, in course of time, restored to an even greater position than before. But the fact that losses of such magnitude could be faced and made good was a form of

s 2

testimonial with which we could have well dispensed. The recovery may be viewed with justifiable pride by those who " followed on " in the management, and its completeness may be gauged by the illustrated table on p. 308 of the Appendix.

By the perversity of fate a few years later and again following upon a transfer of executive responsibility, history repeated itself in an even more serious catastrophe which destroyed the Founder Company, contributed to on this occasion largely by unforeseen events outside the company, which occupied the attention of the Courts, but also by avoidable errors due to a fatuous over-confidence and egotism within the company, which taken together were ultimately expressed in losses to the tune of £4,500,000.

Thus no less than £12,500,000 had been dissipated to an appreciable degree by ignoring the old and well-tried conservative policies upon which the two companies had been founded. After an honourable and historic career of forty years, without one whisper against its good name for fair dealing, the company that founded a world industry deserved a better fate at the hands of its supposedly qualified and competent executive and afterwards at those of its wealthy and, in some cases, partly responsible creditors. It is only to be expected that new executive chiefs, whether drawn from within or without, and given a wide discretion, must prove their fitness to fill the shoes of their predecessors and their ability to distinguish between the substance and the shadow ; but, after making extravagant allowances for exceptional circumstances in these two cases, why, oh why, at a cost of £12,500,000 ? That, however, is another story.

All of which goes to prove that one of the main secrets of success in business is the selection of the right men for the right places : if that could be consistently done the number of millionaires in the business world would gladden the heart of any Chancellor of the Exchequer. But men, like machines, wear out, and these problems will always arise when they come to be replaced.

But despite old time reverses I may turn from these events in the sure knowledge that, so long as the world continues to travel upon wheels, the Dunlop unit will maintain its position in the forefront of its industry. An observer recently writing on the commemoration of the fiftieth anniversary of the Dunlop invention remarked with regard to the foundation of the pneumatic tyre industry, that it was a proud privilege to have been associated with such an enterprise, and that from its earliest beginnings the House of Dunlop had been erected on a firm foundation of integrity. It had been wisely governed by a succession of able and honourable leaders and served by men and women of ability and high principle ; with the name was associated a tradition that is a monument to its founders and an inspiration to those who have followed them.

Fifty Years After

Here muse we of old times, old hopes, old friends—
Old friends: the writing of those words has borne
Our fancy backward to the gracious past.
      . . . The years
Have taught some sweet, some bitter lessons, none
Wiser than this,—to spend in all things else,
But of old friends to be most miserly.

by

ARTHUR ROY DU CROS

THE demise of the Founder Company after forty-one years of adventurous existence was no unworthy one, attracting as it did by its melancholy obsequies the attention of the world. At the same time it afforded the author of this book at long last the opportunity to gratify his love of travel, which he now indulges to the full. Although he was stricken by this avoidable calamity, he was sustained in the knowledge that he and his family stood by the Company to the extent of more than half their fortune, and now finds solace in exploring the world which he and the pioneers of that industry have done so much to change. Whilst he is thus engaged it might be well to ask, at the conclusion of an account such as this of effort and endeavour, those questions which must arise in the mind of the reader, first among which is the inevitable " Why ? " " To what end ? "

The attempt to answer this question in its deeper sense raises at once the whole problem of the meaning of progress and of civilisation, and calls to mind those interminable discussions which devolve as a rule into a conflict between cynicism and optimism, in which defeat is never admitted and victory never won.

It would be profitless indeed to conclude a record of practical achievement with a discourse upon metaphysical values, or with an attempt to decide whether " progress " is but a synonym for " change " or in truth signifies an advance towards the ultimate Destiny of Man. It will be sufficient here to outline the broad effects upon the human race of the actions that have been chronicled and leave the reader to pass judgment, according to his humour and to his temperament.

It is one of the bitter paradoxes of this world that in all which is good there is so large a potentiality for evil, and the realisation of this, as often as not, blinds us to its compensation—the potentiality for good in much that is evil. But certain it is that few inventions of major importance exist which have not resulted in some evil, if not by reason of their own nature, then because they have been put to evil ends ; indeed, the vast majority of them have much to answer for, since they become the blind tools of human nature, which is at once both good and evil. Printing, for example, has spread the doctrines of Christ and Machiavelli with equal indifference : whilst wireless telegraphy warns imperilled ships or directs aeroplanes in war with cold impartiality.

The pneumatic tyre then, in common with most other inventions, has its measure of evil to account for, and little wonder, since coming as it did hand in hand with the internal combustion engine which Carl Benz and Daimler were busy evolving in 1885, it has done more than most things to change the aspect and the tempo of human existence.

Let it be remembered that in 1888 the railway was supreme, whilst the highways were falling into grass-grown disuse : these small islands were full of men and women who lived and died without ever a sight of the sea, and England's monuments and beauties were chiefly known to the rich and leisured, or to the often unappreciative minds of those born and bred near at hand. The pneumatic tyre, first by making popular the cycle, and then the motor car and coach, threw open the glories of the sea and of the English countryside to the whole nation, alike strengthening the people's love of their native land and their appreciation of Nature and of Beauty ; not only in England but all across the world the heart of every country has been revealed to their peoples.

Surely an unalloyed benefit ?

And yet before this invention there were no laws or societies for preventing the desecration of rural England by this mass invasion, no wastes of orange peel and litter, nor was the sweep of the Downs scarred with by-pass roads, its beauties desecrated by advertisements.

The pneumatic tyre has helped to destroy the cloistered seclusion of local life ; the Lotharios of the country village need no longer confine their choice of a bride to the maidens of the same parish, or at the boldest to the " belles " of the hamlet across the hill ; this change is apparently insignificant, yet the family conservatism and the almost ritual-like observance of tradition which was at once the strength and weakness of the English yeoman race is fast breaking down before the influx of ideas garnered by these gallants, adventuring over the length and breadth of the land in search of more remunerative employment, of a fitting bride, or simply for the love of variety and speed.

The population of England has been " liquefied " as never before in its history. The hereditary ignorance which was a characteristic of British agriculture is being dissipated, as were the clouds of mediæval superstition, for it can only survive in semi-insulated communities ; let us hope that the qualities of reverence for the past, contentment with one's lot, of caution and respect may not vanish with them, and let us rejoice in the new spirit of enterprise and initiative which is rapidly being diffused in rural England.

But above all the tyre brought in its train speed, speed on land and in the air ; the sick no longer wait upon the doctor's trap jogging leisurely through the narrow lanes ; men and women and children no longer spend their scant holidays in the familiar environment of their everyday work to save the precious moments wasted by even the shortest journeys. The horizon has been rolled back and the world rendered so small by the advent to it of this speed, that in time all men may even come to realise their own brotherhood.

Not only has time been remeasured for man, but speed has become an end in itself making for courage and endurance and bringing to men a unique sense of rhythm and of harmony, a new ecstasy hitherto unknown. Ecstasy is not infrequently the inspiration of art ; it is too soon to discern fully the effects of speed upon artistic creation, but in music, poetry and literature these effects are already apparent, while even in the more static forms of expression, painting, sculpture, and architecture, speed has had its influence. For even to this last the absence of wind resistance seems to have been illogically extended until it has become a criterion of architectural beauty. No doubt much of this is ephemeral and spurious, but there is equally no doubt that generations of future art critics will have little difficulty in estimating the effect of the pneumatic tyre upon human culture !

Is not this gift of speed one for which men may give thanks with a full heart ?

Here again there is another side to the picture, the vast

mortality of the air and the roads. More than a hundred lives a week, a figure so terrible that one wonders whether, if Thomson in his Edinburgh library, Dunlop in his Belfast stable-yard or Welch in his father's workshop, had had the power to see into the future, they would have fathered and foster-fathered this strange child of theirs. Vain questions these, as well to ask if Papa Daimler would have persevered if he had been granted a vision of the mighty array of tanks and bombing aeroplanes that terrorise the world to-day.

The pneumatic tyre vastly accelerated other things besides motor cars and motor cycles ; for instance, the movement towards the emancipation of women, which was in the early 'nineties but a small and weakly one, rapidly gained health and strength from the opportunities which the air-tyred safety bicycle threw open to it, and in a leading article in the *Irish Times* of 1909 this aspect of the invention is the one most greatly stressed, yet this great change in history is now so much a part of everyday life that its beginnings are already half forgotten.

Are we of the twentieth century to praise the tyre because people no longer need to live huddled together in sunless overcrowded towns, close beside their means of livelihood, or to blame it because our suburbs straggle half across the countryside ? Are we to sympathise with the anxious parson deploring his depleted

ROY DU CROS.

flock, or rejoice with the jocund landlord of the replenished wayside inn ? To welcome the improved aroma of the city streets or to commiserate with the severely rationed sparrows ?

264

Living in this century in which the problem of un-employment has become the constant attending shadow of our social life, it is impossible not to value the inesti-mable work of these pioneers of speed in giving employ-ment and means of livelihood to millions of people.

Millions of people ? Yes ; not only the few thousands of workers in the tyre town of Fort Dunlop with its many tentacles throughout the world, but those other thousands who work on the rubber plantations, in the cotton fields and mills or upon the roads themselves, and to the still greater number who work in the industries which the tyre has made possible, the cycle industry and the motor industry.

All these effects and countless others which will occur to the mind of any who pause to consider, are discernible immediately in our everyday surroundings in England, but in order to comprehend the magnitude of this inven-tion, coming in conjunction with that of the petrol engine, it must be remembered that similar changes were taking place in every country of the world embracing every branch of the human race.

II

The foregoing pages have given some account of the men who have worked these changes, but that account would be incomplete were the work of the author himself not to be amplified beyond the limits to which natural modesty have up to now restricted it. My father began his working life at the age of fifteen upon one of the lowest rungs of the civil service ladder, and indeed this whole family of brothers was actively engaged in an important industry before they had quitted their teens. This in itself indicates a trend of modern society, for science has gradually prolonged the allotted span of human existence, which in the sixteenth century was no more than fifty years or so, but society, by increasing the scope and period of education, has delayed the entry of men and women into the arena, thus compensating in some measure for the addition to the end of their activities by curtailing the beginning.

My father's life is certainly not one which requires either explanation or comment from me, nor would he himself desire it, holding as he does the strict view that a tree should be judged by its fruits. It is enough for me to chronicle very briefly the principal achievements of that life, and with this knowledge the reader will have little difficulty in estimating for himself the part played by such a man in the foregoing events. If it is necessary in order to appreciate these achievements of a Dublin boy of fifteen earning 12s. 6d. a week on an office stool to have some idea of his character, I would say that the most fundamental qualities of his nature are generosity, thoroughness in matters of detail, an open and constructive mind, and a persistency which never admits defeat. Whilst the most apparent quality to an outside observer is a rare combination of dignity and humour.

It is frequently said of men who have originated vast and widespread undertakings that at the time they never realised or foresaw their magnitude ; but of my father, at least, this could never be said, for in business he thought more of the effect upon future transactions than of the outcome of the present one, in politics he showed the same appreciation of the needs of future generations, while even at bridge he seems (to me at least) to have played the hand while others are considering the next card.

266

My father did not long remain a clerk, for during these years he had been steadily building up for himself a reputation of pre-eminence upon the cycle track, and in this field he was to become, before he reached the age of twenty, one of Ireland's cycling champions, a holder of world records and a popular figure not only on the cycle tracks of Ireland but also of England and of France.

To many it was a mystery how so slight a man could achieve mastery in sport. Personally, I have little doubt but that his success was due to the intense *mental* concentration which he brought and still brings to bear upon anything which he undertakes.

When my grandfather became engrossed in the launching of the Pneumatic Tyre Company he handed over his paper business to his son to terminate or continue as he thought best ; my father did not find this trade a congenial one, so he successfully disposed of the family interests in it, and was upon the point of embarking for Australia to seek fame and fortune in that more spacious environment, when he was transferred to Coventry by the Pneumatic Tyre Co. (and at his own request, without any salary) upon a year's trial. At the end of that year he had made such good use of this unique opportunity to prove his merits that he was cordially congratulated upon the progress that had been made, and voted a salary of £600 a year with a bonus of £200, which at that time must have seemed to him magnificent indeed ! With this sum he insisted upon repaying my grandfather the money the latter had advanced him for living expenses for the preceding year, and from that moment his financial future was assured and he proceeded to build up a fortune with an ease and assurance that has never deserted him. He also spent it with equal ease.

One of the strongest traits in his character is a fervent loyalty and patriotism, and it being invariably his custom to translate his feelings into instant practical action he became in 1895 a volunteer and later a territorial. It would not be his wish that I should enlarge upon his activities in this connection, but he must have been endowed with the pioneering spirit, for he concerned himself closely with the initiation of new movements, for instance, flying ; the mechanisation of the army ; the distribution of propaganda in war ; and the introduction of ambulances to the battlefields.

Concurrently with these more military pursuits my father was also building up for himself a reputation in politics. His political career may be said to have begun with his success in the municipal elections of November 1895 in Coventry, but local politics were not long to occupy his sole attention ; in 1905 he was unsuccessful as a Conservative candidate for Parliament, but subsequently contested and won four elections during his fifteen years' membership of the House of Commons. He played some part, too, in the creation of the Junior Imperial League and became the first Chairman of its Committee.

For his national and industrial services he was created a baronet in 1917.

No account of this man would be complete without some mention of his fondness for children to which he hastened to give practical expression, and of his devotion to the family ideal and his interest in art ; the collection of pictures and antiques being one of his favourite hobbies. Also he has a partiality for sporting records and two of his own may be worth relating ; when he sailed his yacht round the world he accomplished the feat " without shipping a single green sea " throughout the entire voyage of just 30,000 miles, and survived an involuntary immersion for thirty long minutes in the Red Sea when he had, on expert advice, slowed down to *fish for shark*. On another occasion he landed a considerable wager through being consistently *unlucky* ! It happened in this way ; a racing friend challenged my father, who took little interest in the sport, to toss to decide which one of them should stake a " pony " on an approaching classic event. My father lost the toss. The friend, relenting, offered to toss double or quits—my father lost. A third time they tossed and a third time he lost. Accordingly he embarked £200 on Winkfield's Pride for the Cæsarewich of 1896, winning for himself and his friend £6,600.

That then in brief is the life of the author of this book, which he has written, despite the burden of ill-health, in order that the work of his friends might not be forgotten with the passing of the generation who knew and appreciated. It is, I know, a source of regret to him that, although there exist isolated memorials to the work of individuals, there is no composite memorial in any country to the five principals who made so many fortunes, built up so rich an industry, and so profoundly affected the lives of their generation.

EARLY MEMBERS OF THE FOUNDER COMPANY

G. H. TUKE.

R. M. HANLON.

E. H. BLAKE.

F. S. GIBBINGS.

A. CUNNINGHAM.

A. H. HUET.

L. V. KENWARD.

W. J. McCORMACK.

D. G. SNODGRASS.

A. MOSSES.

F. J. KEEGAN.

J. E. JAMIESON.

C. G. THISELTON.

F. W. BENNETT.

E. J. MORRISSEY.

R. J. PARK.

W. J. GREER.

HARRY GREER.

A. E. GREEN.

H. L. RICHARDSON.

H. E. HOLMES.

W. T. WHANN.

J. A. TAYLOR.

C. R. OWEN.

W. HIBBERT.

W. H. PAUL.

C. MACBETH.

R. WALKER.

R. H. BAGNALL.

E. A. MURPHY.

J. HALL.

J. EGAN.

F. MACCABE.

S. K. SHELLEY.

W. F. STAFFORD.

G. MURPHY.

T 2

W. George.

F. C. Worsfold.

P. Bradstock.

H. F. Ryan.

C. W. Chandler.

M. MacDonagh.

M. Irving.

W. S. Tinkler.

J. McDowell.

R. D. MUNROE.   W. POULTON.   M. EGAN.

H. WELLS.   W. KINGSBURY.

BEN TUKE.   HARVEY DU CROS.   GEORGE DU CROS.

A CYCLE POLO TEAM OF THE '90's

275

A. HOLROYD

NAMES OF OTHER
EARLY MEMBERS

A. F. Greene, S. Hill, Ronald Jameson, W. H. Kingsbury, C. Sinclair, E. A. Stephens, Tommy Stephens, H. T. Whorlow, E. W. Armstrong, L. Beech, W. Bond, H. H. Camps, H. J. Dymond, E. Fell, H. Gibbins, G. T. Gregory, V. Iliffe, M. C. Johnson, V. J. Leechman, W. A. Llewellyn, E. F. Mitchell, W. Parsons, W. Pearl, G. C. K. Pinnell, W. H. Sharp, H. Stone, S. J. Terry, F. Vivian, T. E. Walker, F. Webb, Harry Wells.

APPENDIX

Extracts reprinted from

" THE IRISH CYCLIST AND MOTOR CYCLIST "

April 16th, 1924

"THE HISTORY OF THE PNEUMATIC TYRE

" Mr. J. B. Dunlop's long-expected Work

" BY T. W. MURPHY

" As long ago as 1905, as I am reminded by an extract from the *Irish Cyclist* which Mr. J. B. Dunlop quotes in ' The History of the Pneumatic Tyre,' the hope was expressed in these pages that, sooner or later, someone thoroughly versed in the facts would publish in book form a history of the pneumatic tyre. As was then said, the subject is an exceedingly interesting one—it is, in fact, one of the many commercial romances of the nineteenth century. It is a matter of no little regret that we have had to wait so long to see our hope fulfilled.

" It is nearly thirty-six years since the date of Mr. Dunlop's patent, and during that time most of the leading actors in the drama have passed the bourne. Mr. Dunlop is dead, and his son, Johnnie, for whom the first tyre was made, has passed away. We looked to the latter,

277

more than to any other man, to undertake the work. He was eminently qualified to do so, not only because of his life-long association with his father's invention and the fact that he had access to all his private papers, but by reason of his literary ability. More than once I discussed the subject with him. I learned that his father had collected most of the material for the work and put it into rough form. My hope that Johnnie Dunlop would write the history of the pneumatic tyre as a monument to the memory of his father was doomed to disappointment. He pre-deceased his father by a year and a half, and it was not until after his son's death that the father seriously tackled the subject and worked at it occasionally during the last years of his life. There were many reasons why those of us who were associated with the period of the introduction of the pneumatic tyre regretted the early demise of the inventor's son. His was a young life of unfulfilled promise; but above all things he should have given us the history of the tyre.

"THE FELL REAPER'S HARVEST

" Other leading personalities associated with the early history of the pneumatic tyre have also passed beyond the range of controversy. Harvey du Cros, its commercial sponsor, is gone; so, too, is John Griffiths, the first secretary of the Pneumatic Tyre Company, Ltd.; and most of those who were associated with the company in its early stages have passed away. Bartlett, of the North British Rubber Co., the inventor of the Clincher beaded-edge tyre, is gone also. Almost alone of the notabilities and inventors of the eighties and nineties is C. K. Welch, the inventor of the wired-on tyre; fortunately he is still amongst us.

"THE OBJECT OF THE BOOK

"While, therefore, we welcome the posthumous publication of Mr. Dunlop's book, we cannot refrain from expressing regret that it did not see the light of day during the lifetime of the author, even if it had been presented to us as a ' first rough sketch,' ' crude and unfinished,' as Mrs. McClintock, his daughter, admits it is in her ' Foreword.' During Mr. Dunlop's lifetime he had frequently to point out certain inaccuracies concerning the invention of the tyre which appeared in the Press. It was with the intention of preventing the possibility of any further inaccuracies that he undertook the writing of a history of the invention, and it is in the belief that she is carrying out his wishes that his daughter has published ' this book, which . . . contains essential true facts.' Despite Mrs. McClintock's statement, that the proofs of all the important facts stated in the book are now in her hands, we doubt if many of Mr. Dunlop's statements and conclusions will be accepted as the last words on the subject. Much that is essential to the full understanding of the history of the pneumatic tyre has been glossed over or altogether omitted. Some of the ' facts ' will be disputed. Had the book been published while Mr. Dunlop was still alive, many points of possible dispute could have been elucidated.

"CRITICISM DISARMED

"Mrs. McClintock's candid description of the book as ' crude and unfinished ' disarms criticism, but one can hardly pass over such a serious blunder as that in the very first lines of the book. ' I was born . . . on the 5th February, 1845, so that I am now in my eightieth year,' writes Mr. Dunlop. A man born in 1845 would not reach his eightieth birthday until 1925. Mr. Dunlop died in 1921. The year of his birth is given twice in the first chapter as 1845 and in another part of the book as 1840, without any reference to the discrepancy. We believe Mr. Dunlop was in his eightieth year when he died ; he would therefore appear to have been born in 1842.*

"THE IMPORTANCE OF DATES

" In a work of history or autobiography dates are of the greatest importance, but in this book no effort seems to have been made to secure accuracy. In one chapter the author writes of having the pleasure for the second time of meeting the Irish Old Timers at Donnybrook ' in June, 1890.' The organisation to which Mr. Dunlop refers was not formed until 1916. The numerous mistakes in the dates of the extracts from the *Irish Cyclist* make it impossible for anyone to check their accuracy ; but attention must be directed to one glaring error. It struck us as extraordinary that on 4th September, 1890, the *Irish Cyclist* should have any doubt as to the advantages of the pneumatic tyre for racing purposes, remembering that R. J. Mecredy had won innumerable races, including the N.C.U. championships at all four distances, in England during the year. Consequently we took the trouble to check the accuracy of the following quotation :—

' Mounted on it (pneumatic), a second-class man can beat a first-class man, as witness Hume's defeat of Arthur du Cros at Banbridge. On a hard cinder or

---

* Dunlop was born in 1840 and died in his 82nd year.

gravel path, we think the ordinary build of safety has the advantage, especially round corners.'

" There was no issue of the *Irish Cyclist* on the 4th September, 1890. The paragraph did not appear in the issue of 3rd September, 1890. It is obviously taken from an issue of the previous year, when the *Irish Cyclist* was not convinced of the advantages of the tyre on smooth racing tracks—a scepticism that the experience of the year quite justified. The error in the date is important, as the paragraph is reproduced as a proof that at that period Mr. Dunlop stood alone in his faith as to the speed potentialities of his tyre. In 1890 the question had been put beyond all debate, mainly by Mecredy's racing successes in England. He could not have any doubt on the subject in face of his unbeaten record in the leading scratch races of the season in England and Ireland.

" Not the Whole Story

" In the chapter which tells of the circumstances which led up to the invention of the tyre, Mr. Dunlop recounts modestly an oft-told tale, and corrects one or two minor inaccuracies which were current during his lifetime.

" In his story of the early history of his invention Mr. Dunlop is not always consistent, and his editor has to call attention to the fact that some of the statements made by him are not in agreement with those he makes in other parts of the book. But the main fault of the book is not the mistakes that Mr. Dunlop makes with regard to his own invention, but the manner in which he glosses over or altogether omits many important facts of first-class importance bearing on the history of the pneumatic tyre. The book is not, be it noted, a history of

Mr. Dunlop's invention. If it was it would end with the 1892 pneumatic. After that date the tyres made by the Pneumatic Tyre Co., while called Dunlops,* were made under the patents of others ; but all the circumstances leading up to this state of affairs are either ignored or passed over lightly as if of no importance.

" FOUR EPOCH-MAKING EVENTS

" From the date of Mr. Dunlop's patent in 1888 to the present time there were four notable events in the history of the pneumatic tyre. They might almost be called epoch-making events. The first was the introduction of the valve invented by Mr. Woods, a brother of one of the original directors of the company. The second was the discovery of the fact that Thomson had anticipated Dunlop by forty years. The third was the practically simultaneous invention of the detachable tyre by two inventors—the wired-on type by Welch and the beaded-edge type by Bartlett—and the fourth was the adoption of the tangential fabric, the invention of an American, J. F. Palmer.† One looks in vain for the facts relating to these important happenings in Mr. Dunlop's story.

" From the formation of the Pneumatic Tyre Co. until the adoption of the wired-on detachable tyre the only real alteration in Mr. Dunlop's original tyre was the fitting of the Woods valve, the type of valve that, unaltered from its original form, is almost universal to-day. Woods' name is not mentioned in the book. The startling discovery that Thomson had patented and made a pneumatic tyre in the forties, and that therefore the principle of an air tyre was not a good patent, is passed over, and the first reference we find to Thomson is a

* Dunlop-Welch.
† Palmer was anticipated in Britain by Moseley.

newspaper extract giving Mr. Dunlop the credit of making the article a practical one. Bartlett's invention—one of the two master patents under which alone any form of pneumatic tyre could be made—is not mentioned at all, and for the first wired-on detachable Mr. Dunlop gives the credit to T. W. Robertson, ignoring the fact that Robertson's tyre could not be made without infringing Welch's patent, the second of the master patents to which we have referred.

"The Invention of the Detachable Tyre

"Mr. J. B. Dunlop's claim to have invented the wired-on detachable tyre can only be described as grotesquely absurd. It is not put forward for the first time. Many years ago, long after Welch and Bartlett's patents had expired, it was advanced and promptly challenged in the pages of the *Irish Cyclist*, and Mr. Dunlop defended himself at great length in a correspondence with Mr. William Stewart. It is not an exaggeration to say that Mr. Dunlop's opponent in the correspondence riddled his arguments, and completely demonstrated the falsity of his pretensions. If we were to regard Mr. Dunlop as the defeated party in a newspaper controversy it would not be surprising to find him re-making in his book a claim he had failed to establish in the Press. In such a work as this there is no one to come forward within seven days of its publication and expose the fallacy of his arguments.

"Settled by Litigation

"But the question of the first inventor of the detachable tyre was not settled in that way. Both the Welch and the Bartlett patents were the subject of prolonged litigation in the courts, in which every patent lawyer of any standing at the English Bar was engaged on one side or the other. There were not one or two actions ; there were figuratively hundreds, and many judges tried the cases in the first instances and on appeal. The net result of that litigation was to establish the fact that no form of pneumatic tyre which relied on an inextensible edge as a means of attachment of the cover to the rim could be made without infringing Welch's patent, and that any form of tyre that was clinched to the rim was an infringement of Bartlett's patent. All these facts were established by law as long ago as 1896. It was their establishment that led E. T. Hooley, of unhappy memory, to buy out the Pneumatic Tyre Co., Ltd., at a price that gave the shareholders £12 10s. per £1 share and to purchase the Bartlett patent from the North British Rubber Co., Ltd., and to pass on the combined purchase to the public for £6,000,000.* It was not until these patents were established by law and amalgamated in one proprietorship that the company had the monopoly of the manufacture of pneumatic tyres—a monopoly which the original company imagined it had secured when in 1889 it purchased Mr. Dunlop's patent of the 31st October, 1888.

" What Dunlop did Invent

" Mr. Dunlop patented a principle that Thomson had invented in the forties. Had he at that time known of the existence of Thomson's patent he would have patented a method of attachment. His patent, as it stood, might have given him a monopoly of making an air tyre by his method ; but by the time the existence of Thomson's patent became known it was already evident that the

* £5,000,000.

pneumatic tyre would never attain a world-wide popularity unless it could be made easily repairable. This
was what Welch's and Bartlett's patents secured.
Dunlop's patent was never defended in a court of law.
Its owners realised it was of no commercial value.

"DUNLOP'S TWO POINTS

"Many of Mr. Dunlop's claims are put forward in
language which is indefinite. Consequently, it is difficult
to understand what he really claims and to refute his
unfounded pretensions. His scattered references to the
detachable tyre are cases in point. As far as I am able to
gather from the book, he bases his claim to the credit of
being the inventor of the detachable tyre on two points.
Describing a patent which he took out on 15th December,
1890, for a detachable tyre, he says :—' This tyre was,
I believe, the first detachable tyre ever made with an
all-rubber tube.' It may have been ; an all-rubber
tube is not an essential element of detachability. The
pneumatic tyre that Welch exhibited to the directors of
the Pneumatic Tyre Co. in May, 1892, had an air tube
which ' was made of cloth and rubber vulcanised
together as shown in the complete specification.' The
first Clincher tyre (Bartlett's patent) was also made with
an inextensible (cloth and rubber) air tube. According
to Mr. du Cros' evidence in a law case in 1895, ' They
[cloth and rubber tubes and all rubber tubes] were
equally efficacious, but the extensible [all rubber] tube
was the faster.' Mr. Dunlop controverts the theory put
forward by Mr. du Cros in the evidence quoted by
saying :—' An inextensible air tube was as fast as an all
rubber tube.' No one would accept such a statement,
even in 1895. To-day it is rank heresy. Would any

racing man of 1924 use a cloth and rubber inner tube ? The idea is laughable.

" The Dunlop-Welch detachable was always made with all rubber air tubes. The North British Rubber Co. in time adopted an all rubber tube also.

" This detachable tyre, the patent of 15th December, 1890, was not a wired-on or beaded-edge tyre. It was made on what is now known as the Constrictor principle.

" TWICE ANTICIPATED

" Mr. Dunlop's second claim to be regarded as the inventor of the detachable tyre is based on a patent of 9th April, 1891, for a detachable tyre held on to the rim by endless wires. ' This is the first patent recorded in the Patent Office for a detachable wired-on tyre having endless wires,' writes Mr. Dunlop. Even if one admits that all Mr. Dunlop claims for this patent can be granted, it does not establish his claim. Five months previously, as Mr. Dunlop admits in his book, he had been shown T. W. Robertson's tyre (patented in the names of Robertson and du Cros), which he describes as ' the first wired-on detachable made.' Robertson therefore anticipated him in (1) the use of wires and (2) detachability.

" But the broad and incontrovertible fact is that Welch had anticipated both Robertson and Dunlop. Neither Robertson or Dunlop could make his tyre without a licence from Welch, or the owners of his patent.

" WHAT CONSTITUTES DETACHABILITY ?

" While on the subject of the detachable tyre, attention may be directed to the following extraordinary statement made in the chapter headed ' The Detachable Tyre ' :—

" No detachable tyre, having an air tube of canvas and rubber, is worthy of the name ' detachable.'

" To say that a tyre is unworthy of being called detachable because its air tube is not all rubber is absurd. The judges who tried the issues arising out of the Bartlett litigation did not think so. Nor does any practical person.

" TYRE AND RIM DESIGN

" Mr. Dunlop claims to have told Welch how to design the rim for his tyre. On the same page of the book there are two contradictory statements on the subject. In the first Mr. Dunlop does not claim to have designed the rim. ' Mr. Welch submitted to me templates for the rim in two sizes which I approved of,' he writes. Later on the same page Mr. Dunlop refers to ' my design of rim and cover.' Under the title of the illustration of one of the templates which is reproduced on the page facing the statements we have quoted the template is described as ' Designed by Mr. Dunlop.' We take it Mr. Dunlop was not responsible for the titles of the illustrations. His editor has accepted the more sweeping of the claims, but Mr. Dunlop's own words leave the point in doubt.

" A MONOPOLY MISSED

" When, however, Mr. Dunlop claims that ' The detachable made according to these templates has never been improved upon,' he makes a statement that few will accept as accurate. The Westwood rim, which was not acquired by the Dunlop Co.,* was so great an advance on the original rim that it was subsequently adopted by the company. Its use is now universal on cycles and motor cycles. Mr. Dunlop proceeds to say : ' It was to be

---

* It was—in 1896. The inside section was not altered.

regretted that my design of rim and cover was not patented over the civilised countries of the Globe. It would have given the company a master patent for wiring on and would have been worth millions.' In Welch's patent they had the master patent covering all types of wired-on tyres, as subsequent litigation proved. Even if Mr. Dunlop improved on Welch's design of rim and cover, such an improvement could not be regarded as a master patent as the ordinary layman understands those words.

" Good Advice

"The only credit that is due to Mr. Dunlop in connection with the detachable tyre (and it is no small one) is that he advised the company to buy Welch's patent. His claim that ' I was responsible ' for ' the introduction of the detachable ' (p. 86) rests on no higher grounds.*

" As I have insisted on the importance of dates, it is well, in the interest of historical accuracy, to remind the modern student of tyre history of the dates of the Welch and Bartlett patents. They are : Welch, 16th September, 1890 ; Bartlett, 14th October, 1890.† All of the patents that Mr. Dunlop cites in support of his claim to the credit of being responsible for the introduction of the detachable tyre are of a later date. It is on the principles covered by these patents that all wired-on and beaded-edge tyres of to-day are made.

" Mr. Dunlop's Sensitiveness

" Mr. Dunlop was always sensitive to criticism. He pilloried the *Irish Cyclist* in 1919, and does so again in his book, for the use of the word ' Mummy ' as descrip-

* See p. 107.
† October 22nd, 1890.

tive of his original stuck-on tyre. (The reference, of course, is to the resemblance of the wrappings of the tyre to those of the dead of the ancient Egyptians.) Yet he twice uses the word himself in a description ' of the earliest or " Mummy " tyre.' The word is descriptive, and was not used as one of contempt. He objects to the original tyres being described by the *Irish Cyclist* (in 1919) as exceedingly heavy, and to the statement that the original canvas was not as fast as the modern fabric on tangential lines. He objects to others describing the original tyre as clumsy. He actually disputes the fact that the addition of pneumatic tyres to the bicycles of 1889 increased their weight ! These objections are so groundless that it would be waste of time to refute them.

" His sensitiveness to criticism, however, does no produce a generosity of feeling to his brother inventors, and many of the references in the book are not in keeping with the kindly nature of the author as I knew him in the later years of his life. I feel sure that were he alive to-day, and were his attention drawn to the reference, he would not sneer at Mr. Welch as one who was ' considered to be an expert.'

" THE HOSE-PIPE MYTH

" Although one of the main objects of the book is to lay for ever the hose-pipe myth, one of the references to the early tyre does much to revive it. Describing the train of thought that led up to his first patent, Mr. Dunlop says :—

' At length it dawned on me that the problem as to light vehicles, at any rate, might be solved by means of a triple tube of rubber, canvas and rubber distended with compressed air. Those were some of the ideas that led up, eventually, to the invention of the pneumatic tyre.'

" If the words ' a triple tube of rubber, canvas and rubber ' do not describe a hose pipe they describe something very like one.

" In his description of his own invention Mr. Dunlop is not always happy. Describing the first tyre made in 1887, he writes : ' The flaps were secured to the wooden rim with solution and the rim slung over the driving wheels of the tricycle with copper wire.' The description is unintelligible to me. Another statement, twice made in the same chapter, does not agree with my recollection of the original tyre. He states : ' The outer end of the air-supply tube was concealed in a recess in the rim.' Our memory suggests that the valve protruded through the rim. It is so shown in the photograph of Johnnie Dunlop on his first pneumatic-tyred bicycle.* The point is not of any importance, save in the interest of historical accuracy, and it could easily be set at rest by an inspection of one of the original tyres which is now in the Royal Scottish Museum at Edinburgh.

" Looking at the Inside

" Another very peculiar statement is that which follows the reference to Mr. Dunlop having ridden one of the original pneumatic-tyred bicycles to the meet of the Irish Old Timers ' in June, 1890.' (The date should be 1918.) After telling that in order to do so he repaired a leak in the inner tube, he adds : ' I never saw an 1892 tyre made, and this was the only one I ever saw opened

* See p. 37.

up.' Whether Mr. Dunlop is referring to the tyres made in the year 1892 or to the original tyres of the stuck-on type, which, subsequent to the introduction of the 1893 tyre (the detachable), were referred to as the 1892 pattern, is not clear. But in its narrowest meaning it is difficult to accept the statement.

" WHERE THE HISTORY FAILS

" There are many other points in connection with the book to which I would like to refer, but the review has already run to an inordinate length. I may return to the subject on another occasion. Frankly, I am greatly disappointed with the book, both as regards its contents and production. It is a contribution to the history of the pneumatic tyre, but it can make no claim to be ' The History.' It is a useful description of Mr. Dunlop's invention and of the earliest years with which he was associated with it ; but even in this respect it loses its value by dwelling to too great an extent and repeating *ad nauseam* the early and, in many cases, trivial episodes. Its worst feature is the manner in which it attempts to belittle everyone who had to do with improvements, and ignores the romance of the commercial development, leaving the ' History ' twenty-five years out of date. The sneer at Welch, the ignoring of Woods, Bartlett, Palmer and Westwood, to mention but a quartette, is only paralleled by the fact that the references to du Cros seem to be animated by a desire to demonstrate his lack of vision as to the potentialities of the tyre and his want of commercial acumen ! "

FURTHER PRESS COMMENTS ON THE MAJORITY CELEBRATION BANQUET

" The immense gathering was representative of every aspect of both the cycle and motor industries—the trade, the sport, and the pastime—throughout the world. It was a truly international gathering and a great and worthy tribute to a distinguished personality. This celebration must be inscribed on the tablets of the allied industries as a remarkable demonstration of the better feeling and higher instincts which animate mankind. All petty feeling was sunk in the determination to commemorate a great event, and the entire proceedings were characterized by a warmth and enthusiasm which left no room for doubt as to the sincerity of the celebrants."—*The Cycle and Motor-Cycle Trader*, November 26th, 1909.

" Mr. J. B. Dunlop, the inventor of the tyre, was present, and it must have been gratifying to himself and to his friends to note with what warmth his name was received. The name of John Boyd Dunlop will be handed down through generations, probably for centuries, as one of the inspired few who have created new eras in the world and in the march of science and civilization. It is true that the idea which made him famous had, forty years earlier, germinated in the brain of another, but nothing came of it, and it had been buried away neglected and forgotten till it was reborn in the mind of Mr. Dunlop. To him and to those who followed him with improvements and modifications all honour is due.

" But of what avail is the greatest invention unless it is taken in hand and commercially exploited by some man of commanding genius. Fortunately for the pneumatic tyre, such a man was at hand in Mr. Harvey du Cros, one of the commercial giants of the age. There is no need to tell here of the oft-told story of Mr. du Cros' invincible faith despite the most disheartening obstacles, of his amazing energy and determination, of his tireless work, of his many disappointments and his ultimate triumph."—*The Motor Trader*, November 24th, 1909.

" There was one other thing about his speech (Mr. du Cros') that pleased everybody. He fairly and freely allotted a full meed of credit to all the old directors. Starting with Mr. Dunlop, he mentioned them each by name. His allusion to the great part Mr. Dunlop had played brought out the best cheer of the night. The long-sustained applause must have rejoiced the heart of the old inventor. If J. B. Dunlop was not pleased with the enthusiasm with which his name was received, then he must be hard to satisfy, but he was pleased and I have no hesitation in saying that he was the happiest man in the room."—*The Irish Cyclist*, November 24th, 1909.

" There was also at that historic gathering ' Johnny ' Dunlop, now grown to manhood, and whose struggles in getting to school on his solid-tyred bicycle over the Belfast tram-lines caused his father, a veterinary surgeon, to think of having a tyre filled with a cushion of air. Little could the boy or his father have dreamt what their makeshift contrivance would come to mean to humanity in both hemispheres in a brief twenty-one years. Yet if ever there was an unpromising thing, it was this invention in its beginnings. The miracle has been wrought so quickly and so many firms have been established in the tyre industry to-day that one is apt to forget that to Ireland, and Ireland alone, we really owe this invention, for even Thomson's patent was issued in that country in 1846, which, curiously, chances to be the year when, as Mr. du Cros puts it : ' I was also issued in Ireland.'

" It wanted a lot of pluck in those days to stake one's all on such an unlikely development, and Mr. du Cros confessed that had they known in 1888 of the existence of the Thomson patent they would never have started the industry. What that means it is hard for the most

293

imaginative among us to picture to-day."—*Illustrated Sporting and Dramatic News*, November 27th, 1909.

" It was a night of recollections ; a night of reflections ; and many undercurrents ran strong and deep through that throng. But all were united in the main respects, to return thanks for an epoch-making invention, and to honour the man who had been the greatest figure in its development. It was pleasant to see all the directors of the original company present ; it was pleasant to hear the tribute to Mr. Thomson, the inventor who was born too soon ; it was pleasant to learn that Mr. Thomson's two sons were there to hear the acknowledgment of their father's posthumous fame ; it was pleasant to hear the grateful acknowledgements to Woods and Bartlett and Welch, and above all it was pleasant to take part in the great burst of cheers which greeted the name of Mr. J. B. Dunlop, the inventor—for as far as he was concerned the Dunlop tyre was an original conception—of a practical tyre, and the name of Mr. Harvey du Cros, the man who spread the gospel of the invention to the ends of the earth.

" In replying to the toast of the evening, ' The old man,' as he is endearingly called, got ' off his mark ' (as he phrased it) splendidly, and charmed us with an oration which was graceful in its terms, full of thoughtful allusions to others who had assisted in the great achievement, and charged with the pent-up thanks of an overflowing heart. It was a great honour gratefully and splendidly acknowledged."—*The Cycle and Motor Trades Review*, November 25th, 1909.

THE MECHANICS' MAGAZINE

August 22nd, 1846

"A BROUGHAM WITH ELASTIC TYRE-WHEELS

"THE attention of the visitors to the parks this week has been much attracted by the appearance among the crowd of gay equipages, of a *brougham* with *silent* wheels—so silent as to suggest a practical inconsistency of a most startling character, between the name and quality of the thing. The tyre of the wheels consists of an elastic tubular ring, made (we believe) of caoutchouc, inclosed in a leather case, and inflated with air to any degree of tightness desired. The motion of the carriage is exceedingly easy. We are informed that it has now gone about a hundred miles, over roads of all sorts, even some that were newly macadamised, and that the outer leather casing is (contrary to what might have been expected) as sound and entire as at first, not exhibiting in any part of it the slightest tendency to rupture. The inventor is Mr. R. W. Thomson, C.E."

THE MECHANICS' MAGAZINE

No. 1233, March 27th, 1847

"THOMSON'S PATENT AERIAL WHEELS

"WE gave a slight notice of these wheels at the time of the first appearance in public of a carriage fitted with them, about six months ago, and since then we have been favoured with a full explanation of their mode of construction, and also had an opportunity of personally testing their capabilities.

" The reader will perhaps recollect that the peculiarity of these wheels consists in their tyres being formed of elastic tubular rings, made of india-rubber (vulcanised) and inflated with air to any degree of tightness required. The most obvious advantage—indeed, the only one which, at first sight, would seem likely to result from the substitution of an elastic for a non-elastic tyre—is a diminution of noise ; and hence it was that we were led in one former notice of the wheels to characterise them as ' silent ' rather than as being distinguished for any other property.

" It has been so long regarded as a settled thing, that friction is least with hard substances, and greatest with soft, that, by a natural, though not perhaps strictly logical, course of induction, we inferred that, though in this case the noise might be less, the friction, and consequently the tractive power required, would be greater. We must candidly own that we little expected to find the very reverse of this to be the fact. Yet so it is. Experiments very carefully conducted, and which we have ourselves repeated and verified, prove incontestably that the friction and draught are diminished to a very great extent by the use of these elastic wheels. The experiments we refer to were made by Messrs. Whitehurst & Co. the eminent coach-builders of Oxford Street and the inventor Mr. R. W. Thomson, C.E., on a piece of road in the Regent's Park, nearly one-half of which is firm and smooth, and the other covered with newly-broken stone. The results are shown in the following table :—

Result of Experiments tried by Messrs. Whitehurst & Co.
and the Patentee, for ascertaining the Comparative
Draught of R. W. Thomson's Patent Aerial Wheels and
the Common Wheels. Tried in Regent's Park,
March 17th, 1847.

Weight of Carriage, 10½ cwts.	Common Wheels. Actual Draught in Pounds.	Patent Wheels. Actual Draught in Pounds.	Saving of Draught by Patent Wheels.
Over a smooth, hard macadamized level road	45	28	Per cent. 60
Over new broken flints . .	120	38½	310

" It stands thus established, that we have here a wheel which not only makes little noise, or, more strictly speaking, perhaps, which is in itself noiseless, for to us it seemed as if all the noise were occasioned by the rumbling of the body of the carriage, and parts in connection with it—but which requires from one to three times less tractive power than a common carriage, and which must consequently be much less subject to wear and last proportionately longer.

" The wheel-tyres of the carriage with which we made our experiments were stated to have travelled upwards of 1,200 miles on all sorts of roads ; yet we could not discern in them the slightest symptoms of deterioration or decay."

THE MECHANICS' MAGAZINE

Vol. 50. 1849

" THOMSON'S PATENT WHEELS

" WE have recently had the pleasure of a drive in a carriage fitted with these wheels. Some improvements have been effected since we gave a description of them in a former number (1233) which are of a very marked character. The leather case for the air tube has been replaced by a case made of a peculiar kind of canvas, manufactured expressly for the purpose ; and on the outside of the canvas, where it is liable to wear from coming in contact with the ground, a band of vulcanised India rubber is placed. The behaviour of the India rubber under this treatment is extraordinary. Not only does it not wear thinner, but the original surface remains wholly undisturbed. A curious proof of this was presented to us, on comparing a piece of new vulcanised rubber with the surface of the rubber on a carriage wheel which had been constantly at work for about two months. The new rubber was marked on its surface by a clearly defined impression of fine cotton cloth (arising, we believe, from its being spread on cloth when in a soft state to form it into sheets) and this marking we found on the wheel as sharply defined as on the new rubber. On examining the two surfaces with a microscope not the slightest difference could be detected between the new rubber and that which had been running through the wet grit and dirt of the London streets for two months. The markings on the surface of the rubber, although clearly defined, have no depth, so that if there had been the slightest wear they would have been at once defaced.

" Despite the opinion most people would form, on first seeing the wheels, that the draught must be greatly increased by a soft and yielding tyre, the draught is unquestionably very much lessened. We ourselves have tried a series of experiments on the draught by a dynamometer, and are perfectly satisfied of the fact.

" The tyres are perfectly *elastic* as well as soft. They do not sink into loose gravel or soft ground as common wheels do. Nor, on paved streets, do they retard the carriage by receiving constant concussions from every paving stone or other obstacle they pass over—they yield to every inequality, permit the carriage to pass over it without rising up, and the elastic tyre expanding as it passes from the obstruction, returns the force borrowed for a moment to compress the tyre.

" *We entertain a confident expectation that these wheels will speedily come into general use.* The perfect stillness with which they roll along, places them above any comparison with common spring carriages. The saving of horse flesh will more than repay their additional cost at first ; and they can be renewed, we believe, at about the same expense as common wheels."

THOMSON'S PATENT SPECIFICATION

A.D. 1845 . . . . . . N°. 10,990

Carriage Wheels

TO ALL TO WHOM THESE PRESENTS SHALL COME, I, ROBERT WILLIAM THOMSON, of Adam Street, Adelphi, in the County of Middlesex, Civil Engineer, send greeting.

WHEREAS Her present most Excellent Majesty Queen Victoria, by Her Royal Letters Patent under the Great Seal of Great Britain, bearing date at Westminster, the Tenth day of December, in the ninth year of Her reign, did, for Herself, Her heirs and successors, give and grant unto me, the said Robert William Thomson, my exors, admors, and assigns, Her especial licence, full power, sole privilege and authority, that I, the said Robert William Thomson, my exors, admors, and assigns, or such others as I, the said Robert William Thomson, my exors, admors, or assigns, should at any time agree with, and no others, from time to time and at all times during the term of years therein expressed, should and lawfully might make, use, exercise, and vend, within England, Wales, and the Town of Berwick-upon-Tweed, my Invention of "AN IMPROVEMENT IN CARRIAGE WHEELS, WHICH IS ALSO APPLICABLE TO OTHER ROLLING BODIES;" in which said Letters Patent is contained a proviso that I, the said Robert William Thomson, shall cause a particular description of the nature of my said Invention, and in what manner the same is to be performed, to be enrolled in Her said Majesty's High Court of Chancery within six calendar months next and immediately after the date of the said in part recited Letters Patent, as in and by the same, reference being thereunto had, will more fully and at large appear.

NOW KNOW YE, that in compliance with the said proviso, I, the said Robert William Thomson, do hereby declare that the nature of my said Invention, and in what manner the same is to be performed, are fully described in and by the present Specification thereof, reference being had to the Drawings hereunto annexed (that is to say) :—

The nature of my said Invention consists in the application of elastic bearings round the tires of the wheels of carriages, for the purpose of lessening the power required to draw the carriages, rendering their motion easier, and diminishing the noise they make when in motion. I prefer employing for the purpose a hollow belt composed of some air and water tight material, such as caoutchouc or gutta percha, and inflating it with air, whereby the wheels will in every part of their revolution present a cushion of air to the ground or rail or track on which they run.

Figure 1 is a side view of a wheel of this description, shewn partly in section. The tire and felly T, T, are made much broader than usual, and project considerably at both sides beyond the supporting spokes, as shewn at T, T, in the cross section of the wheel given in Figure II. The elastic belt is made as follows :—A number of folds of canvas, saturated and covered on both sides with india rubber or gutta percha in a state of solution, are laid one upon the other, and each fold connected to the one immediately below it by a solution of india rubber or gutta percha, or other suitable cement. The belt thus formed is then sulphurised by immersion in melted sulphur or exposure to the fumes of burning sulphur, which renders it more pliable and prevents it getting stiff on exposure to cold ; or the belt may be made of a single thickness of india rubber or gutta percha, in a sheet state and sulphurized, as aforesaid, and then enclosed in a canvas cover. A strong outer casing D, D (Figures I. and II.), in which to hold the elastic belt, is then built up (so to speak) around the tire by rivetting together a series of circular segments of leather and bolting them to the tire, in the manner shewn in Figure 2. The segments at two of their edges *a, a*, Figure 2, are made to overlap each other, as shewn, and then secured in their place by passing bolts G, G (Figure II.) through the tire and felly, and making them fast by nuts *g, g* (Figure II.) The elastic belt (C), Figure II., is then layed upon the portion of the segments D, D, Figure II., thus made fast to the tire and secured in its place by bringing the two remaining and as yet unjoined edges *b, b*, Figure II., of the segments together over the casing, and connecting them together by rivets F, F (Figure II.) A pipe P, Figure I, through which to inflate the elastic belt with air is passed at one place through the tire of the wheel and fitted with an air-tight screw cap. I prefer distending the elastic belt with air, as being more suitable than anything else for the purpose, but they may be distended with various solid substances of an elastic quality, as for instance, metallic springs, sulphurised pieces of caoutchouc or gutta percha, or horse hair, or sponge. If the elastic belt were first stuffed with horse hair or sponge, or other elastic materials, and then inflated by blowing in air to a high degree of tension, the belt would be less liable to be cut by concussion between the tire of the wheel and the roadway. Instead also of the elastic belt being made in either of the modes aforesaid, it might be formed of a number of separate tubes, of smaller dimensions, clustered together and enclosed within a leather cover (D). A wheel with a belt constructed in this manner is shown in Figures III. and IV., the former being a side view partly in section, and the latter a cross section. The tubes are nine in number, and each of length sufficient to go round the wheel. They are represented as tied at the ends, but, for greater convenience of inflation, may be closed by screw caps at one end ; the whole are enclosed in a leather cover D. If the three tubes which are shewn in the cross section Figure IV., as coming next the tire, were filled with air more highly compressed than that contained in the tubes which come in contact with the ground, this would serve to graduate the resiliency of the belt, in a manner highly favorable to the efficiency of its action. Any undue displacement of the air at the bearing points of the wheel may be prevented by tyeing the tubes across at distances of two or three feet apart, so that each tube shall be divided into a number of separate air-tight compartments. Or, instead of any of the preceding modes of construction the belt may be formed of separate and distinct sections, as shewn in Figures V. and VI., each section having its own air pipe (P), in which case the range of expansion and contraction being limited by the extent of the compartments, the belt must necessarily offer at each point of contact with the ground a greater degree of resistance to compression ; and in some cases where, from the nature of the roadway, frequent concussions are likely to take place, a flat strap or band of sulphurized caoutchouc or gutta percha, or other suitable elastic substance, of the width of the tire, and about half an inch in thickness, might be interposed between the tire of the wheel and the elastic belt, so as to render it less liable to rupture in the event of its being jambed between the roadway and the tire. Where the leather cover of the elastic belt is likely to be exposed to much tear and wear, I propose to use a belt of the description shewn on the cross section, Fig. VI. Here one of the pieces D^1 is secured to the tire of the wheel by bolts or screws, and it is bent round and sewed or rivetted to the other piece D^2. The edges of D^1 overlap the edges of D^2, and the outer casing E is secured to those edges by strong leather thongs. This arrangement will permit of the ready removal of the outer casing (E) when worn, and the substitution of a new casing, without disturbing the elastic belt or its attachment to the wheel. And in all cases the outer casing (D or E) may be protected from wear by covering the outer surface with flat-headed metal rivets secured on the inside with small washers. For common passenger carriages the elastic belt will require to be about four or five inches in diameter, and to be inflated to such an extent as to keep the tire of the wheel two and a half or three inches from the ground, a distance which, it is presumed, will be found sufficient to admit of the wheel passing over any stones or other matters projecting beyond the general level of any ordinary turnpike road without the solid tire coming in contact with them. In carriages to which these elastic belts are applied the springs now in use may be dispensed with. In waggons for the carriage of goods the belt ought to be made of stronger materials and of larger diameter than in the case of passenger carriages, and the outer leather cover should be protected by flat-headed metal rivets secured by small washers, as aforesaid. Wheels with elastic belts, such as I have described, may be used with great advantage on timber railways, especially if the modification represented in Figures VII. and VIII. are adopted. The wheels in this case might be of the common form, except they should have a greater width of tire given them, and be without flanges. The carriages are proposed to be kept on the rails by guide wheels (K, K,) working on a shaft L, secured by stays to the carriages, and acting on a raised rail (M) laid between the lines of rails on which the bearing wheels run. The rails (R, R,) are to be made of longitudinal beams of timber, say of twelve inches broad and six inches deep across ; ties of timber (T, T,) are to connect the two longitudinal rails together, and to these cross ties the longitudinal rail on which the guide wheels act is to be fixed. I prefer employing guide wheels to attaching flanges to the bearing wheels, but the latter also may be used. To increase the bite of the driving wheels of the locomotive I insert in the outer cover of the elastic belt a large number of rivets with sharp conical heads.

The Drawing, Figure VIII., shews a side view of a pair of railway wheels on this plan, for running on timber rails, and Figure VII. a cross section and end elevation of the same. The elastic belts are also peculiarly applicable to carriages propelled by steam on common roads. The comparatively small amount of power required to propel carriages, the wheels of which are fitted with these belts, the steadiness of their motion, the absence of all jolting and consequent security of the machinery from injury, the small damage the carriages will do to roads, the absence of nearly all noise, the high speed that may safely be attained, and the great gentleness of the motion, will, I think, enable steam carriages to be run on common roads with great advantage both for carrying passengers and goods.

Among many minor applications which suggest themselves I may mention the great applicability of these elastic bearings for bath chairs, rocking chairs, and other like articles, used commonly either in pleasure grounds or within doors. In the common rocking chair a rolling motion is obtained by resting the legs of the chair on two circular segments. In applying my elastic bearings to this chair I propose to make the circular segments on which the chair rolls about three inches wide on their bearing surfaces, and to secure to these segments an elastic tube of about two inches diameter, so as to interpose the tube between the segments and the floor, so that the chair would roll on and be supported by the elastic tube. I propose further to apply the elastic bearings to rollers for the removal of heavy bodies. Such rollers would be used in the same way that wood or iron rollers are now commonly used, that is, by being placed below the body which is to be moved. The advantage which rollers with elastic bearings would have over hard and metallic rollers are, that a large number of them may be made to bear equally at the same time, even although the ways on which the body is being moved are not quite even.

And having now described the nature of my said Invention, and in what manner the same is to be performed, I declare that what I claim is,—

First, the application of elastic bearings round the tire of carriage wheels, as before described ; and,

Secondly, the application of similar elastic bearings to the surfaces of other rolling bodies, as before exemplified.

> In witness whereof, I, the said Robert William Thomson, have hereunto set my hand and seal, this Tenth day of June, in the year of our Lord One thousand eight hundred and forty-six.

R. W. (L.S.) THOMSON.

AND BE IT REMEMBERED, that on the Tenth day of June, in the year of our Lord 1846, the aforesaid Robert William Thomson, came before our said Lady the Queen in Her Chancery, and acknowledged the Specification aforesaid, and all and every thing therein contained and specified, in form above written. And also the Specification aforesaid was stamped according to the tenor of the Statute made for that purpose.

> Enrolled the Tenth day of June, in the year of our Lord One thousand eight hundred and forty-six.

THE DUNLOP RUBBER CO. LTD.
FOUNDED BY SIR ARTHUR DU CROS, BART.

THIS chart shows companies controlled by the DUNLOP RUBBER COMPANY and the countries in which they have a direct interest through manufacturing or trading companies. Company was registered in 1900 and now has an issued share and loan capital of £16,166,158 and assets, as shown in the last consolidated statement, valued at £31,787,999. Apart from tyres and accessories, four other main groups of articles are made, general rubber manufactures, footwear, garments and sports goods.

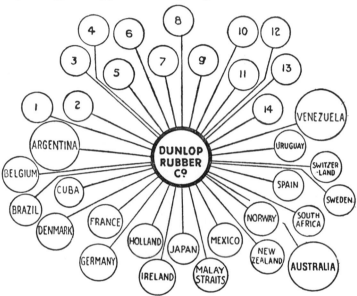

DUNLOP RUBBER COMPANY control the following companies and, except where shown, hold all the capital :—	
1. W. and A. Bates.	7. Tyre Investment Trust (95 per cent of Ord. shares).
2. Dunlop Rim and Wheel Co.	8. Dunlop Tire and Rubber Goods Co. (64 per cent.).
3. W. Goodyear and Sons.	9. Dunlop Cotton Mills (all Ord. shares).
4. Dunlop Tire and Rubber Corporation of America (98 per cent. of common stock).	10. Dunlop Plantations (all Ord. shares).
5. Clipper Tyre Co. (99 per cent.).	11. Dunlop Rubber Co. (India) (controlling interest).
6. Dunlop Rubber Co. (China) (99 per cent.)	12. Campbell Achnach and Co.
	13. Chas. Macintosh and Co.
	14. India Tyre and Rubber Co.

In addition the Company own all the capital of the Dunlop manufacturing and trading companies in the various countries shown on the chart, except that in Ireland only Ordinary shares are held, while in France the company have a majority holding of shares of one class.

By the courtesy of the DAILY EXPRESS.

REX v. CLEWLEY

The postcards which formed the basis of the prosecution in this case were selected from a considerable correspondence of a similar type, in which not only the prosecutor and Welch, but also Bartlett, Dunlop and Harvey du Cros were accused of complicity or knowingly deriving benefits from the alleged theft. When the defendant was asked in cross-examination whether he claimed the wired-on or beaded-edged method, he replied : "All the lot."

It was shown in evidence that at the date of the alleged theft Sir Arthur du Cros, to whom the defendant had apologised, was sixteen years of age, and had never visited England, that Welch was an engineer of twenty-six, in business in Tottenham, and had not been in Oxford, and Bartlett was fifty-seven, and had been educated in America and that he (Bartlett) was totally dissimilar in appearance to Welch. No allegations had been made until 1934—forty-seven years after.

DEFAMATORY LIBELS ON POSTCARDS
Man's Allegation of Stolen Invention

A claim that a pneumatic tyre invention had been stolen from him was mentioned at the Central Criminal Court yesterday when Frederick William Clewley, sixty-four, described as of no occupation, was charged with publishing defamatory libels concerning Sir Arthur Philip du Cros, for many years managing-director of the Dunlop Rubber Company. Clewley pleaded "Not Guilty" and justification.

Mr. Bassett, for the prosecution, said the alleged libels were contained in three postcards sent to Sir Arthur du Cros in July. In the postcards Clewley alleged that his invention, which had brought in millions, had been stolen from him, and he claimed £50,000 or prosecution. Mr. Bassett asserted that there was no shadow of truth in Clewley's allegations.

Sir Arthur du Cros, giving evidence, was asked by Miss Constance Colwill (defending) why he had not prosecuted sooner. Sir Arthur replied : "I have sent many of his communications to the police asking them in mercy to stop him because I did not want to prosecute. I would not have done so had he enclosed his libels in envelopes."

A Wired-on Tyre

The witness said that the Pneumatic Tyre and Booth's Cycling Agency, which later became Dunlops, purchased a wired-on tyre invention from a Mr. Welch in 1891. Formerly the pneumatic tyre was fastened to the wheel, but Mr. Welch's invention allowed it to be detached. The witness added that

309

he was associated with his father in the formation of the Dunlop Company in 1889. The original pneumatic tyre was invented by R. W. Thomson in 1845, and rediscovered by Mr. J. B. Dunlop in 1888.

Miss Colwill read a letter written by Clewley in 1934 in which he alleged that at a boys' club in Oxford in 1887 he sketched an invention of his for Mr. Welch. Welch took it away to see if he could do anything with it, and later said he could not. The defendant alleged that he then found that Welch had taken out a patent and sold it to the Dunlop Company.

Sir Arthur du Cros remarked that this was a serious accusation against a man he had always found to be honourable and straightforward. He had known Mr. Welch from his early days. He was an inventive genius, and never went to Oxford.

DEFENDANT'S EVIDENCE

Clewley, in the witness box, said that in 1887, when he was thirteen years of age and when he was working at a type foundry in Oxford, a workman spoke to him about the old penny-farthing bicycle. The defendant said, " I told him that what was wanted was a low bicycle with two wheels so that one did not have to fall far. I invented one afterwards and with a wind tyre and inner tube. That was the first pneumatic tyre. In 1887, I was in a club called the Oxford Institute, and the founder, the Rev. Mr. Chandler, now Bishop Chandler, brought in the ' thief.' I do not say intentionally."

The Recorder (Mr. Gerald Dodson) asked Sir Arthur du Cros to stand up, and Clewley, after looking at him, said, " That is not the gentleman."

The Recorder : " That is a comfort, Sir Arthur."

Clewley went on to say that he drew a pneumatic tyre in the " thief's " notebook. The man said he would give him something for it, but he never saw the man again and he never got a copper.

The jury returned a verdict of guilty, and found the plea of justification not proved.

Mr. Bassett, having indicated that the prosecutor was not desirous of pressing the case, and the defendant having undertaken not to repeat the offence, the Recorder, in postponing sentence said : " Now, Frederick William Clewley, somehow or other you have got a strange idea in your head, and the sooner you get it out the better, because if you do not, and if you do anything like this again connected either with Sir Arthur du Cros, or any of the relatives of Mr. Bartlett or Mr. Welch, or any member of the Dunlop family, you will go to prison. Whether that is better or worse than the lodging houses in which you spend your precarious life now it is not for me to say, but that is the only way of protecting the members of the community whom you assail in this way, and who are entitled to the protection of the law."

The defendant was then remanded to Brixton Prison until the next Sessions for a report from the Probation Officer.

INDEX